MW01001505

BRAVE NEW FAMILY

BRAVE NEW FAMILY

G. K. Chesterton on
Men and Women, Children, Sex,
Divorce, Marriage & the Family

Edited and with an introduction by
Alvaro de Silva

IGNATIUS PRESS   SAN FRANCISCO

Cover by Roxanne Mei Lum

ISBN 978-0-89870-314-6

Library of Congress catalogue number 90-82989
Printed in the United States of America

Editor's Acknowledgments

I would like to thank the director and staff of the Special Collections at the John J. Burns Library of Boston College, for their assistance. I deeply appreciate the generous help of Katharine Allan, Jay Delahanty, Sean McLaughlin, Mickie Teetor and Ted Wills. Without the encouragement of Stratford Caldecott, at Collins Publishers in London, the idea for this anthology would have long been forgotten.

Alvaro de Silva
May 24, 1990

BRAVE NEW FAMILY

* * *

O, wonder!
How many goodly creatures are there here!
How beauteous mankind is! O brave new world,
That hath such people in't!

Miranda in Shakespeare's *The Tempest*

Love is a constant challenge,
thrown to us by God,
thrown, I think, so that we should challenge fate.

A character in Karol Wojtyla's play *The Jeweler's Shop*

Marriage is like life in this—that it is a field of
battle, and not a bed of roses.

R. L. Stevenson, *Virginibus puerisque*

All that we call modern is already antiquated. All that is called
Futurist is already a part of the past. And the new thing is still too
new to be seen.

G. K. Chesterton, "The World is Dying", *G.K.'s Weekly,*
July 21, 1928, p. 295.

CONTENTS

INTRODUCTION

Gilbert Keith Chesterton once referred to the family as something "now never mentioned in respectable circles".[1] Were he introducing his own anthology on the subject, he could very well say that—judging by the proliferation of *familiologists*—the family is now mentioned everywhere. It is recalled as obsessively as the name of a lost paradise, a bad joke or an obscenity. Perhaps today the family is all three: something lost, laughed about and abused. But the moral and social desolation produced by its decay could bring about a newer and deeper appreciation of its relevance.

> When all the promises of mere traders are perforce broken, when all the praises of mere trade have perforce become a jest, when all that was called practical has turned out to be a practical joke, and all that was called modern is in ruins more useless than Stonehenge—then, there is a real psychological possibility that men may think of things forgotten: of property, of privacy, of piety in the old sense of reverence for the human sanctities; for the family, from the hearthstone to the headstone.[2]

As we turn the leaf of another century, we get closer—in this most central and intimate subject of love and family—to the conditions depicted in Aldous Huxley's cautionary tale of horror *Brave New World*. Indeed, we have left 1984 behind. Lenina, the young woman protagonist of Huxley's novel, feels that the word

---

[1] "On Education", in *All I Survey* (New York: Dodd, Mead, 1933), p. 196.

[2] G. K. Chesterton, "The Day of the Lord", in *G.K.'s Weekly*, Jan. 14, 1933, p. 299.

father is a scatological impropriety and that *mother* is not a joke any more but an obscenity. She "had never seen anything so indecent in her life as young women giving breast to their babies". This bottled baby had never seen a family, not even her own. In this nightmare universe, " 'Father' was not so much obscene as—with its connotation of something at one remove from the loathsomeness and moral obliquity of child-bearing—merely gross, a scatological rather than a pornographic impropriety." And "to say one was a mother—that was past a joke: it was an obscenity".[3]

The home has been devoured by the jungle. It used to take courage—indeed, it was the act of courage par excellence—to leave the comforts of home and family and go out into the world at large seeking adventure. Today there are fewer places to discover, and the real adventure is to stay home. Courage may be on its way to becoming more a domestic virtue than a political one. Nothing probably requires more courage, determination and spirit of adventure. As the French poet Charles Péguy wrote,

> Family life is the most "engaged" life in the world. There is only one adventurer in the world, as can be seen very clearly in the modern world, the father of a family. Even the most desperate adventurers are nothing compared with him. Everything in the modern world ... is organized against that fool, that imprudent, daring fool, ... against the unruly, audacious man who is daring enough to have a wife and family, against the man who dares to *found* a family. Everything is against him. Savagely organized against him. Everything turns and combines against him. Men, events, the events of society, the automatic play of economic laws. And, in short, everything else.[4]

Gilbert K. Chesterton (1874–1936) thought that the Victorians had lost "the sense of the sacredness of the home".[5] The suc-

---

[3] See Aldous Huxley, *Brave New World: A Novel* (New York: Harper and Row, 1932), p. 180.

[4] Clio I (Cahiers), in *Temporal and Eternal,* (New York, 1958), p. 108.

[5] *Sidelights,* in *The Collected Works of G. K. Chesterton,* vol. 21 (San Francisco: Ignatius Press, 1990), p. 511.

ceeding generation tried to get rid of the home altogether. Now we hunger and search for it everywhere. For some, a cat will do, or a dog or an expensive fur or a cheap affair with a stranger. Our name is Lenina, and this a brave new world indeed. We are spiritual barbarians and emotional nomads. In our despair, we put two broken umbrellas together and call it home sweet home. We look for the right thing in the wrong place. And often we manage to turn the right thing into something very wrong. Alongside the modern despair of the family, the cynicism about romance and fidelity, there is an evident craving for what the family is. The despair is only modern; the family, eternal. Thus our expectations of a home have become one of the most important decoys in advertising. Every conceivable commercial product is supposed to remind buyers about the delights and offerings of "family". Respect, caring, understanding, sharing, loyalty, freedom, love, joy and a smile or two are now being offered as readily available outside, at the bank or at the hardware store, because these commodities are found less and less at home. Despite the efforts to find one, there is no alternative to the family.

Those who recognize the malaise judge it our most crucial problem. These wise men complain that nobody seems to do anything about it—but do what? The problem of the family is not a social problem; it is a spiritual problem. Here one may see not only the dangerous extent of the crisis but also the moral solidity and the indispensability of the family. It is something so precious that, once broken, it cannot be easily repaired, not even with a proliferation of profamily laws. Intelligent legislation and social programs can obviously do much good, but the crisis of the family will never be solved by laws. The solution remains within each family, in the mind and heart of every man and woman. It cannot be otherwise. At the root of every crisis in marriage and family life is the problem of one's personal life. In a sense, every honest family is a crisis initiated over the earthquakes and hurricanes of human love and romance. Here we see the gravity and urgency of the crisis but also the challenge of its solution. Getting into marriage is by definition getting into trouble, and if people keep on marrying it is due to the truth that if some happiness is be found in this life, it is to be found at home.

Chesterton was full of compassion for the limitations and sins of men, beginning with his own, but also full of hope in the immense capabilities of their love and self-sacrifice. Chesterton is definitely a writer of the home. He wrote extensively about the subject and, with a few exceptions, what he wrote has always appealed to me as firmly grounded on common sense, rooted in the rich soil of humanity's wisdom, with an abundance of sanity and sanctity. His vision and intuition, his lucid style, his ability to see where practically everyone else saw darkness or saw nothing, even his extraordinary literary production on every possible subject, are a consequence of this central fact: Chesterton felt *at home* in the world. "He had the artist's eye, which could suddenly see, in some quite familiar object, a new value; he had the poet's intuition, which could suddenly detect, in the tritest of phrases, a wealth of new meaning and possibilities. The most salient quality, I think, of his writing is the gift of illuminating the ordinary; of finding in something trivial a type of the eternal. And it was a gift of vision he himself valued."[6]

The family is the thread of Chesterton's work, the lighthouse that guides the ship safely to harbor. Even in his conversion to the Catholic Church, he felt as one finally coming home, "the home of man", as he called it. He saw to his own surprise that the madness of the Gospel was the only sane thing in the world. "The madhouse has been a house to which, age after age, men are continually coming back as to a home."[7] Chesterton had a gift to see in splendid colors what many had always seen in black and white, or in sad gray. He could see what had never been seen before. A guest may look around and admire the bouquet of flowers in the living room or dislike in silence the roughly finished wooden box in the kitchen, but only a member of the

[6] Ronald Knox in his panegyric for G. K. Chesterton: *G.K.'s Weekly*, July 2, 1936, p. 255.

[7] G. K. Chesterton, *The Everlasting Man*, in *The Collected Works of G. K. Chesterton*, vol. 2 (San Francisco: Ignatius Press, 1986), p. 402.

household can see through them. Maybe the flowers adorned the altar on the couple's wedding day. Maybe the box is their little child's first creation, even as she is the loving creation of her parents. Our difficulty with marriage and family may well be precisely this: that we see them as strangers or visitors; they are not really home. We refuse to accept their limitations, which are also ours. "We must see things objectively, as we do a tree; and understand that they exist whether we like them or not. We must not try and turn them into something different by the mere exercise of our own minds, as if we were witches."[8]

Saint Augustine excused the Romans' belief in Romulus' divinity by saying that "it did not spring from a love of error but from an error of love".[9] And something similar could be said about the situation of the family, although it is far from being a complete explanation. At the dawn of the twentieth century Chesterton realized that the decay of the family was not merely due to a lack of traditional morals or mere human weakness but also the rise of a whole new doctrine against the family. He was contending with a new metaphysics, a different vision of life and death on this corner of the galaxy. So he put out his flag and went to war without the slightest doubt of defending a truly great cause: "We fight for the trust and for the tryst; for fixed memories and the possible meeting of men; for all that makes life anything but an uncontrollable nightmare. We fight for the long arm of honour and remembrance; for all that can lift a man above the quicksands of his moods, and give him the mastery of time."[10]

The family was a central element in Chesterton's vision, perhaps a unifying theme of his literary work. He fought for the world because he felt at home in it. For him, the family is a kingdom unto every man and woman so mutually committed as husband and wife. A physical, psychological, moral, intellectual

[8] G. K. Chesterton, *Illustrated London News,* Nov. 22, 1913, in *The Collected Works of G. K. Chesterton,* vol. 29 (San Francisco: Ignatius Press, 1988), p. 589.

[9] *The City of God,* chap. xxii, 6.

[10] *The Appetite of Tyranny,* in *The Collected Works of G. K. Chesterton,* vol. 5 (San Francisco: Ignatius Press, 1987), pp. 252–53.

and spiritual environment where they are sovereign and thus can be themselves but also, and for the same reason, where they can sacrifice and deny themselves. A place where one can give oneself to others without diminishing oneself or one's joy, thus proving true an old evangelical promise. The only place where man can really be free, where to command is to obey, to serve is to reign and to suffer, a joy. The place indeed that solves nearly all the paradoxes of human life, including those that Chesterton invented himself. The family solves the paradox of man, and the paradox that God made man male and female. It also solves the paradox of God, because the warmth of home helps us see that God does not lack that warmth. No wonder the greatest heresy of modern times is the denial of God the Father "of whom the whole family in heaven and earth is named" (Eph 3: 15). We would rather worship God the Grandfather, as Nietzsche described him: old, soft, passive, half-deaf and nearly blind. To accept God's total commitment as our Father, his intervention in history, not to mention the death at Calvary, is more than even believers can take.

Any attempt to help the family must begin with an understanding of what the family is and what it is not. This is at the root of what Chesterton wrote on the subject. The wishes of some editorialists and other vociferous sociologists or psychologists to solve the crisis by simply accepting it as the birth of a new *kind* of family will not do. No doctor will solve the puzzle of a disease by saying that we are merely contemplating a new step in the long process of organic evolution. The doctor, sooner or later, will contemplate a dead man, not a new kind of man. Those who try to persuade us that we are only at the threshold of a new *kind* of family will perhaps enjoy the spiritual atmosphere of Huxley's *Brave New World.* But the horrifying bravura of this new kind of family is largely based on the denial of true love. In that brave world, love and generosity have been replaced with lust and selfishness, and these rations, together with their bitter taste, will be theirs until death or madness do them part. In this brilliant writer, Chesterton saw a return of "something of the spirit of Jonathan Swift". But, Aldous Huxley's recognition of original sin was left somehow without a counterpart, drifting to a state of total depravity, hence his pessimism. Chesterton saw that neither this brutal pessimism nor the naïve optimism that stands at the other end will satisfy man, "for man knows there is that within him that can never be valued too highly, as well as that within him which can never be hated too much; and only a philosophy which emphasizes both, violently and simultaneously, can restore the balance to the brain".[11]

Chesterton saw the family as one of the "human sanctities", more sacred than the state. For him it was an earthly sanctity even before it became a divine sacrament. Only in this philosophy of the family, upon the firm ground of an irrevocable commitment, are reform and even rebellion possible. "The Christian view of marriage", he wrote, "conceives of the home as self-governing in a manner analogous to an independent state; that is, that it may include internal reform and even internal rebellion; but because of the bond, not against it."[12] The union becomes a song and a poem, a human and a divine comedy, even when we insist on having only a tragedy. In this radiant vision, each new family seems to have in its own hands the destiny of the world.

If Christian marriage is one of the great contributions of Christianity to civilization (according to D. H. Lawrence, "the greatest"), divorce is one of civilization's great perils. That is why it came back disguised as progress and liberty. "Divorce by now is prayed for as if it were the proper sequel of marriage", wrote Tertullian, not a contemporary but an ancient Christian writer. So much for progress. Chesterton saw in divorce the barbarous act of "dividing the tune from the words of a song". In a series of articles, later edited and gathered in a book called *The Superstition of Divorce*, he explained why it is such a sentimental superstition. His argument is as valid today as it was yesterday. The only difference is that today he could have said that divorce has become

[11] "The Spirit of the Age in Literature", *Sidelights,* in *The Collected Works of G. K. Chesterton,* vol. 21, p. 611.
[12] Preface to *Divorce versus Democracy,* in *The Collected Works of G. K. Chesterton,* vol. 4 (San Francisco: Ignatius Press, 1987), p. 421.

the very foundation of marriage. And this is a paradox that not even Chesterton would have wanted. The denial of the marriage bond has become its cement. How can anyone not be cynical of marriage if his mind comfortably admits the quick reasonable exit of divorce, preferably the no-fault divorce? What began as an exception has ended as the rule, and a sovereign rule at that! For many men and women the happy ending of their love is divorce. There the curse of marriage is lifted and destroyed at the blessing of divorce. And another marriage. And most likely, another divorce. If this is progress, shall we advance by running in circles? Many will identify divorce with freedom, equality and progress. Some will say that divorce is better than adultery. I rather believe with Charles Williams that "adultery is bad morals but divorce is bad metaphysics".[13] It is exactly what Chesterton insisted upon. And, if there is a lesson history can teach, it is that society's survival and success depend upon true metaphysics more than good morals. The consequences of false metaphysics are worse and beyond the ugly results of bad morals. At the end, not only the morals but even the morale of a people are the ripe fruit of its metaphysics.

This anthology ends with a small selection of the many essays Chesterton penned about Christmas. In the Jewish family of Nazareth, he saw an inexhaustible source of inspiration and strength, since it was the birth of the true family. "A child has been born to us, a son has been given to us." The family has been given to us. With the first Christmas, God entered into the human family, and the family of man entered into the Trinity of God. Saint Paul would later write that the love of man and woman is a figure of the love of Christ for his Church, "the mystical idea that the man and the woman had become one sacramental substance".[14] And Chesterton believed that the modern attack against the family was an attack on Christianity. He would defend the family as he would defend the Church, and the Church as he would his home

---

[13] *The Forgiveness of Sins* (London, 1942), chap. viii, p. 117.

[14] G. K. Chesterton, *The Everlasting Man,* in *The Collected Works of G. K. Chesterton,* vol. 2, p. 326.

and hearth. In Bethlehem the first Christian temple was also, literally, the first Christian home. That is exactly the spirit of Christmas celebration, and the lesson is that "where there is no temple, there shall be no homes", as the choruses sing in T. S. Eliot's *The Rock*.

This book was written by Chesterton, and I have no idea whether he would have approved of its title. Upon reading almost everything he wrote (at least what has been so far published), I collected these poems and essays in the same spirit that moved Chesterton to write in his splendid book on Chaucer: "What matters is not books on Chaucer, but Chaucer." So here I say that what matters is not books on the family but the family. That is why it seems to me important to understand what the title means. The real family is always a brave new family. A new family is needed because not everything was right with the old family. Chesterton was less interested with this or that kind of family — liberal, conservative — than with the family as such. As he put it, "I don't care where the water goes / if it doesn't get into the wine." So with the family. Let times change, let the weather change, but do not invent an adulterated family and drink it as if it were the real nourishing thing.

The attitude to marriage and home should be similar to Innocent Smith's attitude toward the woman he loves in Chesterton's novel *Manalive:* "He seriously sought by a perpetual recapture of his bride to keep alive the sense of her perpetual value, and the perils that should be run for her sake." Chesterton believed that "man is not merely an evolution but rather a revolution".[15] Our nostalgia for the family is even greater because we despair of it. Although many families will manage one way or another, we feel that the family is a thing of the past, something obsolete, impossible after the sexual and the women's revolution. We concede divorce as a necessary element in modern life, a *sine qua non* of freedom and progress. For Chesterton this thinking is simply a lack of thought or thinking upside down or thinking with your

---

[15] *The Everlasting Man,* in *The Collected Works of G. K. Chesterton,* vol. 2, p. 158.

feet. It is putting the cart before the horse: "One very common form of the blunder is to make modern conditions an absolute end, as if they were only means. Thus people say, 'Home life is not suited to the business life of today.' Which is as if they said, 'Heads are not suited to the sort of hats now in fashion.' "[16] He was convinced that whatever freedom and happiness men can attain would first be found at home and everywhere else only secondarily. This great lover and defender of liberty and democracy put liberty's flag on top of every door and in every window of the house, because he saw the home as the source of freedom and democracy.

"And if there is one thing in the world that I hate more than being a Communist, it is being an Individualist."[17] The danger threatening an institution such as the family is not only collectivism but also individualism—not only as political and cultural ideologies that sooner or later destroy the family but also as domestic practices that subtly or violently may run within a particular home. Writing of Robert Browning's marriage, for instance, Chesterton describes the home of Edward Barrett as "the house of a madman", who treated his daughter Elizabeth "as part of the furniture of the house and of the universe", because, Chesterton concludes, "the worst tyrant is not the man who rules by fear; the worst tyrant is he who rules by love and plays on it as on a harp".[18] In some traditional families the well-intentioned claim to authority on the part of the parents may be so pervasive that instead of being home it may more closely resemble a mild concentration camp. Doubtless, there must be authority in a family, but the family is not merely authority or an excuse for authority, for lording over other people. The other extreme may be as pernicious, of course. Thus Chesterton was not defending a particular kind of conservative authoritarian family. Here his position followed common sense: while the family lasts forever,

---

[16] *Illustrated London News,* Dec. 11, 1926, in *The Collected Works of G. K. Chesterton,* vol. 34 (San Francisco: Ignatius Press, 1990).

[17] "The Other Questions", in *G.K.'s Weekly,* Oct. 8, 1932, p. 71.

[18] *Robert Browning* (London, 1903), pp. 73 and 74, respectively.

paternalism is only good for a while, for a very short while indeed. As the wisdom of an exceptional defender of human love and family has it, the cry shall not be, "Family, become what you were", but rather, "Family, become what you are."[19]

If this urgent call is heeded, the family will be even more a "true communion of persons", where husband and wife and children have equal dignity, where all wholeheartedly embrace the true advances that women have recently made, some of them revolutionary. The sacramental vision of marriage and family that Chesterton shared even before he had thought about it offers a rich source of ideas and ideals, of new visions and energies, that could help transform each ordinary family into a brave new family that still remains an ordinary home. It will be brave with another kind of courage but not less bravura. It will be new with the rich flavor of old wine. But, above all, it will be simply family—and its reward a greater joy and wonder than ever Miranda imagined because it will march on to conquer this brave new world and the next.

Alvaro de Silva
May 24, 1990

---

[19] Cfr. John Paul II, *Familiaris consortio:* "The Role of the Christian Family in the Modern World" (Rome, 1981), n. 18. The document underlined "the equal dignity and responsibility of women with men" (n. 22) and the heroic sacrifice that love, marriage and family imply.

PART ONE

THE WILDEST
OF ADVENTURES

* * *

The supreme adventure is being born. There we do walk suddenly into a splendid startling trap. There we do see something of which we have not dreamed before. Our father and mother do lie in wait for us and leap out on us, like brigands from a bush. Our uncle is a surprise. Our aunt is, in the beautiful common expression, a bolt from the blue. When we step into the family, by the act of being born, we do step into a world which is incalculable, into a world which has its own strange laws, into a world which could do without us, into a world that we have not made. In other words, when we step into the family we step into a fairy-tale.

Heretics

A dead thing can go with the stream, but only a living thing can go against it.

The Everlasting Man

Of all human institutions marriage is the one which most depends upon slow development, upon patience, upon long reaches of times, upon magnanimous compromise, upon kindly habit.

Early Notebooks

When we defend the family we do not mean it is always a peaceful family; when we maintain the thesis of marriage we do not mean that it is always a happy marriage. We mean that it is the theatre of the spiritual drama, the place where things happen, especially the things that matter. It is not so much the place where a man kills his wife as the place where he can take the equally sensational step of not killing his wife.

"The Home of the Unities",
in *The New Witness,* January 17, 1919

The family is the test of freedom; because the family is the only thing that the free man makes for himself and by himself.

"The Home of the Unities",
in *The New Witness,* January 17, 1919

There are no rules of architecture for a castle in the clouds.

The Everlasting Man

If we wish to preserve the family we must revolutionize the nation.

What's Wrong with the World

The modern world (intent on anarchy in everything, even in Government) refuses to perceive the permanent element of tragic constancy which inheres in all passion, and which is the origin of marriage. Marriage rests upon the fact that you cannot have your cake and eat it; that you cannot lose your heart and have it.

Introduction to *David Copperfield*

Love is not blind; that is the last thing it is. Love is bound; and the more it is bound the less it is blind.

Orthodoxy

The first of all the marks of love is seriousness: love will not accept sham bulletins or the empty victory of words.

A Denunciation of Patriotism

One thing the marriage ideal did and did alone: it took love seriously: it demanded the payment of the eternal promise of youth. Herein we think, though the trend of today is wholly against such feeling, it inexpressibly increased the vividness, the poetry, the boyish heroism of life. Society associated itself with the worship of the lover, it set on the woman's head a price high enough to satisfy even his imagination. It said "You shall not have this secret and superhuman happiness, unless you give up all for it, unless you bring your life in your hands."

Early Notebooks

For the purpose even of the wildest romance results must be real; results must be irrevocable. Christian marriage is the great example of a real and irrevocable result; and that is why it is the chief subject of all our romantic writing.

Orthodoxy

Creation Day

Between the perfect marriage day
   And that fierce future, proud and furled,
I only stole six days, — six days,
   Enough for God to make the world.

For us is a creation made
   New moon by night, new sun by day,
That ancient elm that holds the heavens
   Sprang to its stature yesterday —
       . . . .

Dearest and first of all things free,
   Alone as bride and queen and friend,
Brute facts may come and bitter truths,
   But here all doubts shall have an end.
       . . . .

Never again with cloudy talk
   Shall life be tricked or faith undone,
The world is many and is mad,
   But we are sane and we are one.

A Marriage Song

Why should we reck of hours that rend
   While we two ride together?
The Heavens rent from end to end
   Would be but windy weather,
The strong stars shaken down in spate
   Would be a shower of spring,

And we should list the trump of fate
  And hear a linnet sing.

We break the line with stroke and luck,
  The arrows run like rain,
If you be struck, or I be struck,
  There's one to strike again.
If you befriend, or I befriend,
  The strength is in us twain,
And good things end and bad things end,
  And you and I remain.

Why should we reck of ill or well
  While we two ride together?
The fires that over Sodom fell
  Would be but sultry weather.
Beyond all ends to all men given
  Our race is far and fell,
We shall but wash our feet in heaven,
  And warm our hands in hell.

Battles unborn and vast shall view
  Our faltered standards stream,
New friends shall come and frenzies new,
  New troubles toil and teem;
New friends shall pass and still renew
  One truth that does not seem,
That I am I, and you are you,
  And Death a morning dream.

Why should we reck of scorn or praise
  While we two ride together?
The icy air of godless days
  Shall be but wintry weather.
If hell were highest, if the heaven
  Were blue with devils blue,

I should have guessed that all was even,
    If I had dreamed of you.

Little I reck of empty prides,
    Of creeds more cold than clay;
To nobler ends and longer rides,
    My lady rides to-day.
To swing our swords and take our sides
    In that all-ending fray
When stars fall down and darkness hides,
    When God shall turn to bay.

Why should we reck of grin and groan
    While we two ride together?
The triple thunders of the throne
    Would be but stormy weather.
For us the last great fight shall roar,
    Upon the ultimate plains,
And we shall turn and tell once more
    Our love in English lanes.

To My Lady

God made you very carefully
He set a star apart for it
He stained it green and gold with fields
And aureoled it with sunshine
He peopled it with kings, peoples, republics
And so made you, very carefully.
All nature is God's book, filled with his rough sketches
    for you.

God Made Thee Mightily, My Love,

God made thee mightily, my love,
He stretched his hands out of his rest
And lit the star of east and west
Brooding o'er darkness like a dove.
God made thee mightily, my love.

God made thee patiently, my sweet,
Out of all stars he chose a star
He made it red with sunset bar
And green with greeting for thy feet.
God made thee mightily, my sweet.

Under How Many Suns

Under how many suns have we embraced
  In what long fields of flowers and streets of stone
In the strong light of summer, interlaced
  And made, like God, a darkness of our own.

Oh when the bitter wind of longing blows,
  And all between us seems an aching space
Think that we hold each other close, so close;
  We cannot even see each other's face.

Marriage and the Modern Mind

I have been requested to write something about Marriage and the Modern Mind. It would perhaps be more appropriate to write about Marriage and the Modern Absence of Mind. In much of their current conduct, those who call themselves "modern" seem to have abandoned the use of reason; they have sunk back into their own subconsciousness, perhaps under the influence of the psychology now most fashionable in the drawing-room; and it is an understatement to say that they act more automatically than the animals. Wives and husbands seem to leave home more in the manner of somnambulists.

If anybody thinks I exaggerate the mindlessness of modern comment on this matter, I am content to refer him to the inscription under a large photograph of a languishing lady, in the newspaper now before me. It states that the lady has covered herself with glory as the inventor of "Companionate Divorce." It goes on to state, in her own words, that she will marry her husband again if he asks her again; and that she has been living with him ever since she was divorced from him. If mortal muddle-headedness can go deeper than that, in this vale of tears, I should like to see it. The newspaper picture and paragraph I can actually see; and stupidity so stupendous as that has never been known in human history before. The first thing to say about marriage and the modern mind, therefore, is that it is natural enough that people with no mind should want to have no marriage.

But there is another simple yet curious illustration of modern stupidity in the matter. And that is that, while I have known thousands of people arguing about marriage, sometimes furiously against it, sometimes rather feebly in favour of it, I have never

known any one of the disputants begin by asking what marriage
is. They nibble at it with negative criticism; they chip pieces off it
and exhibit them as specimens, called "hard cases"; they treat
every example of the rule as an exception to the rule; but they
never look at the rule. They never ask, even in the name of history
or human curiosity, what the thing is, or why it is, or why the
overwhelming mass of mankind believes that it must be. Let us
begin with the alphabet, as one does with infants.

Marriage, humanly considered, rests upon a fact of human
nature, which we may call a fact of natural history. All the higher
animals require much longer parental protection than do the
lower; the baby elephant is a baby much longer than the baby
jellyfish. But even beyond this natural tutelage, man needs something
quite unique in nature. Man alone needs education. I know that
animals train their young in particular tricks; as cats teach kittens
to catch mice. But this is a very limited and rudimentary education.
It is what the hustling millionaires call Business Education; that is,
it is not education at all. Even at that, I doubt whether any pupil
presenting himself for Matriculation or entrance into Standard
VI, would now be accepted if flaunting the stubborn boast of a
capacity to catch mice. Education is a complex and many-sided
culture to meet a complex and many-sided world; and the animals,
especially the lower animals, do not require it. It is said that the
herring lays thousands of eggs in a day. But, though evidently
untouched by the stunt of Birth-Control, in other ways the herring is highly modern. The mother herring has no need to remember her own children, and certainly therefore, no need to remember
her own mate. But then the duties of a young herring, just
entering upon life, are very simple and largely instinctive; they
come, like a modern religion, from within. A herring does not
have to be taught to take a bath; for he never takes anything else.
He does not have to be trained to take off a hat to a lady herring,
for he never puts on a hat, or any other Puritanical disguise to
hamper the Greek grace of his movements. Consequently his
father and mother have no common task or responsibility; and
they can safely model their union upon the boldest and most

advanced of the new novels and plays. Doubtless the female herring does say to the male herring, "True marriage must be free from the dogmas of priests; it must be a thing of one exquisite moment." Doubtless the male herring does say to the female herring, "When Love has died in the heart, Marriage is a mockery in the home."

This philosophy, common among the lower forms of life, is obviously of no use among the higher. This way of talking, however suitable for herrings, or even for rats and rabbits, who are said to be so prolific, does not meet the case of the creature endowed with reason. The young of the human species, if they are to reach the full possibilities of the human culture, so various, so laborious, so elaborate, must be under the protection of responsible persons through very long periods of mental and moral growth. I know there are some who grow merely impatient and irrational at this point; and say they could do just as well without education. But they lie; for they could not even express that opinion, if they had not laboriously learnt one particular language in which to talk nonsense. The moment we have realized this, we understand why the relations of the sexes normally remain static; and in most cases, permanent. For though, taking this argument alone, there would be a case for the father and mother parting when the children were mature, the number of people who at the age of fifty really wish to bolt with the typist or be abducted by the chauffeur is less than is now frequently supposed.

Well, even if the family held together as long as that, it would be better than nothing; but in fact even such belated divorce is based on bad psychology. All the modern licence is based on bad psychology; because it is based on the latest psychology. And that is like knowing the last proposition in Euclid without knowing the first. It is the first elements of psychology that the people called "modern" do not know. One of the things they cannot comprehend is the thing called "atmosphere"; as they show by shrieking with derision when anybody demands "a religious atmosphere" in the schools. The atmosphere of something safe and settled can only exist where people see it in the future as well as in the past. Children know exactly what is meant by having really come home; and the happier of them keep something of the feeling as they grow up. But they cannot keep the feeling for ten minutes, if there is an assumption that Papa is only waiting for Tommy's twenty-first birthday to carry the typist off to Trouville; or that the chauffeur actually has the car at the door, that Mrs. Brown may go off the moment Miss Brown has "come out."

That is, in practical experience, the basic idea of marriage; that the founding of a family must be on a firm foundation; that the rearing of the immature must be protected by something patient and enduring. It is the common conclusion of all mankind; and all common sense is on its side. A small minority of what may be called the idle Intelligentsia, have, just recently and in our corner of the world, criticized this idea of Marriage in the name of what they call the Modern Mind. The first obvious or apparent question is how they deal with the practical problem of children. The first apparent answer is that they do not deal with it at all.

At best, they propose to get rid of babies, or the problem of babies, in one of three typically modern ways. One is to say that there shall be no babies. This suggestion may be addressed to the individual; but it is addressed to every individual. Another is that the father should instantly send the babies, especially if they are boys, to a distant and inaccessible school, with bounds like a prison, that the babies may become men, in a manner that is considered impossible in the society of their own father. But this is rapidly ceasing to be a Modern method; and even the Moderns have found that it is rather behind the times. The third way, which is unimpeachably Modern, is to imitate Rousseau, who left his baby on the door-step of the Foundling Hospital. It is true that, among the Moderns, it is generally nothing so human or traditional as the Foundling Hospital. The baby is to be left on the door-step of the State Department for Education and Universal Social Adjustment. In short, these people mean, with various degrees of vagueness, that the place of the Family can now be taken by the State.

The difficulty of the first method, and so far, of the second and third, is that they may be carried out. The suggestion is made to everybody in the hope that it will not be accepted by everybody; it is offered to all in the hope that it may not be accepted by all. If *nobody* has any children, everybody can still be satisfied by Birth-Control methods and justified by Birth-Control arguments. Even the reformers do not want this; but they cannot offer any objection to any individual—or every individual. In somewhat the same way, Rousseau may act as an individual and not as a social philosopher; but he could not prevent all the other individuals acting as individuals. And if all the babies born in the world were left on the door-step of the Foundling Hospital, the Hospital, and the door-step, would have to be considerably enlarged. Now something like this is what has really happened, in the vague and drifting centralization of our time. The Hospital has been enlarged into the School and then into the State; not the guardian of some abnormal children, but the guardian of all normal children. Modern mothers and fathers, of the emancipated sort, could not do their quick-change acts of bewildering divorce and scattered polygamy, if they did not believe in a big benevolent Grandmother, who could ultimately take over ten million children by very grandmotherly legislation.

This modern notion about the State is a delusion. It is not founded on the history of real States, but entirely on reading about unreal or ideal States, like the Utopias of Mr. Wells. The real State, though a necessary human combination, always has been and always will be, far too large, loose, clumsy, indirect and even insecure, to be the "home" of the human young who are to be trained in the human tradition. If mankind had not been organized into families, it would never have had the organic power to be organized into commonwealths. Human culture is handed down in the customs of countless households; it is the only way in which human culture can remain human. The households are right to confess a common loyalty or federation under some king or republic. But the king cannot be the nurse in every nursery; or even the government become the governess in every schoolroom. Look at the real story of States, modern as well as ancient, and you will see a dissolving view of distant and uncontrollable things, making up most of the politics of the earth. Take the most populous centre. China is now called a Republic. In consequence it is ruled by five contending armies and is much less settled than when it was an Empire. What has preserved China has been its domestic religion. South America, like all Latin lands, is full of domestic graces and gaieties; but it is governed by a series of revolutions. We ourselves may be governed by a Dictator; or by a General Strike; or by a banker living in New York. Government grows more elusive every day. But the traditions of humanity support humanity; and the central one is this tradition of Marriage. And the essential of it is that a free man and a free woman choose to found on earth the only voluntary state; the only state which creates and which loves its citizens. So long as these real responsible beings stand together, they can survive all the vast changes, deadlocks and disappointments which make up mere political history. But if they fail each other, it is as certain as death that "the State" will fail them.

On Certain Modern Writers
and the Institution of the Family

The family may fairly be considered, one would think, an ultimate human institution. Every one would admit that it has been the main cell and central unit of almost all societies hitherto, except, indeed, such societies as that of Lacedaemon, which went in for "efficiency," and has, therefore, perished, and left not a trace behind. Christianity, even enormous as was its revolution, did not alter this ancient and savage sanctity; it merely reversed it. It did not deny the trinity of father, mother, and child. It merely read it backwards, making it run child, mother, father. This it called, not the family, but the Holy Family, for many things are made holy by being turned upside down. But some sages of our own decadence have made a serious attack on the family. They have impugned it, as I think wrongly; and its defenders have defended it, and defended it wrongly. The common defence of the family is that, amid the stress and fickleness of life, it is peaceful, pleasant, and at one. But there is another defence of the family which is possible, and to me evident; this defence is that the family is not peaceful and not pleasant and not at one.

It is not fashionable to say much nowadays of the advantages of the small community. We are told that we must go in for large empires and large ideas. There is one advantage, however, in the small state, the city, or the village, which only the wilfully blind can overlook. The man who lives in a small community lives in a much larger world. He knows much more of the fierce varieties and uncompromising divergences of men. The reason is obvious. In a large community we can choose our companions. In a small community our companions are chosen for us. Thus in all extensive and highly civilized societies groups come into existence founded upon what is called sympathy, and shut out the real world more sharply than the gates of a monastery. There is nothing really narrow about the clan; the thing which is really narrow is the clique. The men of the clan live together because they all wear the same tartan or are all descended from the same sacred cow; but in their souls, by the divine luck of things, there will always be more colours than in any tartan. But the men of the clique live together because they have the same kind of soul, and their narrowness is a narrowness of spiritual coherence and contentment, like that which exists in hell. A big society exists in order to form cliques. A big society is a society for the promotion of narrowness. It is a machinery for the purpose of guarding the solitary and sensitive individual from all experience of the bitter and bracing human compromises. It is, in the most literal sense of the words, a society for the prevention of Christian knowledge.

We can see this change, for instance, in the modern transformation of the thing called a club. When London was smaller, and the parts of London more self-contained and parochial, the club was what it still is in villages, the opposite of what it is now in great cities. Then the club was valued as a place where a man could be sociable. Now the club is valued as a place where a man can be unsociable. The more the enlargement and elaboration of our civilization goes on the more the club ceases to be a place where a man can have a noisy argument, and becomes more and more a place where a man can have what is somewhat fantastically called a quiet chop. Its aim is to make a man comfortable, and to make a man comfortable is to make him the opposite of sociable. Sociability, like all good things, is full of discomforts, dangers, and renunciations. The club tends to produce the most degraded of all combinations—the luxurious anchorite, the man who combines the self-indulgence of Lucullus with the insane loneliness of St. Simeon Stylites.[1]

If we were to-morrow morning snowed up in the street in which we live, we should step suddenly into a much larger and much wilder world than we have ever known. And it is the whole effort of the typically modern person to escape from the street in which he lives. First he invents modern hygiene and goes to Margate. Then he invents modern culture and goes to Florence. Then he invents modern imperialism and goes to Timbuctoo. He goes to the fantastic borders of the earth. He pretends to shoot tigers. He almost rides on a camel. And in all this he is still essentially fleeing from the street in which he was born; and of this flight he is always ready with his own explanation. He says he is fleeing from his street because it is dull; he is lying. He is really fleeing from his street because it is a great deal too exciting. It is exciting because it is exacting; it is exacting because it is alive. He can visit Venice because to him the Venetians are only Venetians; the people in his own street are men. He can stare at the Chinese because for him the Chinese are a passive thing to be stared at; if he stares at the old lady in the next garden, she becomes active. He is forced to flee, in short, from the too stimulating society of his equals—of free men, perverse, personal, deliberately different from himself. The street in Brixton is too glowing and overpowering. He has to soothe and quiet himself among tigers and vultures, camels and crocodiles. These creatures are indeed very different from himself. But they do not put their shape or colour or custom into a decisive intellectual competition with his own. They do not seek to destroy his principles and assert their own; the stranger monsters of the suburban street do seek to do this. The camel does not contort his features into a fine sneer because Mr. Robinson has

[1] One of the best examples of extravagant austerity and asceticism, St. Simeon the Elder is the best known of the "pillar hermits". He lived on a platform on top of a pillar nine feet above the ground. See *Catholic Encyclopedia,* vol. 13, p. 795.

not got a hump; the cultured gentleman at No. 5 does exhibit a
sneer because Robinson has not got a dado. The vulture will not
roar with laughter because a man does not fly; but the major at
No. 9 will roar with laughter because a man does not smoke. The
complaint we commonly have to make of our neighbours is that
they will not, as we express it, mind their own business. We do
not really mean that they will not mind their own business. If our
neighbours did not mind their own business they would be asked
abruptly for their rent, and would rapidly cease to be our
neighbours. What we really mean when we say that they cannot
mind their own business is something much deeper. We do not
dislike them because they have so little force and fire that they
cannot be interested in themselves. We dislike them because they
have so much force and fire that they can be interested in us as
well. What we dread about our neighbours, in short, is not the
narrowness of their horizon, but their superb tendency to broaden it.
And all aversions to ordinary humanity have this general character.
They are not aversions to its feebleness (as is pretended), but to
its energy. The misanthropes pretend that they despise humanity
for its weakness. As a matter of fact, they hate it for its strength.

Of course, this shrinking from the brutal vivacity and brutal
variety of common men is a perfectly reasonable and excusable
thing as long as it does not pretend to any point of superiority. It
is when it calls itself aristocracy or aestheticism or a superiority to
the bourgeoisie that its inherent weakness has in justice to be
pointed out. Fastidiousness is the most pardonable of vices; but it
is the most unpardonable of virtues. Nietzsche, who represents
most prominently this pretentious claim of the fastidious, has a
description somewhere—a very powerful description in the purely
literary sense—of the disgust and disdain which consume him at
the sight of the common people with their common faces, their
common voices, and their common minds. As I have said, this
attitude is almost beautiful if we may regard it as pathetic. Nietzsche's
aristocracy has about it all the sacredness that belongs to the weak.
When he makes us feel that he cannot endure the innumerable
faces, the incessant voices, the overpowering omnipresence which

belongs to the mob, he will have the sympathy of anybody who has ever been sick on a steamer or tired in a crowded omnibus. Every man has hated mankind when he was less than a man. Every man has had humanity in his eyes like a blinding fog, humanity in his nostrils like a suffocating smell. But when Nietzsche has the incredible lack of humour and lack of imagination to ask us to believe that his aristocracy is an aristocracy of strong muscles or an aristocracy of strong wills, it is necessary to point out the truth. It is an aristocracy of weak nerves.

We make our friends; we make our enemies; but God makes our next-door neighbour. Hence he comes to us clad in all the careless terrors of nature; he is as strange as the stars, as reckless and indifferent as the rain. He is Man, the most terrible of the beasts. That is why the old religions and the old scriptural language showed so sharp a wisdom when they spoke, not of one's duty towards humanity, but one's duty towards one's neighbour. The duty towards humanity may often take the form of some choice which is personal or even pleasurable. That duty may be a hobby; it may even be a dissipation. We may work in the East End because we are peculiarly fitted to work in the East End, or because we think we are; we may fight for the cause of international peace because we are very fond of fighting. The most monstrous martyrdom, the most repulsive experience, may be the result of choice or a kind of taste. We may be so made as to be particularly fond of lunatics or specially interested in leprosy. We may love negroes because they are black or German Socialists because they are pedantic. But we have to love our neighbour because he is *there* — a much more alarming reason for a much more serious operation. He is the sample of humanity which is actually given us. Precisely because he may be anybody he is everybody. He is a symbol because he is an accident.

Doubtless men flee from small environments into lands that are very deadly. But this is natural enough; for they are not fleeing from death. They are fleeing from life. And this principle applies to ring within ring of the social system of humanity. It is perfectly reasonable that men should seek for some particular variety of the human type, so long as they are seeking for that variety of the human type, and not for mere human variety. It is quite proper that a British diplomat should seek the society of Japanese generals, if what he wants is Japanese generals. But if what he wants is people different from himself, he had much better stop at home and discuss religion with the housemaid. It is quite reasonable that the village genius should come up to conquer London if what he wants is to conquer London. But if he wants to conquer something fundamentally and symbolically hostile and also very strong, he had much better remain where he is and have a row with the rector. The man in the suburban street is quite right if he goes to Ramsgate for the sake of Ramsgate—a difficult thing to imagine. But if, as he expresses it, he goes to Ramsgate "for a change," then he would have a much more romantic and even melodramatic change if he jumped over the wall into his neighbour's garden. The consequences would be bracing in a sense far beyond the possibilities of Ramsgate hygiene.

Now, exactly as this principle applies to the empire, to the nation within the empire, to the city within the nation, to the street within the city, so it applies to the home within the street. The institution of the family is to be commended for precisely the same reasons that the institution of the nation, or the institution of the city, are in this matter to be commended. It is a good thing for a man to live in a family for the same reason that it is a good thing for a man to be besieged in a city. It is a good thing for a man to live in a family in the same sense that it is a beautiful and delightful thing for a man to be snowed up in a street. They all force him to realize that life is not a thing from outside, but a thing from inside. Above all, they all insist upon the fact that life, if it be a truly stimulating and fascinating life, is a thing which, of its nature, exists in spite of ourselves. The modern writers who have suggested, in a more or less open manner, that the family is a bad institution, have generally confined themselves to suggesting, with much sharpness, bitterness, or pathos, that perhaps the family is not always very congenial. Of course the family is a good institution because it is uncongenial. It is wholesome precisely because it

contains so many divergencies and varieties. It is, as the sentimentalists say, like a little kingdom, and, like most other little kingdoms,
is generally in a state of something resembling anarchy. It is
exactly because our brother George is not interested in our religious difficulties, but is interested in the Trocadero Restaurant,
that the family has some of the bracing qualities of the commonwealth. It is precisely because our uncle Henry does not approve
of the theatrical ambitions of our sister Sarah that the family is like
humanity. The men and women who, for good reasons and bad,
revolt against the family, are, for good reasons and bad, simply
revolting against mankind. Aunt Elizabeth is unreasonable, like
mankind. Papa is excitable, like mankind. Our youngest brother is
mischievous, like mankind. Grandpapa is stupid, like the world;
he is old, like the world.

Those who wish, rightly or wrongly, to step out of all this, do
definitely wish to step into a narrower world. They are dismayed
and terrified by the largeness and variety of the family. Sarah
wishes to find a world wholly consisting of private theatricals;
George wishes to think the Trocadero a cosmos. I do not say, for a
moment, that the flight to this narrower life may not be the right
thing for the individual, any more than I say the same thing about
flight into a monastery. But I do say that anything is bad and
artificial which tends to make these people succumb to the strange
delusion that they are stepping into a world which is actually
larger and more varied than their own. The best way that a man
could test his readiness to encounter the common variety of mankind would be to climb down a chimney into any house at random,
and get on as well as possible with the people inside. And that
is essentially what each one of us did on the day that he was born.

This is, indeed, the sublime and special romance of the family.
It is romantic because it is a toss-up. It is romantic because it is
everything that its enemies call it. It is romantic because it is
arbitrary. It is romantic because it is there. So long as you have
groups of men chosen rationally, you have some special or sectar-
ian atmosphere. It is when you have groups of men chosen irra-
tionally that you have men. The element of adventure begins to

exist; for an adventure is, by its nature, a thing that comes to us. It is a thing that chooses us, not a thing that we choose. Falling in love has been often regarded as the supreme adventure, the supreme romantic accident. In so much as there is in it something outside ourselves, something of a sort of merry fatalism, this is very true. Love does take us and transfigure and torture us. It does break our hearts with an unbearable beauty, like the unbearable beauty of music. But in so far as we have certainly something to do with the matter; in so far as we are in some sense prepared to fall in love and in some sense jump into it; in so far as we do to some extent choose and to some extent even judge—in all this falling in love is not truly romantic, is not truly adventurous at all. In this degree the supreme adventure is not falling in love. The supreme adventure is being born. There we do walk suddenly into a splendid and startling trap. There we do see something of which we have not dreamed before. Our father and mother do lie in wait for us and leap out on us, like brigands from a bush. Our uncle is a surprise. Our aunt is, in the beautiful common expression, a bolt from the blue. When we step into the family, by the act of being born, we do step into a world which is incalculable, into a world which has its own strange laws, into a world which could do without us, into a world that we have not made. In other words, when we step into the family we step into a fairy-tale.

This colour as of a fantastic narrative ought to cling to the family and to our relations with it throughout life. Romance is the deepest thing in life; romance is deeper even than reality. For even if reality could be proved to be misleading, it still could not be proved to be unimportant or unimpressive. Even if the facts are false, they are still very strange. And this strangeness of life, this unexpected and even perverse element of things as they fall out, remains incurably interesting. The circumstances we can regulate may become tame or pessimistic; but the "circumstances over which we have no control" remain god-like to those who, like Mr. Micawber, can call on them and renew their strength. People wonder why the novel is the most popular form of literature; people wonder why it is read more than books of science or books of metaphysics. The reason is very simple; it is merely that the novel is more true than they are. Life may sometimes legitimately appear as a book of science. Life may sometimes appear, and with a much greater legitimacy, as a book of metaphysics. But life is always a novel. Our existence may cease to be a song; it may cease even to be a beautiful lament. Our existence may not be an intelligible justice, or even a recognizable wrong. But our existence is still a story. In the fiery alphabet of every sunset is written, "to be continued in our next." If we have sufficient intellect, we can finish a philosophical and exact deduction, and be certain that we are finishing it right. With the adequate brain-power we could finish any scientific discovery, and be certain that we were finishing it right. But not with the most gigantic intellect could we finish the simplest or silliest story, and be certain that we were finishing it right. That is because a story has behind it, not merely intellect which is partly mechanical, but will, which is in its essence divine. The narrative writer can send his hero to the gallows if he likes in the last chapter but one. He can do it by the same divine caprice whereby he, the author, can go to the gallows himself, and to hell afterwards if he chooses. And the same civilization, the chivalric European civilization which asserted freewill in the thirteenth century, produced the thing called "fiction" in the eighteenth. When Thomas Aquinas asserted the spiritual liberty of man, he created all the bad novels in the circulating libraries.

But in order that life should be a story or romance to us, it is necessary that a great part of it, at any rate, should be settled for us without our permission. If we wish life to be a system, this may be a nuisance; but if we wish it to be a drama, it is an essential. It may often happen, no doubt, that a drama may be written by somebody else which we like very little. But we should like it still less if the author came before the curtain every hour or so, and forced on us the whole trouble of inventing the next act. A man has control over many things in his life; he has control over enough things to be the hero of a novel. But if he had control over everything, there would be so much hero that there would be no novel. And the reason why the lives of the rich are at bottom so tame and uneventful is simply that they can choose the events. They are dull because they are omnipotent. They fail to feel adventures because they can make the adventures. The thing which keeps life romantic and full of fiery possibilities is the existence of these great plain limitations which force all of us to meet the things we do not like or do not expect. It is vain for the supercilious moderns to talk of being in uncongenial surroundings. To be in a romance is to be in uncongenial surroundings. To be born into this earth is to be born into uncongenial surroundings, hence to be born into a romance. Of all these great limitations and frameworks which fashion and create the poetry and variety of life, the family is the most definite and important. Hence it is misunderstood by the moderns, who imagine that romance would exist most perfectly in a complete state of what they call liberty. They think that if a man makes a gesture it would be a startling and romantic matter that the sun should fall from the sky. But the startling and romantic thing about the sun is that it does not fall from the sky. They are seeking under every shape and form a world where there are no limitations—that is, a world where there are no outlines; that is, a world where there are no shapes. There is nothing baser than that infinity. They say they wish to be as strong as the universe, but they really wish the whole universe as weak as themselves.

"I Will"

Some of the same sort of social thinkers, who enlighten us in the daily Press, have more than once observed that the Marriage Service contradicts everything in the Modern Spirit. It contradicts everything in the world now around us and the way the world is going. So it does; and it contradicts them in two words: "I will."

For it is precisely on that point of the power to say "I will," about Marriage or about anything else, that the real war of the world is being waged today. For the typical modern man, or rather the typical man who calls himself modern, always prefers to say "I must," whether he says it as an anarchist or as a man of the Servile State. He says "I must," whether he means that he must obey a passion or that he must obey a policeman. He always represents himself as driven by some sort of irresistible compulsion, whether it is that of lawless love or an emphatically loveless law. Whether he is obeying the State, or the Boss, or the brute force of Nature, he equally excuses himself on the plea that the power is stronger than his own will. Sometimes he says that his anarchical behavior is due to heredity. In other words, he will not have his love-affairs arranged by his father and mother; but he will have them arranged by his great-great-grandfather, and his great-great-grandmother. Sometimes he says that everything is due to environment and education; which is a sort of lawless parody of the Indian infant marriage. But in all cases he talks as if he himself had really nothing to do with it; and he very naturally finds something annoying in an antiquated and superstitious formula that requires him to pronounce the words "I will."

A Defence of Rash Vows

If a prosperous modern man, with a high hat and a frock-coat, were to solemnly pledge himself before all his clerks and friends to count the leaves on every third tree in Holland Walk, to hop up to the City on one leg every Thursday, to repeat the whole of Mill's 'Liberty' seventy-six times, to collect 300 dandelions in fields belonging to anyone of the name of Brown, to remain for thirty-one hours holding his left ear in his right hand, to sing the names of all his aunts in order of age on the top of an omnibus, or make any such unusual undertaking, we should immediately conclude that the man was mad, or, as it is sometimes expressed, was 'an artist in life.' Yet these vows are not more extraordinary than the vows which in the Middle Ages and in similar periods were made, not by fanatics merely, but by the greatest figures in civic and national civilization—by kings, judges, poets, and priests. One man swore to chain two mountains together, and the great chain hung there, it was said, for ages as a monument of that mystical folly. Another swore that he would find his way to Jerusalem with a patch over his eyes, and died looking for it. It is not easy to see that these two exploits, judged from a strictly rational standpoint, are any saner than the acts above suggested. A mountain is commonly a stationary and reliable object which it is not necessary to chain up at night like a dog. And it is not easy at first sight to see that a man pays a very high compliment to the Holy City by setting out for it under conditions which render it to the last degree improbable that he will ever get there.

But about this there is one striking thing to be noticed. If men behaved in that way in our time, we should, as we have said, regard them as symbols of the 'decadence.' But the men who did these things were not decadent; they belonged generally to the most robust classes of what is generally regarded as a robust age. Again, it will be urged that if men essentially sane performed such insanities, it was under the capricious direction of a superstitious religious system. This, again, will not hold water; for in the purely terrestrial and even sensual departments of life, such as love and lust, the medieval princes show the same mad promises and performances, the same misshapen imagination and the same monstrous self-sacrifice. Here we have a contradiction, to explain which it is necessary to think of the whole nature of vows from the beginning. And if we consider seriously and correctly the nature of vows, we shall, unless I am much mistaken, come to the conclusion that it is perfectly sane, and even sensible, to swear to chain mountains together, and that, if insanity is involved at all, it is a little insane not to do so.

The man who makes a vow makes an appointment with himself at some distant time or place. The danger of it is that himself should not keep the appointment. And in modern times this terror of one's self, of the weakness and mutability of one's self, has perilously increased, and is the real basis of the objection to vows of any kind. A modern man refrains from swearing to count the leaves on every third tree in Holland Walk, not because it is silly to do so (he does many sillier things), but because he has a profound conviction that before he had got to the three hundred and seventy-ninth leaf on the first tree he would be excessively tired of the subject and want to go home to tea. In other words, we fear that by that time he will be, in the common but hideously significant phrase, *another man*. Now, it is this horrible fairy tale of a man constantly changing into other men that is the soul of the decadence. That John Paterson should, with apparent calm, look forward to being a certain General Barker on Monday, Dr. Macgregor on Tuesday, Sir Walter Carstairs on Wednesday, and Sam Slugg on Thursday, may seem a nightmare; but to that nightmare we give the name of modern culture. One great decadent, who is now dead, published a poem some time ago, in which he powerfully summed up the whole spirit of the movement by declaring that he could stand in the prison yard and entirely comprehend the feelings of a man about to be hanged:

> 'For he that lives more lives than one
> More deaths than one must die.'

And the end of all this is that maddening horror of unreality which descends upon the decadents, and compared with which physical pain itself would have the freshness of a youthful thing. The one hell which imagination must conceive as most hellish is to be eternally acting a play without even the narrowest and dirtiest greenroom in which to be human. And this is the condition of the decadent, of the aesthete, of the free-lover. To be everlastingly passing through dangers which we know cannot scathe us, to be taking oaths which we know cannot bind us, to be defying enemies who we know cannot conquer us—this is the grinning tyranny of decadence which is called freedom.

Let us turn, on the other hand, to the maker of vows. The man who made a vow, however wild, gave a healthy and natural expression to the greatness of a great moment. He vowed, for example, to chain two mountains together, perhaps a symbol of some great relief, or love, or aspiration. Short as the moment of his resolve might be, it was, like all great moments, a moment of immortality, and the desire to say of it *exegi monumentum aere perennius*[1] was the only sentiment that would satisfy his mind. The modern aesthetic man would, of course, easily see the emotional opportunity; he would vow to chain two mountains together. But, then, he would quite as cheerfully vow to chain the earth to the moon. And the withering consciousness that he did not mean what he said, that he was, in truth, saying nothing of any great import, would take from him exactly that sense of daring actuality which is the excitement of a vow. For what could be more maddening than an existence in which our mother or aunt received the information that we were going to assassinate the King or build a temple on Ben Nevis with the genial composure of custom?

---

[1] "I have built a monument more lasting than bronze."

The revolt against vows has been carried in our day even to the extent of a revolt against the typical vow of marriage. It is most amusing to listen to the opponents of marriage on this subject. They appear to imagine that the ideal of constancy was a yoke mysteriously imposed on mankind by the devil, instead of being, as it is, a yoke consistently imposed by all lovers on themselves. They have invented a phrase, a phrase that is a black and white contradiction in two words—'free-love'—as if a lover ever had been, or ever could be, free. It is the nature of love to bind itself, and the institution of marriage merely paid the average man the compliment of taking him at his word. Modern sages offer to the lover, with an ill-flavoured grin, the largest liberties and the fullest irresponsibility; but they do not respect him as the old Church respected him; they do not write his oath upon the heavens, as the record of his highest moment. They give him every liberty except the liberty to sell his liberty, which is the only one that he wants.

In Mr. Bernard Shaw's brilliant play 'The Philanderer,' we have a vivid picture of this state of things. Charteris is a man perpetually endeavouring to be a free-lover, which is like endeavouring to be a married bachelor or a white negro. He is wandering in a hungry search for a certain exhilaration which he can only have when he has the courage to cease from wandering. Men knew better than this in old times—in the time, for example, of Shakespeare's heroes. When Shakespeare's men are really celibate they praise the undoubted advantages of celibacy, liberty, irresponsibility, a chance of continual change. But they were not such fools as to continue to talk of liberty when they were in such a condition that they could be made happy or miserable by the moving of someone else's eyebrow. Suckling classes love with debt in his praise of freedom.

> 'And he that's fairly out of both
> Of all the world is blest.
> He lives as in the golden age,
> When all things made were common;
> He takes his pipe, he takes his glass,
> He fears no man or woman.'

This is a perfectly possible, rational and manly position. But what have lovers to do with ridiculous affectations of fearing no man or woman? They know that in the turning of a hand the whole cosmic engine to the remotest star may become an instrument of music or an instrument of torture. They hear a song older than Suckling's, that has survived a hundred philosophies. 'Who is this that looketh out of the window, fair as the sun, clear as the moon, terrible as an army with banners?'

As we have said, it is exactly this back-door, this sense of having a retreat behind us, that is, to our minds, the sterilizing spirit in modern pleasure. Everywhere there is the persistent and insane attempt to obtain pleasure without paying for it. Thus, in politics the modern Jingoes practically say, 'Let us have the pleasures of conquerors without the pains of soldiers: let us sit on sofas and be a hardy race.' Thus, in religion and morals, the decadent mystics say: 'Let us have the fragrance of sacred purity without the sorrows of self-restraint; let us sing hymns alternately to the Virgin and Priapus.' Thus in love the free-lovers say: 'Let us have the splendour of offering ourselves without the peril of committing ourselves; let us see whether one cannot commit suicide an unlimited number of times.'

Emphatically it will not work. There are thrilling moments, doubtless, for the spectator, the amateur, and the aesthete; but there is one thrill that is known only to the soldier who fights for his own flag, to the ascetic who starves himself for his own illumination, to the lover who makes finally his own choice. And it is this transfiguring self-discipline that makes the vow a truly sane thing. It must have satisfied even the giant hunger of the soul of a lover or a poet to know that in consequence of some one instant of decision that strange chain would hang for centuries in the Alps among the silences of stars and snows. All around us is the city of small sins, abounding in backways and retreats, but surely, sooner or later, the towering flame will rise from the harbour announcing that the reign of the cowards is over and a man is burning his ships.

The Drift from Domesticity

In the matter of reforming things, as distinct from deforming them, there is one plain and simple principle; a principle which will probably be called a paradox. There exists in such a case a certain institution or law; let us say, for the sake of simplicity, a fence or gate erected across a road. The more modern type of reformer goes gaily up to it and says, "I don't see the use of this; let us clear it away." To which the more intelligent type of reformer will do well to answer: "If you don't see the use of it, I certainly won't let you clear it away. Go away and think. Then, when you can come back and tell me that you *do* see the use of it, I may allow you to destroy it."

This paradox rests on the most elementary common sense. The gate or fence did not grow there. It was not set up by somnambulists who built it in their sleep. It is highly improbable that it was put there by escaped lunatics who were for some reason loose in the street. Some person had some reason for thinking it would be a good thing for somebody. And until we know what the reason was, we really cannot judge whether the reason was reasonable. It is extremely probable that we have overlooked some whole aspect of the question, if something set up by human beings like ourselves seems to be entirely meaningless and mysterious. There are reformers who get over this difficulty by assuming that all their fathers were fools; but if that be so, we can only say that folly appears to be a hereditary disease. But the truth is that nobody has any business to destroy a social institution until he has really seen it as an historical institution. If he knows how it arose, and what purposes it was supposed to serve, he may really be able to say that they were bad purposes, or that they have since become bad

53

purposes, or that they are purposes which are no longer served.
But if he simply stares at the thing as a senseless monstrosity that
has somehow sprung up in his path, it is he and not the traditionalist
who is suffering from an illusion. We might even say that he is
seeing things in a nightmare. This principle applies to a thousand
things, to trifles as well as true institutions, to convention as well
as to conviction. It was exactly the sort of person, like Joan of Arc,
who did know why women wore skirts, who was most justified
in not wearing one; it was exactly the sort of person, like St.
Francis, who did sympathise with the feast and the fireside, who
was most entitled to become a beggar on the open road. And
when, in the general emancipation of modern society, the Duchess says she does not see why she shouldn't play leapfrog, or the
Dean declares that he sees no valid canonical reason why he
should not stand on his head, we may say to these persons with
patient benevolence: "Defer, therefore, the operation you contemplate until you have realised by ripe reflection what principle or
prejudice you are violating. Then play leapfrog and stand on your
head and the Lord be with you."

Among the traditions that are being thus attacked, not intelli-
gently but most unintelligently, is the fundamental human creation called the Household or the Home. That is a typical thing
which men attack, not because they can see through it, but
because they cannot see it at all. They beat at it blindly, in a
fashion entirely haphazard and opportunist; and many of them
would pull it down without even pausing to ask why it was ever
put up. It is true that only a few of them would have avowed this
object in so many words. That only proves how very blind and
blundering they are. But they have fallen into a habit of mere drift
and gradual detachment from family life; something that is often
merely accidental and devoid of any definite theory at all. But
though it is accidental it is none the less anarchical. And it is all the
more anarchical for not being anarchist. It seems to be largely
founded on individual irritation; an irritation which varies with
the individual. We are merely told that in this or that case a
particular temperament was tormented by a particular environment;

but nobody even explained how the evil arose, let alone whether the evil is really escaped. We are told that in this or that family Grandmamma talked a great deal of nonsense, which God knows is true; or that it is very difficult to have intimate intellectual relations with Uncle Gregory without telling him he is a fool, which is indeed the case. But nobody seriously considers the remedy, or even the malady; or whether the existing individualistic dissolution is a remedy at all. Much of this business began with the influence of Ibsen, a very powerful dramatist and an exceedingly feeble philosopher. I suppose that Nora of The Doll's House was intended to be an inconsequent person; but certainly her most inconsequent action was her last. She complained that she was not yet fit to look after children, and then proceeded to get as far as possible from the children, that she might study them more closely.

There is one simple test and type of this neglect of scientific thinking and the sense of a social rule; the neglect which has now left us with nothing but a welter of exceptions. I have read hundreds and thousands of times, in all the novels and newspapers of our epoch, certain phrases about the just right of the young to liberty, about the unjust claim of the elders to control, about the conception that all souls must be free or all citizens equal, about the absurdity of authority or the degradation of obedience. I am not arguing those matters directly at the moment. But what strikes me as astounding, in a logical sense, is that not one of these myriad novelists and newspaper-men ever seems to think of asking the next and most obvious question. It never seems to occur to them to enquire what becomes of the opposite obligation. If the child is free from the first to disregard the parent, why is not the parent free from the first to disregard the child? If Mr. Jones, Senior, and Mr. Jones, Junior, are only two free and equal citizens, why should one citizen sponge on another citizen for the first fifteen years of his life? Why should the elder Mr. Jones be expected to feed, clothe and shelter out of his own pocket another person who is entirely free of any obligations to him? If the bright young thing cannot be asked to tolerate her grandmother, who has become something of a bore, why should the grandmother or the mother have tolerated the bright young thing at a period of her life when she was by no means bright? Why did they laboriously look after her at a time when her contributions to the conversation were seldom epigrammatic and not often intelligible? Why should Jones Senior stand drinks and free meals to anybody so unpleasant as Jones Junior, especially in the immature phases of his existence? Why should he not throw the baby out of the window; or at any rate, kick the boy out of doors? It is obvious that we are dealing with a real relation, which may be equality, but is certainly not similarity.

Some social reformers try to evade this difficulty, I know, by some vague notions about the State or an abstraction called Education eliminating the parental function. But this, like many notions of solid scientific persons, is a wild illusion of the nature of mere moonshine. It is based on that strange new superstition, the idea of infinite resources of organisation. It is as if officials grew like grass or bred like rabbits. There is supposed to be an endless supply of salaried persons, and of salaries for them; and they are to undertake all that human beings naturally do for themselves; including the care of children. But men cannot live by taking in each other's baby-linen. They cannot provide a tutor for each citizen; who is to tutor the tutors? Men cannot be educated by machinery; and though there might be a Robot bricklayer or scavenger, there will never be a Robot schoolmaster or governess. The actual effect of this theory is that one harassed person has to look after a hundred children, instead of one normal person looking after a normal number of them. Normally that normal person is urged by a natural force, which costs nothing and does not require a salary; the force of natural affection for his young, which exists even among the animals. If you cut off that natural force, and substitute a paid bureaucracy, you are like a fool who should pay men to turn the wheel of his mill, because he refused to use wind or water which he could get for nothing. You are like a lunatic who should carefully water his garden with a watering-can, while holding up an umbrella to keep off the rain.

It is now necessary to recite these truisms; for only by doing so can we begin to get a glimpse of that *reason* for the existence of the family, which I began this essay by demanding. They were all familiar to our fathers, who believed in the links of kinship and also in the links of logic. To-day our logic consists mostly of missing links; and our family largely of absent members. But, anyhow, this is the right end at which to begin any such enquiry; and *not* at the tail-end or the fag-end of some private muddle, by which Dick has become discontented or Susan has gone off on her own. If Dick or Susan wish to destroy the family because they do not see the use of it, I say as I said in the beginning; if they do not see the use of it, they had much better preserve it. They have no business even to think of destroying it until they have seen the use of it.

But it has other uses, besides the obvious fact that it means a necessary social work being done for love when it cannot be done for money; and (one might almost dare to hint) presumably to be repaid with love since it is never repaid in money. On that simple side of the matter the general situation is easy to record. The existing and general system of society, subject in our own age and industrial culture to very gross abuses and painful problems, is nevertheless a normal one. It is the idea that the commonwealth is made up of a number of small kingdoms, of which a man and a woman become the king and queen and in which they exercise a reasonable authority, subject to the common sense of the common-wealth, until those under their care grow up to found similar kingdoms and exercise similar authority. This is the social structure of mankind, far older than all its records and more universal than any of its religions; and all attempts to alter it are mere talk and tomfoolery.

But the other advantage of the small group is now not so much neglected as simply not realised. Here again we have some extraor-dinary delusions spread all over the literature and journalism of our time. Those delusions now exist in such a degree that we may say, for all practical purposes, that when a thing has been stated about a thousand times as obviously true, it is almost certain to be obviously false. One such statement may be specially noted here. There is undoubtedly something to be said against domesticity and in favour of the general drift towards life in hotels, clubs, colleges, communal settlements and the rest; or for a social life organised on the plan of the great commercial systems of our time. But the truly extraordinary suggestion is often made that this escape from the home is an escape into greater freedom. The change is actually offered as favourable to liberty.

To anybody who can think, of course, it is exactly the opposite. The domestic division of human society is not perfect, being human. It does not achieve complete liberty; a thing somewhat difficult to do or even to define. But it is a mere matter of arithmetic that it puts a larger number of people in supreme control of something, and able to shape it to their personal liking, than do the vast organisations that rule society outside; whether those systems are legal or commercial or even merely social. Even if we were only considering the parents, it is plain that there are more parents than there are policemen or politicians or heads of big businesses or proprietors of hotels. As I shall suggest in a moment, the argument actually applies indirectly to the children as well as directly to the parents. But the main point is that the world *outside* the home is now under a rigid discipline and routine and it is only inside the home that there is really a place for individuality and liberty. Anyone stepping out of the front-door is obliged to step into a procession, all going the same way and to a great extent even obliged to wear the same uniform. Business, especially big business, is now organised like an army. It is, as some would say, a sort of mild militarism without bloodshed; as I should say, a militarism without the military virtues. But anyhow, it is obvious that a hundred clerks in a bank or a hundred waitresses in a teashop are more regimented and under rule than the same individuals when each has gone back to his or her own dwelling or lodging, hung with his or her favourite pictures or fragrant with his or her favourite cheap cigarettes. But this, which is so obvious in the commercial case, is no less true even in the social case. In practice, the pursuit of pleasure is merely the pursuit of fashion. The pursuit of fashion is merely the pursuit of convention; only that it happens to be a new convention. The jazz dances, the joy rides, the big pleasure parties and hotel entertainments, do not make any more provision for a *really* independent taste than did any of the fashions of the past. If a wealthy young lady wants to do what all the other wealthy young ladies are doing, she will find it great fun, simply because youth is fun and society is fun. She will enjoy being modern exactly as her Victorian grand-mother enjoyed being Victorian. And quite right too; but it is the enjoyment of convention, not the enjoyment of liberty. It is perfectly healthy for all young people of all historic periods to herd together, to a reasonable extent, and enthusiastically copy each other. But in that there is nothing particularly fresh and certainly nothing particularly free. The girl who likes shaving her head and powdering her nose and wearing short skirts will find the world organised for her and will march happily with the procession. But a girl who happened to like having her hair down to her heels or loading herself with barbaric gauds and trailing garments or (most awful of all) leaving her nose in its natural state—she will still be well advised to do these things on her own premises. If the Duchess does want to play leapfrog, she must not start suddenly leaping in the manner of a frog across the ballroom of the Babylon Hotel, when it is crowded with the fifty best couples professionally practising the very latest dance, for the instruction of society. The Duchess will find it easier to practise leapfrog to the admiration of her intimate friends in the old oak-panelled hall of Fitzdragon Castle. If the Dean must stand on his head, he will do it with more ease and grace in the calm atmosphere of the Deanery than by attempting to interrupt the programme of some social entertainment already organised for philanthropic purposes.

If there is this impersonal routine in commercial and even in social things, it goes without saying that it exists and always must exist in political and legal things. For instance, the punishments of the State must be sweeping generalisations. It is only the punish-ments of the home that can possibly be adapted to the individual case; because it is only there that the judge can know anything of the individual. If Tommy takes a silver thimble out of a work-basket, his mother may act very differently according as she knows that he did it for fun or for spite or to sell to somebody, or to get somebody into trouble. But if Tomkins takes a silver thimble out of a shop, the law not only can but must punish him according to the rule made for all shoplifters or stealers of silver. It is only the domestic discipline that can show any sympathy or especially any humour. I do not say that the family always does do this; but I say that the State never ought to attempt it. So that even if we consider the parents alone as independent princes, and the children merely as subjects, the relative freedom of the family can and often does work to the advantage of those subjects. But so long as the children are children, they will always be the subjects of somebody. The question is whether they are to be distributed naturally under their natural princes, as the old phrase went, who normally feel for them what nobody else will feel, a natural affection. It seems to me clear that this normal distribution gives the largest amount of liberty to the largest number of people.

My complaint of the anti-domestic drift is that it is unintelligent. People do not know what they are doing; because they do not know what they are undoing. There are a multitude of modern manifestations, from the largest to the smallest, ranging from a divorce to a picnic party. But each is a separate escape or evasion; and especially an evasion of the point at issue. People ought to decide in a philosophical fashion whether they desire the traditional social order or not; or if there is any particular alternative to be desired. As it is they treat the public question merely as a mess or medley of private questions. Even in being anti-domestic they are much too domestic in their test of domesticity. Each family considers only its own case and the result is merely narrow and negative. Each case is an exception to a rule that does not exist. The family, especially in the modern state, stands in need of considerable correction and reconstruction; most things do in the modern state. But the family mansion should be preserved or destroyed or rebuilt; it should not be allowed to fall to pieces brick by brick because nobody has any historic sense of the object of bricklaying. For instance, the architects of the restoration should rebuild the house with wide and easily opened doors, for the practice of the ancient virtue of hospitality. In other words, private property should be distributed with sufficiently decent equality to allow of a margin for festive intercourse. But the hospitality of a house will always be different from the hospitality of a hotel. And it will be different in being more individual, more independent, more interesting than the hospitality of a hotel. It is perfectly right that the young Browns and the young Robinsons should meet and mix and dance and make asses of themselves, according to the design of their Creator. But there will always be some difference between the Browns entertaining the Robinsons and the Robinsons entertaining the Browns. And it will be a difference to the advantage of variety, of personality, of the potentialities of the mind of man; or, in other words, of life, liberty and the pursuit of happiness.

PART TWO

THE POETRY OF
THE HOME

* * *

The human house is a paradox, for it is larger inside than out.

Fancies versus Fads

On the whole, I am rather less interested in what people do than in why they do it.

Illustrated London News, December 1, 1928

To me this whole strange world is homely, because in the heart of it there is a home.

The Ball and the Cross

The old-fashioned Englishman, like my father, sold houses for his living but filled his own house with his life.

Autobiography

A bird who never makes a nest is not a complete bird; a man who does not regard the home as more native even than the native land is not a complete man.

G.K.'s Weekly, June 30, 1928

Anyhow, that simple image of a house that is our home, that is rightly loved as our home, but of which we hardly know the best or the worst, and must always wait for the one and watch against the other.

George MacDonald and His Wife
Introduction by Greville M. MacDonald, p. 11

Many of us live publicly with featureless public puppets, images of the small public abstractions. It is when we pass our own private gate, and open our own secret door, that we step into the land of the giants.

Charles Dickens

It is right that men should have houses, right that they should have land, right that they should have laws to protect the land; but all these things are only machinery to make leisure for the labouring soul. The house is only a stage set up by stage carpenters for the acting of what Mr. W. B. Yeats has called "the drama of the home." All the most dramatic things happen at home, from being born to being dead. What a man thinks about these things is his life: and to substitute for them a bustle of electioneering and legislation is to wander about among screens and pulleys on the wrong side of pasteboard scenery; and never to act the play. And that play is always a miracle play; and the name of its hero is Everyman.

Irish Impressions

Homesick at Home

One, seeming to be a traveller, came to me and said, "What is the shortest journey from one place to the same place?"

The sun was behind his head, so that his face was illegible.

"Surely," I said, "to stand still."

"That is no journey at all," he replied. "The shortest journey from one place to the same place is round the world." And he was gone.

White Wynd had been born, brought up, married and made the father of a family in the White Farmhouse by the river. The river enclosed it on three sides like a castle: on the fourth side there were stables and beyond that a kitchen-garden and beyond that an orchard and beyond that a low wall and beyond that a road and beyond that a pinewood and beyond that a cornfield and beyond that slopes meeting the sky, and beyond that—but we must not catalogue the whole earth, though it is a great temptation. White Wynd had known no other home but this. Its walls were the world to him and its roof the sky.

This is what makes his action so strange.

In his later years he hardly ever went outside the door. And as he grew lazy he grew restless: angry with himself and everyone. He found himself in some strange way weary of every moment and hungry for the next.

His heart had grown stale and bitter towards the wife and children whom he saw every day, though they were five of the good faces of the earth. He remembered, in glimpses, the days of his toil and strife for bread, when, as he came home in the

Chesterton wrote this story in 1896, when he was 22.

evening, the thatch of his home burned with gold as though angels were standing there. But he remembered it as one remembers a dream.

Now he seemed to be able to see other homes, but not his own. That was merely a house. Prose had got hold of him: the sealing of the eyes and the closing of the ears.

At last something occurred in his heart: a volcano; an earthquake; an eclipse; a daybreak; a deluge; an apocalypse. We might pile up colossal words, but we should never reach it.

Eight hundred times the white daylight had broken across the bare kitchen as the little family sat at breakfast. And the eight hundred and first time the father paused with the cup he was passing in his hand.

"That green cornfield through the window," he said dreamily, "shining in the sun. Somehow, somehow it reminds me of a field outside my own home."

"Your own home?" cried his wife. "This is your home."

White Wynd rose to his feet, seeming to fill the room. He stretched forth his hand and took a staff. He stretched it forth again and took a hat. The dust came in clouds from both of them.

"Father," cried one child. "Where are you going?"

"Home," he replied.

"What can you mean? This is your home. What home are you going to?"

"To the White Farmhouse by the river."

"This is it."

He was looking at them very tranquilly when his eldest daughter caught sight of his face.

"Oh, he is mad!" she screamed, and buried her face in her hands.

He spoke calmly. "You are a little like my eldest daughter," he said. "But you haven't got the look, no, not the look which is a welcome after work."

"Madam," he said, turning to his thunderstruck wife with a stately courtesy. "I thank you for your hospitality, but indeed I fear I have trespassed on it too long. And my home—"

"Father, father, answer me! Is not this your home?"

The old man waved his stick.

"The rafters are cobwebbed, the walls are rain-stained. The doors bind me, the rafters crush me. There are littlenesses and bickerings and heartburnings here behind the dusty lattices where I have dozed too long. But the fire roars and the door stands open. There is bread and raiment, fire and water and all the crafts and mysteries of love. There is rest for heavy feet on the matted floor, and for starved heart in the pure faces, far away at the end of the world, in the house where I was born."

"Where, where?"

"In the White Farmhouse by the river."

And he passed out of the front door, the sun shining on his face.

And the other inhabitants of the White Farmhouse stood staring at each other.

White Wynd was standing on the timber bridge across the river, with the world at his feet.

And a great wind came flying from the opposite edge of the sky (a land of marvellous pale golds) and met him. Some may know what that first wind outside the door is to a man. To this man it seemed that God had bent back his head by the hair and kissed him on the forehead.

He had been weary with resting, without knowing that the whole remedy lay in sun and wind and his own body. Now he half believed that he wore the seven-leagued boots.

He was going home. The White Farmhouse was behind every wood and beyond every mountain wall. He looked for it as we all look for fairyland, at every turn of the road. Only in one direction he never looked for it, and that was where, only a thousand yards behind him, the White Farmhouse stood up, gleaming with thatch and whitewash against the gusty blue of morning.

He looked at the dandelions and crickets and realised that he was gigantic. We are too fond of reckoning always by mountains. Every object is infinitely vast as well as infinitely small.

He stretched himself like one crucified in an uncontainable greatness.

"Oh God, who hast made me and all things, hear four songs of praise. One for my feet that Thou hast made strong and light upon Thy daisies. One for my head, which Thou hast lifted and crowned above the four corners of Thy heaven. One for my heart, which Thou hast made a heaven of angels singing Thy glory. And one for that pearl-tinted cloudlet far away above the stone pines on the hill."

He felt like Adam newly created. He had suddenly inherited all things, even the suns and stars.

Have you ever been out for a walk?

The story of the journey of White Wynd would be an epic. He was swallowed up in huge cities and forgotten: yet he came out on the other side. He worked in quarries, and in docks in country after country. Like a transmigrating soul, he lived a series of existences: a knot of vagabonds, a colony of workmen, a crew of sailors, a group of fishermen, each counted him a final fact in their lives, the great spare man with eyes like two stars, the stars of an ancient purpose.

But he never diverged from the line that girdles the globe.

On a mellow summer evening, however, he came upon the strangest thing in all his travels. He was plodding up a great dim down, that hid everything, like the dome of the earth itself.

Suddenly a strange feeling came over him. He glanced back at the waste of turf to see if there were any trace of boundary, for he felt like one who has just crossed the border of elfland. With his head a belfry of new passions, assailed with confounding memories, he toiled on the brow of the slope.

The setting sun was raying out a universal glory. Between him and it, lying low on the fields, there was what seemed to his swimming eyes a white cloud. No, it was a marble palace. No, it was the White Farmhouse by the river.

He had come to the end of the world. Every spot on earth is either the beginning or the end, according to the heart of man. That is the advantage of living on an oblate spheroid.

It was evening. The whole swell of turf on which he stood was turned to gold. He seemed standing in fire instead of grass. He stood so still that the birds settled on his staff.

All the earth and the glory of it seemed to rejoice round the madman's homecoming. The birds on their way to their nests knew him, Nature herself was in his secret, the man who had gone from one place to the same place.

But he leaned wearily on his staff. Then he raised his voice once more.

"O God, who hast made me and all things, hear four songs of praise. One for my feet, because they are sore and slow, now that they draw near the door. One for my head, because it is bowed and hoary, now that Thou crownest it with the sun. One for my heart, because Thou hast taught it in sorrow and hope deferred that it is the road that makes the home. And one for that daisy at my feet."

He came down over the hillside and into the pinewood. Through the trees he could see the red and gold sunset settling down among the white farm-buildings and the green apple-branches. It was his home now. But it could not be his home till he had gone out from it and returned to it. Now he was the Prodigal Son.

He came out of the pinewood and across the road. He surmounted the low wall and tramped through the orchard, through the kitchen garden, past the cattle-sheds. And in the stony courtyard he saw his wife drawing water.

The True Victorian Hypocrisy

The most essential educational product is Imagination. It is a wandering and even wild Imagination that all schools should chiefly instruct all school-children. For Imagination will teach them how to live a quiet and humdrum life.

This simple truth is now much neglected both by the fashionable and the old-fashioned. The way to make people contented is to make them creative, not to make them barren. I have no desire to lock people up in the parlour or the pantry, or deny them excursions and excitements. But it is strictly true that the larger is their Imagination, the less they will mind being locked up in the parlour; or, for that matter, in the coal-cellar. The child who can see the pictures in the fire will need less to see the pictures on the film. The man who can make up stories about the next-door neighbour will be the less dependent upon the next day's newspaper. So long as the minds of the poor were perpetually stirred and enlivened by ghost-stories, fairy-stories and legends of wild and wonderful things, they remained comparatively contented; possibly too contented, but still contented. The moment modern science and instruction stopped all these things, we had a Labour Question and the huge discontent of today. Both for good and evil, but especially for good, it is Imagination that keeps people quiet.

On the other hand, dull people always want excitement. Three-quarters of the real luxury or prodigality or profligacy, that is complained of just now, is due to the dullness of people who cannot imagine anything they do not experience. They are so miserably and dismally stupid that they actually have to do things. They are so poor in spirit that they have to have things. They have to have a flying-machine fitted up with every luxury, because they cannot send their souls up while flying a kite. They have to be in a racing car in order to believe that it really races. If this principle of the inner life were understood, we might today restore the sanity of civilization; and especially the poetry of the home.

I have already explained the object of these essays: it is to suggest a criticism of the new generation, that shall not merely suggest a complacency about my own generation. I am not a venerable Victorian objecting to plus-fours because they are different from peg-top trousers; but rather because they are not different enough. I should not complain of Oxford bags because they would have caused a mild surprise to Tom Brown at Oxford; but because they would have caused a mild surprise to almost anybody else. Alexander about to conquer the world, Alfred called upon to reconquer the Wessex kingdom, would certainly have received them with the fervent expression; "Not in these trousers." But it is less true of trifles than of serious truths. And this distinction especially applies to the blunders made by both generations about the fundamental human institution called the Family or the Household.

Half the trouble has arisen from two falsehoods; both of them current, not so much among those who are young enough to be troublesome, as among those who are old enough to know better. But in both generations there is a fixed idea; first, that what is called the Victorian Age was a golden age of domestic respectability and unity; and second, that there was something specially British about this solid and conventional family life. The very name of Queen Victoria is supposed in some way to stamp a sacred domesticity upon the period and the place, and to suggest that the idea of the family was at its highest or strongest in that age and in that country.

Both these ideas are quite false. The Victorian age was not one in which domesticity was at its highest. On the contrary, it was one at which domesticity was at its lowest. Half the present evil arises from the fact that the Victorians never did understand the virtues that they were vaguely supposed to defend. It is as if we were to say that the Catholic religion and the French monarchy were at their healthiest and most hopeful moment in the time of Voltaire. In the eighteenth century there were still bishops for Voltaire to make fun of, as in the nineteenth century there were still British matrons for Bernard Shaw to make fun of. But the matron no more embodied all that was meant by the Mother or the Madonna than an Abbé who was a sycophant was like an Abbot who was a saint. Mrs. Grundy was not really a good wife. We know it—because we never hear of Mr. Grundy. The Age of Mrs. Caudle's Curtain Lectures was not a noble summit of the noble sacrament of matrimony, towering over such monuments of marriage as the Taj Mahal and Charing Cross.

Now the Victorians were people who had *lost* the sense of the sacredness of the home. They still believed in the respectability of the home; but that is only another way of saying that they wanted to be respected by other people for reverencing what they did not really reverence. If we compare Victorian customs with the customs of the mass of mankind, the first thing that will strike us is that the purely domestic customs have been cut down to next to nothing; that they are duller and not brighter, colder and not more convivial. It is as if we were to say that because a Victorian banker generally disapproved of walking about naked, therefore his age was the golden age of glorious and flamboyant costume. The truth is that he had cut down costume to something meaner and more prosaic and less significant and important than costume had ever been before. He wore chimney-pot hats and mutton-chop whiskers because he thought less and not more about the possibilities of dress than did a gallant of Giorgione or a cavalier of Van Dyck. He preferred the chimney-pot hats as he preferred the chimney-pots to the Tower of Giotto. He tolerated the mutton-chop whiskers as he tolerated the mutton-chops; because he despised French cookery along with French culture. It is quite possible for a sympathetic imagination to see something manly and bracing about such a Philistine. But nobody, however sympathetic, would say that he understood the real meaning and possibilities of dress. Nor did he understand the meaning and possibilities of domesticity.

To begin at the beginning, we can invoke not merely the Christian but the Pagan idea of the family. The Pagans actually had Household Gods. They worshipped the house; they treated it as a temple; not metaphorically but literally. They sacrificed to gods who were conceived as present in that place, as distinct from other places. The gods presided over the most material and even grotesque features of domestic life. Now the more modern man of the Manchester School did not go on like that. He did it less than any other man of any other school. He was never tempted to bow down in worship to the door-scraper. He was never known to offer sacrifices to the umbrella-stand. But in the old heathen culture, the door-scraper would really have been an idol or the umbrella-stand a god. The umbrella-stand would at least have been dedicated to some deity who might be supposed to be interested in umbrellas; presumably Jupiter Pluvius. The door-scraper would have stood for a ceremony; and the ceremony of scraping the feet would have been one of purification or lustration; of discarding the dust and mire of the world. So far from the Victorian heavy father having these traditional feelings, he had them far less than the majority of mankind. The satirists who poked fun at him talked about his furniture as his household gods. But the satirists who poked fun at him paid him far too fine a compliment. He did not see any special significance, artistic or religious, in the Victorian furniture around him. He did not have mahogany tables because his dreams brooded on the dark red forests filled with the mysterious red men of the West. He did not have black horse-hair sofas because there rushed through his imagination a gallop of wild black horses. He did not even have cut-glass chandeliers to express his lofty meditations on the mystery of the Prism, which shatters the daylight into colours and stains the white radiance of eternity. Any inquiry addressed to a prosperous banker about the year 1855, upon these points, would substantiate my statement. The banker was not thinking poetically about his furniture; and he was not really thinking mystically about his home. He wrote letters to *The Times,* or read letters in *The Times,* in which was conventionally used the phrase, "The sanctity of the home." But he never really meant sanctity; he only meant security. I mean that he had not the idea of sacredness as compared with his own Christian forefathers, or his own Pagan forefathers or even his own Pagan contemporaries. When he went to China (which he did occasionally, in search of money) he saw a Pagan civilization very like the old Greek and Roman civilization. There also the house was a temple. There the religion of the family flowered or flamed into all sorts of fantastic expressions which the British merchant thought very ridiculous. Coloured lanterns glowed on days of domestic festivity and gorgeous paper dragons were waved like banners. But the Victorian did not want to wave any dragon. The Victorian was never known to dance about with a coloured lantern. The notion of the *poetry* of private life had faded from him and his generation, and seemed to be something not merely alien but barbarous. In order to understand what can be made of the religion of the family, he would have had to learn from a yellow Chinaman; the last thing he would be likely to do. True; he had something at home called Family Prayers; and the mere memory of them has murdered religion for two generations.

This was the real Victorian hypocrisy; at least, this was the real falsity of the Victorian claim. They did to some extent pose to their children and grandchildren as the traditionalists. But they had in fact been the great anti-traditionalists; and it was their time that destroyed a thousand traditions. They did sometimes quote Horace or Virgil about hearth and altar; but there was never any flame upon their altar, even if there were a dying fire upon their hearth. They did sometimes talk about household gods, as if their houses had been full of holy images. But in truth it was they and not their children, who were the iconoclasts. Nineteenth-century England had destroyed the last legends of the fireside, long before twentieth-century England had a chance of feeling the full poetry of the legend. The Philistines were the image breakers; they shattered the household gods and the patron saints. Puritanism combined with Industrialism threw away the Lares and Penates like the disused dolls of a dead infancy and went on to what was counted the manhood of the Manchester School; with what results we see today. And so completely did they dry up that fountain of fairy-tales which flows from China to Peru, that I shall now probably be charged with uttering a "paradox," because I say something so self-evident as that it is the homestead and the inner chamber, the dwelling-place of Imagination.

The generation in revolt fled from a cold hearth and a godless shrine. That is the historical fact that is really hidden by both sides in this controversy. It is supposed that they revolted against what their elders called religion and they called superstition; against what their elders called domesticity and they called drudgery. But those elders were not really religious; they were not even really domestic. This was notably the case in the English middle class, which puffed itself out with preposterous spiritual pride about its domesticity. It actually had the impudence to talk about French immorality; when the French sense of the family was twenty times stronger than the English. The English had their own special merits of sport and adventure; but they were definitely undomestic as compared with nearly everybody else. They exiled all their children to boarding-school; and thought any boy a milksop who admitted any affection for his mother. The chief reason for regarding a Frenchman as a fool (a thing essential to the national self-respect) was that he confessed to a certain respect for his mother. It was from *this* sort of chilly and half-inhabited house that the rebels escaped to conduct their revels in hotels and night-clubs. In my next essay I shall take them in their turn; and affectionately explain to them what fools they are, for doing anything of the sort.

The Wildness of Domesticity

In the course of this crude study we shall have to touch on what is called the problem of poverty, especially the dehumanised poverty of modern industrialism. But in this primary matter of the ideal the difficulty is not the problem of poverty, but the problem of wealth. It is the special psychology of leisure and luxury that falsifies life. Some experience of modern movements of the sort called "advanced" has led me to the conviction that they generally repose upon some experience peculiar to the rich. It is so with that fallacy of free love of which I have already spoken; the idea of sexuality as a string of episodes. That implies a long holiday in which to get tired of one woman, and a motor car in which to wander looking for others; it also implies money for maintenances. An omnibus conductor has hardly time to love his own wife, let alone other people's wives. And the success with which nuptial estrangements are depicted in modern "problem plays" is due to the fact that there is only one thing that a drama cannot depict — that is a hard day's work. I could give many other instances of this plutocratic assumption behind progressive fads. For instance, there is a plutocratic assumption behind the phrase "Why should woman be economically dependent upon man?" The answer is that among poor and practical people she isn't; except in the sense in which he is dependent upon her. A hunter has to tear his clothes; there must be somebody to mend them. A fisher has to catch fish; there must be somebody to cook them. It is surely quite clear that this modern notion that woman is a mere "pretty clinging parasite," "a plaything," etc., arose through the sombre contemplation of some rich banking family, in which the banker at least went to the city and pretended to do something,

76

while the banker's wife went to the Park and did not pretend to do anything at all. A poor man and his wife are a business partnership. If one partner in a firm of publishers interviews the authors while the other interviews the clerks, is one of them economically dependent? Was Hodder a pretty parasite clinging to Stoughton? Was Marshall a mere plaything for Snelgrove?

But of all the modern notions generated by mere wealth the worst is this: the notion that domesticity is dull and tame. Inside the home (they say) is dead decorum and routine; outside is adventure and variety. This is indeed a rich man's opinion. The rich man knows that his own house moves on vast and soundless wheels of wealth: is run by regiments of servants, by a swift and silent ritual. On the other hand, every sort of vagabondage or romance is open to him in the streets outside. He has plenty of money and can afford to be a tramp. His wildest adventure will end in a restaurant, while the yokel's tamest adventure may end in a police-court. If he smashes a window he can pay for it; if he smashes a man he can pension him. He can (like the millionaire in the story) buy an hotel to get a glass of gin. And because he, the luxurious man, dictates the tone of nearly all "advanced" and "progressive" thought, we have almost forgotten what a home really means to the overwhelming millions of mankind.

For the truth is, that to the moderately poor the home is the only place of liberty. Nay, it is the only place of anarchy. It is the only spot on the earth where a man can alter arrangements suddenly, make an experiment or indulge in a whim. Everywhere else he goes he must accept the strict rules of the shop, inn, club, or museum that he happens to enter. He can eat his meals on the floor in his own house if he likes. I often do it myself; it gives a curious, childish, poetic, picnic feeling. There would be considerable trouble if I tried to do it in an A.B.C. tea-shop. A man can wear a dressing-gown and slippers in his house; while I am sure that this would not be permitted at the Savoy, though I never actually tested the point. If you go to a restaurant you must drink some of the wines on the wine list, all of them if you insist, but certainly some of them. But if you have a house and garden you can try to make hollyhock tea or convolvulus wine if you like. For a plain, hard-working man the home is not the one tame place in the world of adventure. It is the one wild place in the world of rules and set tasks. The home is the one place where he can put the carpet on the ceiling or the slates on the floor if he wants to. When a man spends every night staggering from bar to bar or from music-hall to music-hall, we say that he is living an irregular life. But he is not; he is living a highly regular life, under the dull, and often oppressive laws of such places. Sometimes he is not allowed even to sit down in the bars; and frequently he is not allowed to sing in the music-halls. Hotels may be defined as places where you are forced to dress; and theatres may be defined as places where you are forbidden to smoke. A man can only picnic at home.

Now I take, as I have said, this small human omnipotence, this possession of a definite cell or chamber of liberty, as the working model for the present inquiry. Whether we can give every Englishman a free home of his own or not, at least we should desire it; and he desires it. For the moment we speak of what he wants, not of what he expects to get. He wants, for instance, a separate house; he does not want a semi-detached house. He may be forced in the commercial race to share one wall with another man. Similarly he might be forced in a three-legged race to share one leg with another man; but it is not so that he pictures himself in his dreams of elegance and liberty. Again, he does not desire a flat. He can eat and sleep and praise God in a flat; he can eat and sleep and praise God in a railway train. But a railway train is not a house; because it is a house on wheels. And a flat is not a house; because it is a house on stilts. An idea of earthy contact and foundation, as well as an idea of separation and independence, is a part of this instructive human picture.

I take, then, this one institution as a test. As every normal man desires a woman, and children born of a woman, every normal man desires a house of his own to put them into. He does not merely want a roof above him and a chair below him; he wants an objective and a visible kingdom; a fire at which he can cook what food he likes, a door he can open to what friends he chooses. This is the normal appetite of men; I do not say there are not exceptions. There may be saints above the need and philanthropists below it. Opalstein, now he is a duke, may have got used to more than this; and when he was a convict may have got used to less. But the normality of the thing is enormous. To give nearly everybody ordinary houses would please nearly everybody; that is what I assert without apology. Now in modern England (as you eagerly point out) it is very difficult to give nearly everybody houses. Quite so; I merely set up the *desideratum;* and ask the reader to leave it standing there while he turns with me to a consideration of what really happens in the social wars of our time.

On Household Gods and Goblins

Sometime ago I went with some children to see Maeterlinck's fine and delicate fairy play about the Blue Bird that brought everybody happiness. For some reason or other it did not bring me happiness, and even the children were not quite happy. I will not go so far as to say that the Blue Bird was a Blue Devil, but it left us in something seriously like the blues. The children were partly dissatisfied with it because it did not end with a Day of Judgment; because it was never revealed to the hero and heroine that the dog had been faithful and the cat faithless. For children are innocent and love justice; while most of us are wicked and naturally prefer mercy.

But there was something wrong about the Blue Bird, even from my more mature and corrupt point of view. There were several incidental things I did not like. I did not like the sentimental passage about the love-affair of two babes unborn; it seemed to me a piece of what may be called bad Barrie; and logically it spoilt the only meaning of the scene, which was that the babes were looking to all earthly experiences as things inconceivable. I was not convinced when the boy exclaimed, "There are no dead," for I am by no means sure that he (or the dramatist) knew what he meant by it. "I heard a voice from Heaven cry: Blessed are the dead. . . . " I do not know all that is meant in that; but I think the person who said it knew. But there was something more continuous and clinging in the whole business which left me vaguely restless. And I think the nearest to a definition was that I felt as if the poet was condescending to everything; condescending to pots and pans and birds and beasts and babies.

The one part of the business which I really felt to be original and suggestive was the animation of all the materials of the household, as if with familiar spirits; the spirit of fire, the spirit of water and the rest. And even here I felt a faint difference which moved me to an imaginary comparison. I wonder that none of our medievalists has made a Morality or allegorical play founded on the Canticle of Saint Francis, which speaks somewhat similarly of Brother Fire and Sister Water. It would be a real exercise in Gothic craftsmanship and decoration to make these symbolic figures at once stiff and fantastic. If nobody else does this I shall be driven to spoil the idea myself, as I have spoiled so many other rather good ideas in my time. But the point of the parallel at the moment is merely this: that the medieval poet does strike me as having felt about fire like a child while the modern poet felt about it like a man talking to children.

Few and simple as are the words of the older poem, it does somehow convey to me that when the poet spoke of fire as untameable and strong, he felt it as something that might conceivably be feared as well as loved. I do not think the modern poet feared the nursery fire as a child who loved it might fear it. And this elemental quality in the real primitives brought back to my mind something I have always felt about this conception, which is the really fine conception in the Blue Bird: I mean something like that which the heathens embodied in the images of the household gods. The household gods, I believe, were carved out of wood; which makes them even more like the chairs and tables.

The nomad and the anarchist accuse the domestic ideal of being merely timid and prim. But this is not because they themselves are bolder or more vigorous, but simply because they do not know it well enough to know how bold and vigorous it is. The most nomadic life to-day is not the life of the desert but of the industrial cities. It is by a very accurate accident that we talk about a Street-Arab; and the Semitic description applies to not a few gutter-snipes whose gilded chariots have raised them above the gutter. They live in clubs and hotels and are often simply ignorant, I might almost say innocent, of the ancient life of the family, and certainly of the ancient life on the farm.

When a townsman first sees these things directly and intimately, he does not despise them as dull but rather dreads them as wild, as he sometimes takes a tame cow for a wild bull. The most obvious example is the hearth which is the heart of the home. A man living in the lukewarm air of centrally-heated hotels may be said to have never seen fire. Compared to him the housewife at the fireside is an Amazon wrestling with a flaming dragon. The same moral might be drawn from the fact that the watch-dog fights while the wild dog often runs away. Of the husband, as of the house-dog, it may often be said that he has been tamed into ferocity.

This is especially true of the sort of house represented by the country cottage. It is only in theory that the things are petty and prosaic; a man realistically experiencing them will feel them to be things big and baffling and involving a heavy battle with nature. When we read about cabbages or cauliflowers in the papers, and especially the comic papers, we learn to think of them as commonplace. But if a man of any imagination will merely consent to walk round the kitchen-garden for himself, and really looks at the cabbages and cauliflowers, he will feel at once that they are vast and elemental things like the mountains in the clouds. He will feel something almost monstrous about the size and solidity of the things swelling out of that small and tidy patch of ground. There are moods in which that everyday English kitchen plot will affect him as men are affected by the reeking wealth and toppling rapidity of tropic vegetation; the green bubbles and crawling branches of a nightmare.

But whatever his mood, he will see that things so large and work so laborious cannot possibly be merely trivial. His reason no less than his imagination will tell him that the fight here waged between the family and the field is of all things the most primitive and fundamental. If that is not poetical, nothing is poetical, and certainly not the dingy Bohemianism of the artists in the towns. But the point for the moment is that even by the purely artistic test the same truth is apparent. An artist looking at these things with a free and a fresh vision will at once appreciate what I mean by calling them wild rather than tame. It is true of fire, of water, of vegetation, of half a hundred other things. If a man reads about a pig, he will think of something comic and commonplace, chiefly because the word "pig" sounds comic and commonplace. If he looks at a real pig in a real pigsty, he will have the sense of something too large to be alive, like a hippopotamus at the Zoo.

This is not a coincidence or a sophistry; it rests on the real and living logic of things. The family is itself a wilder thing than the State; if we mean by wildness that it is born of will and choice as elemental and emancipated as the wind. It has its own laws, as the wind has; but properly understood it is infinitely less subservient than things are under the elaborate and mechanical regulations of legalism. Its obligations are love and loyalty, but these are things quite capable of being in revolt against merely human laws; for merely human law has a great tendency to become merely inhuman law. It is concerned with events that are in the moral world what cyclones and earthquakes are in the material world.

People are not born in an infant-school any more than they die in an undertaker's shop. These prodigies are private things; and take place in the tiny theatre of the home. The public systems, the large organisation, are a mere machinery for the transport and distribution of things; they do not touch the intrinsic nature of the things themselves. If a birthday present is sent from one family to another all the legal system, and even all that we call the social system, is only concerned with the present so long as it is a parcel. Nearly all our modern sociology might be called the philosophy of parcels. For that matter, nearly all our modern descriptions of Utopia or the Great State might be called the paradise of postmen. It is in the inner chamber that the parcel becomes a present; that it explodes, so to speak, into its own radiance and real popularity; and it is equally true, so far as that argument is concerned, whether it is a bon-bon or a bomb. The essential message is always a personal message; the important business is always private business. And this is, of course, especially with the first of all birthday presents which presents itself at birth; and it is no exaggeration to talk of a bomb as the symbol of a baby. Of course, the same is true of the tragic as of the beatific acts of the domestic drama; of the spadework of the struggle for life or the Damoclean sword of death.

The defence of domesticity is not that it is always happy, or even that it is always harmless. It is rather that it does involve, like all heroic things, the possibilities of calamity and even of crime. Old Mother Hubbard may find that the cupboard is bare; she may even find a skeleton in the cupboard. All that is involved here is the insistence on the true case for this intimate type of association; that in itself it is certainly not commonplace and most certainly is not conventional. The conventions belong rather to those wider worldly organisations which are now set up as rivals to it; to the club, to the school and above all to the State. You cannot have a successful club without rules; but a family will really do without rules exactly in proportion as it is a successful family. What somebody said about the songs of a people could be said much more truly about the jokes of a household. And a joke is in its nature a wild and spontaneous thing; even the modern fanaticism for organisation has never really attempted to organise laughter like a chorus. Therefore, we may truly say that these external emblems or examples of something grotesque and extravagant about our private possessions are not mere artistic exercises in the incongruous; they are not, as the phrase goes, mere paradoxes. They are really related to the aboriginal nature of the institution itself and the idea that is behind it. The real family is something as wild and elemental as a cabbage.

To Frances

. . . I am looking over the sea and endeavouring to reckon up the state I have to offer you. As far as I can make out my equipment for starting on a journey to fairyland consists of the following items.

1st. A Straw Hat. The oldest part of this admirable relic shows traces of pure Norman work. The vandalism of Cromwell's soldiers has left us little of the original hat-band.

2nd. A Walking Stick, very knobby and heavy: admirably fitted to break the head of any denizen of Suffolk who denies that you are the noblest of ladies, but of no other manifest use.

3rd. A Copy of Walt Whitman's poems, once nearly given to Salter, but quite forgotten. It has his name in it still with an affectionate inscription from his sincere friend Gilbert Chesterton. I wonder if he will ever have it.

4th. A number of letters from a young lady, containing everything good and generous and loyal and holy and wise that isn't in Walt Whitman's poems.

5th. An unwieldy sort of pocket knife, the blades mostly having an edge of a more varied and picturesque outline than is provided by the prosaic cutler. The chief element however is a thing "to take stones out of a horse's hoof." What a beautiful sensation of security it gives one to reflect that if one should ever have money enough to buy a horse and should happen to buy one and the horse should happen to have a stone in his hoof—that one is ready; one stands prepared, with a defiant smile!

6th. Passing from the last miracle of practical foresight, we come to a box of matches. Every now and then I strike one of these, because fire is beautiful and burns your fingers. Some people think this a waste of matches: the same people who object to the building of Cathedrals.

7th. About three pounds in gold and silver, the remains of one Mr. Unwin's bursts of affection: those explosions of spontaneous love for myself, which, such is the perfect order and harmony of his mind, occur at startlingly exact intervals of time.

8th. A book of Children's Rhymes, in manuscript, called the "Weather Book" about 3/4 finished, and destined for Mr. Nutt. I have been working at it fairly steadily, which I think jolly creditable under the circumstances. One can't put anything interesting in it. They'll understand those things when they grow up.

9th. A tennis racket—nay, start not. It is a part of the new régime, and the only new and neat-looking thing in the Museum. We'll soon mellow it—like the straw hat. My brother and I are teaching each other lawn tennis.

10th. A soul, hitherto idle and omnivorous but now happy enough to be ashamed of itself.

11th. A body equally idle and quite equally omnivorous, absorbing tea, coffee, claret, sea-water and oxygen to its own perfect satisfaction. It is happiest swimming, I think, the sea being about a convenient size.

12th. A Heart—mislaid somewhere. And that is about all the property of which an inventory can be made at present. After all, my tastes are stoically simple. A straw hat, a stick, a box of matches and some of his own poetry. What more does man require? . . .

When we set up a house, darling (honeysuckle porch, yew clipt hedge, bees, poetry and eight shillings a week), I think you will have to do the shopping. Particularly at Felixstowe. There was a great and glorious man who said, "Give us the luxuries of life and we will dispense with the necessities." That I think would be a splendid motto to write (in letters of brown gold) over the porch of our hypothetical home. There will be a sofa for you, for example, but no chairs, for I prefer the floor. There will be a select store of chocolate-creams (to make you do the Carp with) and the rest will be bread and water. We will each retain a suit of evening dress for great occasions, and at other times clothe ourselves in the skins of wild beasts (how pretty you would look) which would fit your taste in furs and be economical.

I have sometimes thought it would be very fine to take an ordinary house, a very poor, commonplace house in West Kensington, say, and make it symbolic. Not artistic—Heaven—O Heaven forbid. My blood boils when I think of the affronts put by knock-kneed pictorial epicures on the strong, honest, ugly, patient shapes of necessary things: the brave old bones of life. There are aesthetic pottering prigs who can look on a saucepan without one tear of joy or sadness: mongrel decadents that can see no dignity in the honourable scars of a kettle. So they concentrate all their house decoration on coloured windows that nobody looks out of, and vases of lilies that everybody wishes out of the way. No: my idea (which is much cheaper) is to make a house really *allegoric:* really explain its own essential meaning. Mystical or ancient sayings should be inscribed on every object, the more prosaic the object the better; and the more coarsely and rudely the inscription was traced the better. "Hast thou sent the Rain upon the Earth?" should be inscribed on the Umbrella-Stand: perhaps on the Umbrella. "Even the Hairs of your Head are all numbered" would give a tremendous significance to one's hairbrushes: the words about "living water" would reveal the music and sanctity of the sink: while "Our God is a consuming Fire" might be written over the kitchen-grate, to assist the mystic musings of the cook—Shall we ever try that experiment, dearest. Perhaps not, for no words would be golden enough for the tools you had to touch: you would be beauty enough for one house. . . .

By all means let us have bad things in our dwelling and make them good things. I shall offer no objection to your having an occasional dragon to dinner, or a penitent Griffin to sleep in the spare bed. The image of you taking a Sunday school of little Devils is pleasing. They will look up, first in savage wonder, then in vague respect; they will see the most glorious and noble lady that ever lived since their prince tempted Eve, with a halo of hair and great heavenly eyes that seem to make the good heart of things almost too terribly simple and naked for the sons of flesh: and as they gaze, their tails will drop off, and their wings will sprout: and they will become Angels in six lessons. . . .

I cannot profess to offer any elaborate explanation of your mother's disquiet but I admit it does not wholly surprise me. You see I happen to know one factor in the case, and one only, of which you are wholly ignorant. I know you. . . . I know one thing which has made me feel strange before your mother—I know the value of what I take away. I feel (in a weird moment) like the Angel of Death.

You say you want to talk to me about death: my views about death are bright, brisk and entertaining. When Azrael takes a soul it may be to other and brighter worlds: like those whither you and I go together. The transformation called Death may be something as beautiful and dazzling as the transformation called Love. It may make the dead man "happy," just as your mother knows that you are happy. But none the less it is a transformation, and sad sometimes for those left behind. A mother whose child is dying can hardly believe that in the inscrutable Unknown there is anyone who can look to it as well as she. And if a mother cannot trust her child easily to God Almighty, shall I be so mean as to be angry because she cannot trust it easily to me? I tell you I have stood before your mother and felt like a thief. I know you are not going to part: neither physically, mentally, morally nor spiritually. But she sees a new element in your life, wholly from outside—is it not natural, given her temperament, that you should find her perturbed? Oh, dearest, dearest Frances, let us always be very gentle to older people. Indeed, darling, it is not they who are the tyrants, but we. They may interrupt our building in the scaffolding stages: we turn their house upside down when it is their final home and rest. Your mother would certainly have worried if you had been engaged to the Archangel Michael (who, indeed, is bearing his disappointment very well): how much more when you are engaged to an aimless, tactless, reckless, unbrushed, strange-hatted, opinionated scarecrow who has suddenly walked into the vacant place. I could have prophesied her unrest: wait and she will calm down all right, dear. God comfort her: I dare not. . . .

One pleasant Sunday afternoon Lucian said to him, "I am going to take you to see the Bloggs." "The what?" said the unhappy man. "The Bloggs," said the other, darkly. Naturally assuming that it was the name of a public-house he reluctantly followed his friend. He came to a small front-garden; if it was a public house it was not a businesslike one. They raised the latch— they rang the bell (if the bell was not in the close time just then). No flower in the pots winked. No brick grinned. No sign in Heaven or earth warned him. The birds sang on the trees. He went in.

The first time he spent an evening at the Bloggs there was no one there. That is to say there was a worn but fiery little lady in a grey dress who didn't approve of "catastrophic solutions of social problems." That, he understood, was Mrs. Blogg. There was a long, blonde, smiling young person who seemed to think him quite off his head and who was addressed as Ethel. There were two people whose meaning and status he couldn't imagine, one of whom had a big nose and the other hadn't. . . . Lastly, there was a Juno-like creature in a tremendous hat who eyed all the time half wildly, like a shying horse, because he said he was quite happy. . . .

But the second time he went there he was plumped down on a sofa beside a being of whom he had a vague impression that brown hair grew at intervals all down her like a caterpillar. Once in the course of conversation she looked straight at him and he said to himself as plainly as if he had read it in a book: "If I had anything to do with this girl I should go on my knees to her: if I spoke with her she would never deceive me: if I depended on her she would never deny me: if I loved her she would never play with me: if I trusted her she would never go back on me: if I remembered her she would never forget me. I may never see her again. Goodbye." It was all said in a flash: but it was all said. . . .

Two years, as they say in the playbills, is supposed to elapse. And here is the subject of this memoir sitting on a balcony above the sea. The time, evening. He is thinking of the whole bewildering record of which the foregoing is a brief outline: he sees how far he has gone wrong and how idle and wasteful and wicked he has often been: how miserably unfitted he is for what he is called upon to be. Let him now declare it and hereafter for ever hold his peace.

But there are four lamps of thanksgiving always before him. The first is for his creation out of the same earth with such a woman as you. The second is that he has not, with all his faults, "gone after strange women." You cannot think how a man's self-restraint is rewarded in this. The third is that he has tried to love everything alive: a dim preparation for loving you. And the fourth is—but no words can express that. Here ends my previous existence. Take it: it led me to you.

PART THREE

MEN & WOMEN, HUSBANDS & WIVES

* * *

Common sense, that extinct branch of psychology.

"The Unpsychological Age", in Sidelights

For in all legends men have thought of women as sublime separately, but horrible in a crowd.

What's Wrong with the World

Men are men, but Man is a woman.

The Napoleon of Notting Hill

The relations of the sexes are mystical, are and ought to be irrational. Every gentleman should take off his head to a lady.

Notebook

Keeping to one woman is a small price for so much as seeing one woman.

Orthodoxy

Justice, or rather human equality, does demand that a man and a woman should alike have social dignity and social power. It does not in the least demand acceptance of a certain psychological dogma about the effects of sex. Of course these people never state their own dogma clearly; but it might be stated clearly, somewhat thus: that sex only affects sexuality, and that sex can cause no other variation in social functions. This is very far from being self-evident; and is quite the reverse of a rational deduction from human equality. I believe it to be quite untrue; and its professors cannot prove it to be true.

The New Witness, September 5, 1919

The chief difference between the average man and the average woman is simply that the woman is a ruler and the man is not.

Illustrated London News, January 27, 1906

I remember an artistic and eager lady asking me in her grand green drawing-room whether I believed in comradeship between the sexes, and why not. I was driven back on offering the obvious and sincere answer "Because if I were to treat you for two minutes like a comrade you would turn me out of the house."

What's Wrong with the World

Many a man has been lucky in marrying the woman he loves. But he is luckier in loving the woman he marries.

The Princess in *The Surprise*

. . . dreamy old bachelor notion—that notion that the unity of marriage, the being one flesh, has something to do with being perfectly happy, or being perfectly good, or even with being perfectly and continuously affectionate! I tell you, an ordinary honest man is part of his wife even when he wishes he wasn't. I tell you, an ordinary good woman is part of her husband even when she wishes him at the bottom of the sea. I tell you that, whether the two people are for the moment friendly or angry, happy or unhappy, the Thing marches on, the great four-footed Thing, the quadruped of the home. They are a nation, a society, a machine. I tell you they are one flesh, even when they are not one spirit.

Early Notebooks

There is only one timid sort of man that is not afraid of women.

What's Wrong with the World

There is no hope for men who do not boast that their wives bully them.

Alarms and Discursions

The two things that a healthy person hates most between heaven and hell are a woman who is not dignified and a man who is.

All Things Considered

Laughter and love are everywhere. The cathedrals, built in the ages that loved God, are full of blasphemous grotesques. The mother laughs continually at the child, the lover laughs continually at the lover, the wife at the husband, the friend at the friend.

The Napoleon of Notting Hill

It is true that all sensible women think all studious men mad. It is true, for the matter of that, all women of any kind think all men of any kind mad. But they do not put it in telegrams any more than they wire to you that grass is green or God all-merciful. These things are truisms and often private ones at that.

The Club of Queer Trades

The Marchioness really has all the characteristics, the entirely heroic characteristics, which make a woman respected by a man. She is female—that is, she is at once incurably candid and incurably loyal, she is full of terrible common sense, she expects little pleasure for herself and yet she can enjoy bursts of it; above all, she is physically timid and yet she can face anything.

Introduction to *The Old Curiosity Shop*

Suddenly in the Midst

Suddenly in the midst of friends,
Of brothers known to me more and more,
And their secrets, histories, tastes, hero-worships,
Schemes, love-affairs, known to me
    Suddenly I felt lonely.
Felt like a child in a field with no more games to play
Because I have not a lady
    to whom to send my thought at that hour
    that she might crown my piece.

Madonna Mia

About Her whom I have not yet met
    I wonder what she is doing
    Now, at this sunset hour,
Working perhaps, or playing, worrying or laughing,
Is she making tea, or singing a song, or writing,
  or praying, or reading
Is she thoughtful, as I am thoughtful
    Is she looking now out of the window
    As I am looking out of the window?

On Love

There used to be, and possibly is, a mysterious institution for young ladies known as a finishing-school. The chief case against it was that, in certain instances, it meant finishing an education without ever beginning it. In any case, this is what is the matter with a great many modern institutions, and with none more than those delivering judgment on the history of feminine education and generally of feminine affairs. The curse of nearly all such judgments is the journalistic curse of having heard the latest news; that is, of having heard the end of the story without having even heard of the beginning. We talk of people not knowing the A B C of a subject, but the trouble with these people is that they do know the X Y Z of a subject without knowing the A B C.

This morning I read an article in a very serious magazine in which the writer quoted the remark of Byron that a certain sort of romantic love "is woman's whole existence." The writer then said that the first people who ever challenged this view were the revolutionary Suffragettes at the end of the nineteenth century. The truth is that the first people who ever maintained this view were the revolutionary Romantics at the beginning of the nineteenth century. The habit of giving to romantic love this extravagant and exclusive importance in human life was itself an entirely modern and revolutionary thing, and dates from the romantic movement commonly traced to Rousseau, but I think much more truly to be traced to the influence of the German sentimentalists. Most people who curse Rousseau have never read Rousseau, or have only read the *Confessions* and not the *Contrat Social.* The critics read the *Confessions,* if only to condemn them; because the critics themselves are modern romantics and sentimentalists; men

who like Confessions and dislike Contracts. The critics hate or
avoid the *Contrat Social,* not because it is sloppy and sentimental
(for it is not), but because it is hard and clear and lucid and logical.
Rousseau had his emotional weaknesses as an individual, like
other individuals, but he was not an eighteenth-century philosopher for nothing. What the moderns dislike about him is not the
silliness of his confessions, but the solidity of his convictions,
and the fact that, like the old theologians, he could hold general
ideas in a hard-and-fast fashion. When it comes to defining his
fundamentals, Rousseau is as definite as Calvin. They were both
ruthless theorists from Geneva, though one preached the theory
of pessimism and the other the theory of optimism. I am not
maintaining that I agree with either, but Rousseau would be as
useful as Calvin, in teaching some of his critics how to criticize.

But Rousseau is a parenthesis. Wherever the real Romantic
Movement came from, whether from the German forests or the
Genevan lake, it was a recent and revolutionary business as compared
with history as a whole. But it is obvious that the ordinary modern
critic is entirely ignorant of history as a whole. He knows that
his mother read Tennyson and his grandmother read Byron. Beyond
that, he can imagine nothing whatever; he supposes that his great-
great-grandmothers and their great-great-great-grandmothers had
gone on reading Byron from the beginning of the world. He
imagines that Byron, who was a disinherited and disreputable
rebel to the last, has been an established and conventional authority
from the first. He therefore supposes that all women, in all ages,
would have accepted the prehistoric Byronic commandment: that
the Byronic sort of romantic passion was the sole concern of
their lives. Yet it is certain that women have had a great many
other concerns, and have been attached to a great many other
convictions. They have been priestesses, prophetesses, empresses,
queens, abbesses, mothers, great housewives, great letter-writers,
lunatics founding sects, blue-stockings keeping salons, and all sorts
of things. If you had said to Deborah the mother in Israel, or
Hypatia the Platonist of Alexandria, or Catherine of Siena, or
Joan of Arc, or Isabella of Spain, or Maria Theresa of Austria, or

even to Hannah More or Joanna Southcott, that Byronic love was
"woman's whole existence," they would all have been very indignant and most of them flown into a towering passion. They
would have asked in various ways whether there was no such
thing as honour, no such thing as duty, no such thing as glory, no
such thing as great studies or great enterprises, no such thing as
normal functions and necessary labours; incidentally, we may add,
no such thing as babies. They differed a great deal in their type of
vocation and even in their theory of virtue, but they all had some
theory of virtue that went a little further than that. Up to a
particular moment in the eighteenth century, practically every
thinking person would have accepted the colossal common sense
expressed by a French poet of the seventeenth century: *"L'amour
est un plaisir; l'honneur est un devoir."*[1]

Then came the extreme emphasis on romance among the
Victorians; for the Victorians were not notable for their emphasis
on virtue, but for their emphasis on romance. But Queen Victoria
lived so long, and the Victorian Age was such an unconscionably
long time dying, that by the time Mr. Bernard Shaw and others
began what they called a realistic revolt against romance, the
sentimental German movement seemed to be not only as old as
Victoria, but as old as Boadicea. It is highly typical, for instance,
that Mr. Bernard Shaw, in one of his earliest criticisms, complained
of the convention according to which anybody was supposed to
have "penetrated into the Holy of Holies" so long as he was
content to say that "Love is Enough." But, as a matter of fact, the
very phrase "Love is Enough" did not come to him from any
conventional or classical authority; not even from any conventional or conservative Victorian. It came from a book by a Social-
ist and Revolutionist like himself; from a book recently published
by William Morris, who held then the exact position that Mr.
Shaw himself holds now: the position of the Grand Old Man of
Socialism.

Of course, the anti-romantic movement led by Shaw, like the

---

[1] "Love is a pleasure; honor is a duty."

romantic movement led by Byron, had gone forward blindly and blundered in every sort of way. The modern world seems to have no notion of preserving different things side by side, of allowing its proper and proportionate place to each, of saving the whole varied heritage of culture. It has no notion except that of simplifying something by destroying nearly everything; whether it be Rousseau breaking up kingdoms in the name of reason, or Byron breaking up families in the name of romance, or Shaw breaking up romances in the name of frankness and the formula of Ibsen. I myself value very highly the great nineteenth-century illumination of romantic love, just as I value the great eighteenth-century ideal of right reason and human dignity, or the seventeenth-century intensity, or the sixteenth-century expansion, or the divine logic and dedicated valour of the Middle Ages. I do not see why any of these cultural conquests should be lost or despised, or why it is necessary for every fashion to wash away all that is best in every other. It may be possible that one good custom would corrupt the world, but I never could see why the second good custom should deny that the first good custom was good. As it is, those who have no notion except that of breaking away from romance are being visibly punished by breaking away from reason. Every new realistic novel serves to show that realism, when entirely emptied of romance, becomes utterly unreal. For romance was only the name given to a love of life which was something much larger than a life of love, in the Byronic sense. And anything from which it has passed is instantly corrupt and crawling with worms of death.

The Equality of Sexlessness

In almost all the modern opinions on women it is curious to observe how many lies have to be assumed before a case can be made. A young lady flies from England to Australia; another wins an air race; a Duchess creates a speed record in reaching India; others win motoring trophies; and now the King's prize for marksmanship has gone to a woman. All of which is very interesting and possibly praiseworthy as means of spending one's leisure; and if it were left at that, even if no more were added than the perfectly plain statement that such feats could not have been achieved by their mothers or their grandmothers, we would be content to doff our hats to the ladies with all the courtesy and respect which courage, endurance and ability have always rightly demanded.

But it is not left at that; and considerably more is added. It is suggested, for example, that the tasks were beyond the mothers and the grandmothers, not for the very obvious reason that they had no motorcars and airplanes in which to amuse their leisure hours, but because women were then enslaved by the convention of natural inferiority to man. Those days, we are told, "in which women were held to be incapable of positive social achievements are gone for ever." It does not seem to have occurred to this critic that the very fact of being a mother and a grandmother indicates a certain positive social achievement; the achievement of which, indeed, probably left little leisure for travelling airily about the hemispheres. The same critic goes on to state, with all the solemn emphasis of profound thought, that "the important thing is not that women are the same as men—that is a fallacy—but that they are just as valuable to society as men.... Equality of citizenship means that there are twice as many heads to solve present-day problems as there were to solve the problems of the past. And two heads are better than one." And the dreadful proof of the modern collapse of all that was meant by man and wife and the family council, is that this sort of imbecility can be taken seriously.

The *Times,* in a studied leading article, points out that the first emancipators of women (whoever they were) had no idea of what lay in store for future generations. "Could they have foreseen it they might have disarmed much opposition by pointing to the possibilities, not only of freedom, but of equality and fraternity also." And we ask—what does it all mean? What in the name of all that is graceful and dignified does fraternity with women mean? What nonsense, or worse, is indicated by the freedom and the equality of the sexes? We mean something quite definite when we speak of a man being a little free with the ladies. What definite freedom is meant when the freedom of women is proposed? If it merely means the right to free opinions; the right to vote independently of husbands or fathers; what possible connection has it with the freedom to fly to Australia or score bulls-eyes at Bisley? If it really means, as we fear it does, freedom from the responsibility of managing a home and a family, an equal right with men in business and social careers, at the expense of home and family, then such progress we can only call a progressive deterioration.

And for men too, there is, according to a famous authoress, a hope of freedom. Men are beginning to revolt, we are told, against the old tribal custom of desiring fatherhood. The male is casting off the shackles of being a creator and a man. When all are sexless there will be equality. There will be no women and no men. There will be but a fraternity, free and equal. The only consoling thought is that it will endure but for one generation.

Two Points of View

In discussing such a proposal as that of the co-education of the sexes it is very desirable first of all to realise clearly what it is that we want the thing to do. The thing might be upheld for quite opposite reasons. It might be supposed to increase delicacy or to decrease it. It might be valued because it was a sphere for sentiment or because it was a damper for sentiment. My sympathies would move me in a discussion entirely according to what difference its upholders thought it would make. For myself, I doubt whether it would make much difference at all. Everyone must agree with co-education for very young children; and I cannot believe that even for elder children it would do any great harm. But that is because I think the school is not so important as people think it nowadays. The home is the really important thing, and always will be. People talk about the poor neglecting their children; but a little boy in the street has more traces of having been brought up by his mother than of having been taught ethics and geography by a pupil teacher. And if we take this true parallel of the home we can see, I think, exactly what co-education can do and what it cannot do. The school will never make boys and girls ordinary comrades. The home does not make them that. The sexes can work together in a schoolroom just as they can breakfast together in a breakfast-room; but neither makes any difference to the fact that the boys go off to a boyish companionship which the girls would think disgusting, while the girls go off to a girl companionship which the boys would think literally insane. Co-educate as much as you like, there will always be a wall between the sexes until love or lust breaks it down. Your co-educative playground for pupils in their teens will not be a place of sexless camaraderie. It will be a place where boys go about in fives sulkily growling at the girls, and where the girls go about in twos turning up their noses at the boys.

Now if you accept this state of things and are content with it as the result of your co-education, I am with you; I accept it as one of the mystical first facts of Nature. I accept it somewhat in the spirit of Carlyle when somebody told him that Harriet Martineau had "accepted the Universe", and he said, "By God, she'd better." But if you have any idea that co-education would do more than parade the sexes in front of each other twice a day, if you think it would destroy their deep ignorance of each other or start them on a basis of rational understanding, then I say first that this will never happen, and second that I (for one) should be horribly annoyed if it did.

I can reach my meaning best by another route. Very few people ever state properly the strong argument in favour of marrying for love or against marrying for money. The argument is not that all lovers are heroes and heroines, nor is it that all dukes are profligates or all millionaires cads. The argument is this, that the differences between a man and a woman are at the best so obstinate and exasperating that they practically cannot be got over unless there is an atmosphere of exaggerated tenderness and mutual interest. To put the matter in one metaphor, the sexes are two stubborn pieces of iron; if they are to be welded together, it must be while they are red-hot. Every woman has to find out that her husband is a selfish beast, because every man is a selfish beast by the standard of a woman. But let her find out the beast while they are both still in the story of "Beauty and the Beast". Every man has to find out that his wife is cross—that is to say, sensitive to the point of madness: for every woman is mad by the masculine standard. But let him find out that she is mad while her madness is more worth considering than anyone else's sanity.

This is not a digression. The whole value of the normal relations of man and woman lies in the fact that they first begin really to criticise each other when they first begin really to admire each other. And a good thing, too. I say, with a full sense of the responsibility of the statement, that it is better that the sexes should misunderstand each other until they marry. It is better that they should not have the knowledge until they have the reverence and the charity. We want no premature and puppyish "knowing all about girls". We do not want the highest mysteries of a Divine distinction to be understood before they are desired, and handled before they are understood. That which Mr. Shaw calls the Life Force, but for which Christianity has more philosophical terms, has created this early division of tastes and habits for that romantic purpose, which is also the most practical of all purposes. Those whom God has sundered, shall no man join.

It is, therefore, a question of what are really the co-educators' aims. If they have small aims, some convenience in organisation, some slight improvement in manners, they know more about such things than I. But if they have large aims, I am against them.

On Dependence and Independence

I came across a lady quite lately who leapt up in a flame of noble indignation at the suggestion that her husband should pay for her dresses, though she did not apparently object to his paying for her dinners. I admit that there was something fine and generous about such perversity, and that she was an improvement on other ladies who leap up in a flame of indignation because their husbands will *not* pay for a hundred dresses a month. It is sometimes the husband who leaps up in a flame of indignation, and in neither case is the indignation so noble. All the same, it seems to me an instance of the queer welter of inconsequent and inconclusive notions that make it so difficult for the modern world to establish a normal social rule.

Some of us (who cannot be called conservative in the sense of content with social conditions, and who have even been called revolutionary for our attempts to improve those conditions) have nevertheless come to have a profound suspicion of what is called Progress. And the reason is this: that there does not seem to be a principle, but only principles, and these conflicting principles, of Progress. There is not a stream, but a sort of eddy or whirlpool. There could not be a stronger case than this particular ideal of Independence. It is not made the principle of social reform. Even the social reformers would be the first to say that they depend on dependence; on the mutual dependence of comrades and fellow-citizens, as distinct from the individualistic independence they would denounce as mere isolation. It is not made the ideal of the proletarian or wage-earner, either by the Communist or the Capitalist system. Both the Communist and the Capitalist are alike in *not* thinking of the individual worker as independent. They will discuss whether he is well paid, whether he is well treated, whether he works under good or bad conditions, whether he is dependent on a good or bad business or a good or bad government; but *not* whether he is independent. Independence is not made the ideal of the normal man. It is only suddenly and abruptly introduced, in one particular relation, in the case of the exceptional woman. She is only independent of her husband; not independent in any other real relation of life. She is only independent of the home—and not of the workshop or the world. And it is supremely characteristic of this confusion that one well-meaning individual should make a yet finer distinction, and resolve to be independent in the dressing-room, but not in the dining-room.

Now, the modern trouble is that moral scraps and fragments of this sort are floating about like icebergs, and nobody knows when he will bump into one of them. In one case somebody will make an excuse of the ideal of Service, even if it means servility. In another case somebody will make an excuse of the ideal of Individuality, even if it means insanity. People will make attempts at despotism, or demands for freedom, successively or even simultaneously, according to a quite arbitrary program of opportunism. And we feel that they are not submitting a variety of actions to one test; they are applying a variety of tests to one action, which is for them already a fixed and settled action. They do what they want, and make up reasons for it afterwards; but even the reasons are rather too cunning to be reasonable. In a word, it is this chaos, in the creed and code of conduct, that prevents a man from finding in it any sort of guide, even a guide to progress. Thus, in the present case, we could at least settle down to discussing seriously the Independence of Woman, if it were regarded by anybody as part of a real philosophy of the Independence of Man. What we find, as in the case mentioned, is that one woman has made one claim to one curious and rather capricious form of independence. She is independent of the breadwinner, but not of the bank or the employer—not to mention the moneylender.

Thus, to begin with, it would be well to note what economic

independence means: as distinct, that is, from what it ought to mean. It might mean that the lady went out into a primeval forest to slay lions and leopards and clothe herself with their skins, like Diana. It might mean that she sewed together the leaves of the forest and made herself a green garment, like Eve. It might mean that she held herself independent in owning her own spinning-wheel and her own store of thread, and weaving strips of simple drapery, like Mr. Gandhi. In a word, she might be really independent of the dress allowance, in the sense of being independent of the dressmaker. It is not very likely that it does mean this; but it is not the dependence on the dressmaker that is the serious inconsistency in the idea. It is the fact that modern woman, in the condition of modern society, will herself have to work, if not for a dressmaker, then probably for somebody else who is primarily the moneymaker. And the question is, why is it any better to be a proletarian in the shop than to be a Communist in the home? For the only truly and legitimately Communist institution is the home. "With all my worldly goods I thee endow" is the only satisfactory Bolshevist proclamation that has ever been made about property. It is, therefore, of course, the one proclamation which Bolshevists would be the first to attack. The twisted and unnatural posture of the modern controversy, like that of a serpent with its tail in its mouth, biting and tearing at itself, is excellently illustrated in this queer revolt of Communism in the wrong place against Communism in the right place. We no longer make the normal attempt to break up society into homes. We only make an attempt to break up homes, and even that by a principle of division which we dare not apply to anything else in society. The crack or fissure is to run across the hearth or the roof-tree, but to be concealed as far as possible from the forum or the street.

We hear a great deal of the evil passions of Class War and the suggestion that the master and man must of necessity be natural enemies. But surely there is a far more perverse implication pervading the modern world; that the wife and the husband are natural enemies. They are, apparently, such mortal enemies that it is enough for one of them to be freed from the other, even in one trumpery particular, though she is not freed from anything or anybody else. The whole of the rest of the world in which she lives, whether for good or evil, is one network of necessitarian dependence. People have left off even talking the language of independence; the old language about the thrift that leads to independence or the self-respect that comes from independence. Anybody may find himself almost abjectly dependent upon anybody; any woman may do the same. And apparently it does not matter, so long as it is not her own husband and not concerned with her own hats. I should very much like to see some of these good-natured groping people draw up something like a plan or table of their real conception of a social structure, and of the necessary commandments of society. The newspapers talk about the danger of Bolshevism, and the Red Peril. But I am afraid of the Patchwork Peril, which is all colours and none; I am afraid of bits of Bolshevism and bits of insane individualism and bits of independence in the wrong place, floating hither and thither and colliding with they know not what; the icebergs whose very shapelessness, or incalculable shape, has always been the cause of shipwreck.

The Emancipation of Domesticity

And it should be remarked in passing that this force upon a man to develop one feature has nothing to do with what is commonly called our competitive system, but would equally exist under any rationally conceivable kind of Collectivism. Unless the Socialists are frankly ready for a fall in the standard of violins, telescopes and electric lights, they must somehow create a moral demand on the individual that he shall keep up his present concentration on these things. It was only by men being in some degree specialist that there ever were any telescopes; they must certainly be in some degree specialist in order to keep them going. It is not by making a man a State wage-earner that you can prevent him thinking principally about the very difficult way he earns his wages. There is only one way to preserve in the world that high levity and that more leisurely outlook which fulfils the old vision of universalism. That is, to permit the existence of a partly protected half of humanity; a half which the harassing industrial demand troubles indeed, but only troubles indirectly. In other words, there must be in every centre of humanity one human being upon a larger plan; one who does not "give her best," but gives her all.

Our old analogy of the fire remains the most workable one. The fire need not blaze like electricity nor boil like boiling water; its point is that it blazes more than water and warms more than light. The wife is like the fire, or to put things in their proper proportion, the fire is like the wife. Like the fire, the woman is expected to cook: not to excel in cooking, but to cook; to cook better than her husband who is earning the coke by lecturing on botany or breaking stones. Like the fire, the woman is expected to tell tales to the children, not original and artistic tales, but tales—

better tales than would probably be told by a first-class cook. Like the fire, the woman is expected to illuminate and ventilate, not by the most startling revelations or the wildest winds of thought, but better than a man can do it after breaking stones or lecturing. But she cannot be expected to endure anything like this universal duty if she is also to endure the direct cruelty of competitive or bureaucratic toil. Woman must be a cook, but not a competitive cook; a school-mistress, but not a competitive school-mistress; a house-decorator, but not a competitive house-decorator; a dressmaker, but not a competitive dressmaker. She should have not one trade but twenty hobbies; she, unlike the man, may develop all her second bests. This is what has been really aimed at from the first in what is called the seclusion, or even the oppression, of women. Women were not kept at home in order to keep them narrow; on the contrary, they were kept at home in order to keep them broad. The world outside the home was one mass of narrowness, a maze of cramped paths, a madhouse of monomaniacs. It was only by partly limiting and protecting the woman that she was enabled to play at five or six professions and so come almost as near to God as the child when he plays at a hundred trades. But the woman's professions, unlike the child's, were all truly and almost terribly fruitful; so tragically real that nothing but her universality and balance prevented them being merely morbid.

This is the substance of the contention I offer about the historic female position. I do not deny that women have been wronged and even tortured; but I doubt if they were ever tortured so much as they are tortured now by the absurd modern attempt to make them domestic empresses and competitive clerks at the same time. I do not deny that even under the old tradition women had a harder time than men; that is why we take off our hats. I do not deny that all these various female functions were exasperating; but I say that there was some aim and meaning in keeping them various. I do not pause even to deny that woman was a servant; but at least she was a general servant.

The shortest way of summarising the position is to say that woman stands for the idea of Sanity; that intellectual home to which the mind must return after every excursion on extravagance. The mind that finds its way to wild places is the poet's; but the mind that never finds its way back is the lunatic's. There must in every machine be a part that moves and a part that stands still; there must be in everything that changes a part that is unchangeable. And many of the phenomena which moderns hastily condemn are really parts of this position of the woman as the centre and pillar of health. Much of what is called her subservience, and even her pliability, is merely the subservience and pliability of a universal remedy; she varies as medicines vary, with the disease. She has to be an optimist to the morbid husband, a salutary pessimist to the happy-go-lucky husband. She has to prevent the Quixote from being put upon, and the bully from putting upon others. The French King wrote—

> "Toujours femme varie
> Bien fol qui s'y fie,"

but the truth is that woman always varies, and that is exactly why we always trust her. To correct every adventure and extravagance with its antidote in common sense is not (as the moderns seem to think) to be in the position of a spy or a slave. It is to be in the position of Aristotle or (at the lowest) Herbert Spencer, to be a universal morality, a complete system of thought. The slave flatters; the complete moralist rebukes. It is, in short, to be a Trimmer in the true sense of that honourable term; which for some reason or other is always used in a sense exactly opposite to its own. It seems really to be supposed that a Trimmer means a cowardly person who always goes over to the stronger side. It really means a highly chivalrous person who always goes over to the weaker side; like one who trims a boat by sitting where there are few people seated. Woman is a Trimmer; and it is a generous, dangerous and romantic trade.

The final fact which fixes this is a sufficiently plain one. Supposing it to be conceded that humanity has acted at least not unnaturally in dividing itself into two halves, respectively typifying the ideals of special talent and of general sanity (since they are genuinely difficult to combine completely in one mind), it is not difficult to see why the line of cleavage has followed the line of sex, or why the female became the emblem of the universal and the male of the special and superior. Two gigantic facts of nature fixed it thus: first, that the woman who frequently fulfilled her functions literally *could* not be specially prominent in experiment and adventure; and second, that the same natural operation surrounded her with very young children, who require to be taught not so much anything as everything. Babies need not to be taught a trade, but to be introduced to a world. To put the matter shortly, woman is generally shut up in a house with a human being at the time when he asks all the questions that there are, and some that there aren't. It would be odd if she retained any of the narrowness of a specialist. Now if anyone says that this duty of general enlightenment (even when freed from modern rules and hours, and exercised more spontaneously by a more protected person) is in itself too exacting and oppressive, I can understand the view. I can only answer that our race has thought it worth while to cast this burden on women in order to keep common sense in the world. But when people begin to talk about this domestic duty as not merely difficult but trivial and dreary, I simply give up the question. For I cannot with the utmost energy of imagination conceive what they mean. When domesticity, for instance, is called drudgery, all the difficulty arises from a double meaning in the word. If drudgery only means dreadfully hard work, I admit the woman drudges in the home, as a man might drudge at the Cathedral of Amiens or drudge behind a gun at Trafalgar. But if it means that the hard work is more heavy because it is trifling, colourless and of small import to the soul, then, as I say, I give it up; I do not know what the words mean. To be Queen Elizabeth within a definite area, deciding sales, banquets, labours and holidays; to be Whiteley within a certain area, providing toys, boots, sheets, cakes and books; to be Aristotle within a certain area, teaching morals, manners, theology, and hygiene; I can understand how this might exhaust the mind, but I cannot imagine how it could narrow it. How can it be a large career to tell other people's children about the Rule of Three, and a small career to tell one's own children about the universe? How can it be broad to be the same thing to everyone, and narrow to be everything to someone? No; a woman's function is laborious, but because it is gigantic, not because it is minute. I will pity Mrs. Jones for the hugeness of her task; I will never pity her for its smallness.

But though the essential of the woman's task is universality, this does not, of course, prevent her from having one or two severe though largely wholesome prejudices. She has, on the whole, been more conscious than man that she is only one half of humanity; but she has expressed it (if one may say so of a lady) by getting her teeth into the two or three things which she thinks she stands for. I would observe here in parentheses that much of the recent official trouble about women has arisen from the fact that they transfer to things of doubt and reason that sacred stubbornness only proper to the primary things which a woman was set to guard. One's own children, one's own altar, ought to be a matter of principle—or, if you like, a matter of prejudice. On the other hand, who wrote Junius's Letters ought not to be a principle or a prejudice, it ought to be a matter of free and almost indifferent inquiry. But make an energetic modern girl secretary to a league to show that George III. wrote Junius, and in three months she will believe it too, out of mere loyalty to her employers. Modern women defend their office with all the fierceness of domesticity. They fight for desk and typewriter as for hearth and home, and develop a sort of wolfish wifehood on behalf of the invisible head of the firm. That is why they do office work so well; and that is why they ought not to do it.

To Frances: Another Sort of Woman

There are two broad classes of women a man comes across. The first are the "outdoor" women, people . . . who would remain outdoor if they were locked in the Black Hole of Calcutta. They are made physically as sisters of the Sun and Wind, they develop all the virtues that are the children of Fresh Air: humour, courage, self-reliance, Faith, Hope and Charity. They are very jolly people; for their virtues are easy to them.

The second class are the "delicate" women, who cannot bear loud voices and live behind drawn blinds. They are mostly concerned with their own souls and the people who have not called on them. They are either church people and live in South Kensington or Theosophists and live in West Kensington. They are sometimes very silly people, particularly if they have a little money: their very affections, though deep and pathetic, have a tendency to stagnate into bitterness and poison. But a man who should be rude or cold or satiric about them would be a brute. They have much to bear, pains borne in silence and loneliness, when every day is like the last, pains which, real or unreal, organic or nervous, are equally painful. They have physical troubles which I have not, therefore I should be a cur not to respect them. And to their dusty old failures and disappointments, to their fantastic illnesses and needless aversions, — yes, even their microscopic vanities and grievances, I for one would always take off my hat. Lord, as the ancient writer said, count unto them their tears.

And lastly, outside both of these classes a man may happen to come upon another sort of woman—if he does he will probably be a higher and humbler man for ever.

A woman who, fated physically to have the virtues of the

weaker woman, has rebelled and taken the virtues of the stronger—a woman whom Nature, making war, has been unable to defeat, whose body may be in the sickroom but whose soul is in the playground, who has a heart so great that she can *hate* the privileges of her calamity and the excuses of her depression: who spurns the philosophy that would justify and smooth her down and elects the philosophy that can only knock her about: who would rather conceal her disadvantages and be third in the free race for life, than first in a paradise of poetic egoism: a woman who, to add one last supreme touch, shall have even the faults of a tougher physical type, and while she suffers inwardly from the collapses and clouding pains that make other women pessimists, shall be challenged and rebuked outwardly for her too dogmatic cheerfulness, her too cloudless philosophy, her too arrogant faith.

If one had ever met it in a hotel that would have been a valiant and splendid figure. To me it is simply you. Even you will, I fancy, admit it is something like your ideal for yourself: isn't it, dearest?

And now you want to spoil it all by having a lot of beastly, fat, physical health. And the worst of it is that I am quite inconsistent and want it for you too, for I can't bear you to have three minutes discomfort—which is a medieval superstition and a jolly fine thing. But it is perfectly true, as I say, that you could never have been the influence you are, never have given the object lesson you do of the great soul that conceals its wounds that it may serve in the battle, if those wounds did not exist. Oh you dear, dear discontented saint—don't you see that we do want something to love and adore and go on our knees to, something that really shows that courage is not a bundle of nerves—nor optimism a good breakfast. Won't you be patient on the chilly pedestal, for a little while? We are selfish—but you are not. No, by the sun and moon and all the stars—

—You are not—

All of which, I am afraid, doesn't alter the fact that if by taking up the carving-knife now lying beside me and cutting off my right hand with my left, I could guarantee you perfect health for life, I would do it and whistle all the time. But then, you see, that is a man talking about his own dear, true-hearted and beautiful girl whose face gets into his dreams: as a philosopher, speaking of the social influence of a good woman, I am sure the world has reason to bless your bad health.

I do not think, brave heart, that I could praise you better than by writing this odd letter. There are not many women in whose case, when a man has to comfort them in sickness, it would occur to him to point out the good they were doing to the world, as any comfort at all. But to you I *know* it is a comfort. . . .

Woman and the Philosophers

The title of the work before us is *Woman: a Scientific Study and Defence*. It never occurred to us before that woman stood in need of a defence of any kind; and what the women of our acquaintance would think of being made the subject of a "scientific defence" we shudder to conceive. The work which Mr. Seed has adapted from M. Fouillée contains a considerable amount of sound and suggestive argument against the scientific theories of the inferiority of woman; but the plan of the book is a mistake. Instead of attempting to base the equality of the sexes on the domestic habits of some wretched amoeba in the primeval twilight, the author should have turned on the men of science and told them, with all possible respect, that they have nothing whatever to do with questions of superiority and inferiority. Obviously they have not. Whether woman is structurally different to man is a matter of physical science, whether she is superior or inferior or equal is not a matter of physical science; it is a question of what you happen to want. Science does its duty in saying that monkeys have tails and men have not; but as for saying that it is better not to have tails, that is a matter of taste and imagination, and by no means certain even at that.

The author himself quotes incidentally a remarkable instance of this in a citation from Herbert Spencer, but he does not seem to see the full fallacy that he is trying to expose. Herbert Spencer says, truly enough, that the interest of women is generally directed rather to persons than to ideas, and gives this as showing their inferiority, since the last products of human evolution are "abstract reasoning and the abstract emotion of justice." Here we have in full operation that strange religious dogma which crept into the minds of so many evolutionists—the notion that the last thing must be the highest. In this case it is clearly untrue. To understand a man (as many women do) is to understand one of the most complex and untranslatable cryptograms conceivable, to understand a "cause" is to understand the clumsiest thing created, a mere alphabet of thought. What is "abstract justice"? Personally we know nothing about it, except that in proportion as it becomes abstract it generally becomes unjust. If a preference for personal over abstract criticism be a mark of inferiority, the great novelist must be inferior to the political wirepuller. But all this staring common sense is swept away by the philosopher who wishes to make biology prove what it can never prove and the sole test he applies is to ask what is the last product of human evolution. By that argument playing on the typewriter would be superior to playing on the organ.

In any discussion of philosophic strictures upon women it was inevitable that Schopenhauer should be involved, though we fancy most women and most believers in womanhood would be much more annoyed by Schopenhauer's approval than by his denunciation. When a gentleman wishes for the destruction of the human race, and may therefore, presumably, reserve his affections for such things as assassination and typhoid fever, to be regarded by him with a loving smile would be rather disquieting than complimentary. But the particular passage quoted in this book is so remarkable an instance of Schopenhauer's astonishing literary ingenuity and still more astonishing unreality of experience and outlook, that it is worth a moment's consideration. Women, says Schopenhauer, in effect, are the best guardians of children, because they are themselves children, "puerile, futile, limited." Now we know what women do for children; they nearly kill themselves over them with work and anxiety; the simple and obvious way, therefore, of testing the truth of Schopenhauer's comparison is to ask what children do for children. If the "futility" and "limitation" of a little boy of seven lead him naturally to martyr himself for another little boy of seven, then the comparison is sound. But as we all know that they lead him to kick his shins and run away with his toys, the comparison is nonsense. It is surely strange that the name of philosopher should ever have given to a literary man, however brilliant, who was capable of basing an argument upon the amazing notion that people love what is like themselves. In fact, the whole of Schopenhauer's theory of the childishness of women is capable of the shortest and simplest answer. If women are childish because they love children, it follows that men are womanish because they love women.

The author speaks with just contempt of these efforts to discredit women by biological parallels. If it be true that certain baboons have a large amount of the maternal instinct, rational ethics have nothing to say to it except, "So much the better for the baboons." They may be inferior to us in other respects; so are the birds of the air. But a mortal with the wings of a bird is an angel, and a mortal with the maternal instinct is a mother.

We think this book would have been better if it had been purely scientific or purely poetic and moral. Its biological thesis, that from the earliest dawn of life the two sexes have certain types and functions which may still be traced in their moral and mental attitudes, may be true and is very probable. The scope of the book and its dallyings with other matters, however, leave no space for the serious scientific demonstration of this. But while we suspend our judgment on the truth of the biological contention we are heartily in agreement with the moral contention, and cannot see that it requires any biological machinery at all. The divinity of woman is to be decided by what she is, not by how she was made. It has always seemed to us truly extraordinary that Christians should have raised such a shriek of disgust at the "degrading" notion that man was made out of the lower animals, when the very Bible they defended described him, with splendid common sense, as made out of red mud. But it is stranger still that philosophers who have accepted in a healthier spirit the genial fact of our kinship with the other creatures, should try to revive the silly and vulgar prejudice against the animal world in order to throw discredit on the moral dignity of man or woman. To refuse to judge of souls, laws, creeds or tendencies on their own merits is the perfection of cosmic snobbery. To inquire whether a man's father did not keep a shop is far less snobbish than to inquire whether his ancestor did not keep a tail.

The question is far too large a one to be treated here, but we have a strong conviction that the world will gradually, by a beneficent revolution, turn this idea upside down. Hitherto it seems to have been thought that in proportion as a phenomenon detached itself from the background, ceased to be serene, inevitable and obvious and became strange, diverse and audacious, an interesting development, it became less sacred and more profane. We venture to prophesy that the tendency now in progress to show everything, no matter how fundamental, as a growth, an experiment, a choice among alternatives, will at length result in a religious sense of wonder passing all the religions of the earth. The age of miracles will have returned; for a man come from the womb will be as strange as a man risen from the dead and the sun rising in its season as startling as the sun standing still upon Gibeon.

This is at least the true light in which to regard woman. If it were proved to us ten thousand times over (it has not yet been proved once) that woman laboured under eternal mental as well as physical disadvantages, it would not make us think less but rather more of that brilliant instinct of chivalry which saw in her peculiar possibilities and put her to higher uses. The whole romance of life and all the romances of poetry lie in this motion of the utterly weak suddenly developing advantages over the strong. It is the curse of the modern philosophy of strength that it is ridden with the fallacy that there is only one kind of strength and one kind of weakness. It forgets that size is a weakness as well as littleness; that the camel is just as weak for the purpose of going through the eye of a needle as the microbe for carrying a load of hay.

As to what form this peculiar dignity of woman is to take at the present day, a question to which many pages of this book are devoted, we think it a matter for much more serious consideration than it has yet received. We do not mean that we are out of sympathy with the modern movements. We believe firmly in the equality of the sexes, and we agree, moreover, that to use woman merely as a wooden idol is as bad as to use her as a wooden broom. But, in the interests of equality, we must say that we doubt whether the mere equalisation of sports and employments will bring us much further. There is nothing so certain to lead to inequality as identity. A mere struggle between the sexes as to who will make the best tinkers, tailors, or soldiers, is very likely indeed to result in a subordination of women infinitely more gross and heartless than that which disgraced the world up to now. What we really require is a revised and improved division of labour. Whatever solution may be best (we do not pretend for a moment to have decided) it must emphatically not be based upon any idea so paltry and small-minded as the idea that there is anything noble in professional work or anything degrading in domestic. Woman must not be elevated as the worst type of working man is elevated, merely (to use the silly phrase) "to a better kind of work," to choke the memory of his own class in a stick-up collar. If this is the only end of the noble promise of female emancipation, the intellectual woman's lot will certainly be an ironic one, for she will have toiled to reach the haughtiest eminence from which she can look down upon the housemaid, only to discover that world has become sane and discovered that the housemaid is as good as she.

The Macbeths

In studying any general tragedy the first question necessarily is what part of tragedy is eternal. If there be any element in man's work which is in any sense permanent it must have this characteristic, that it rebukes first one generation and then another, but rebukes them always in opposite directions and for opposite faults. The ideal world is always sane. The real world is always mad. But it is mad about a different thing every time; all the things that have been are changing and inconstant. The only thing that is really reliable is the thing that has never been. All very great classics of art are a rebuke to extravagance not in one direction but in all directions. The figure of a Greek Venus is a rebuke to the fat women of Rubens and also a rebuke to the thin women of Aubrey Beardsley. In the same way, Christianity, which in its early years fought the Manicheans because they did not believe in anything but spirit, has now to fight the Manicheans because they do not believe in anything but matter. This is perhaps the test of a very great work of classic creation, that it can be attacked on inconsistent grounds, and that it attacks its enemies on inconsistent grounds. Here is a broad and simple test. If you hear a thing being accused of being too tall and too short, too red and too green, too bad in one way and too bad also in the opposite way, then you may be sure that it is very good.

This preface is essential if we are to profit by the main meaning of *Macbeth.* For the play is so very great that it covers much more than it appears to cover; it will certainly survive our age as it has survived its own; it will certainly leave the twentieth century behind as calmly and completely as it has left the seventeenth century behind. Hence if we ask for the meaning of this classic we must necessarily ask the meaning for our own time. It might have another shade of meaning for another period of time. If, as is possible, there should be a barbaric return and if history is any kind of guide, it will destroy everything else before it destroys great literature. The high and civilized sadness of Virgil was enjoyed literally through the darkest instant of the Dark Ages. Long after a wealthier generation has destroyed Parliament they will retain Shakespeare. Men will enjoy the greatest tragedy of Shakespeare even in the thick of the greatest tragedy of Europe.

It is quite possible that Shakespeare may come to be enjoyed by men far simpler than the men for whom he wrote. Voltaire called him a great savage; we may come to the time far darker than the Dark Ages when he will really be enjoyed by savages. Then the story of Macbeth will be read by a man in the actual position of Macbeth. Then the Thane of Glamis may profit by the disastrous superstitions of the Thane of Cawdor. Then the Thane of Cawdor may really resist the impulse to be King of Scotland. There would be a very simple but a real moral if Macbeth could read *Macbeth.* "Do not listen to evil spirits; do not let your ambition run away with you; do not murder old gentlemen in bed; do not kill other people's wives and children as a part of diplomacy; for if you do these things it is highly probable that you will have a bad time." That is the lesson that Macbeth would have learnt from *Macbeth;* that is the lesson that some barbarians of the future may possibly learn from *Macbeth.* And it is a true lesson. Great work has something to say quite simply to the simple. The barbarians would understand *Macbeth* as a solid warning against vague and violent ambition; and it is such a warning, and they would take along with it this lesson also, which is none the worse because perhaps only the barbarians could adequately understand it. "Distrust those malevolent spirits who speak flatteringly to you. They are not benevolent spirits; if they were they would be more likely to beat you about the head."

Before we talk then of the lesson of a great work of art, let us realize that it has a different lesson for different ages, because it is itself eternal. And let us realize that such a lesson will be in our own day not absolute but suited to the particular vices or particular misfortunes of that day. We are not in any danger at the moment of the positive and concrete actions which correspond to those of *Macbeth*. The good old habit of murdering kings (which was the salvation of so many commonwealths in the past) has fallen into desuetude. The idea of such a play must be for us (and for our sins) more subtle. The idea is more subtle but it is almost inexpressibly great. Let us before reading the play consider if only for a moment what is the main idea of *Macbeth* for modern men.

One great idea on which all tragedy builds is the idea of the continuity of human life. The one thing a man cannot do is exactly what all modern artists and free lovers are always trying to do. He cannot cut his life up into separate sections. The case of the modern claim for freedom in love is the first and most obvious that occurs to the mind; therefore I use it for this purpose of illustration. You cannot have an idyll with Maria and an episode with Jane; there is no such thing as an episode. There is no such thing as an idyll. It is idle to talk about abolishing the tragedy of marriage when you cannot abolish the tragedy of sex. Every flirtation is a marriage; it is a marriage in this frightful sense; that it is irrevocable. I have taken this case of sexual relations as one out of a hundred; but of any case in human life the thing is true. The basis of all tragedy is that man lives a coherent and continuous life. It is only a worm that you can cut in two and leave the severed parts still alive. You can cut a worm up into episodes and they are still living episodes. You can cut a worm up into idylls and they are quite brisk and lively idylls. You can do all this to him precisely because he is a worm. You cannot cut a man up and leave him kicking, precisely because he is a man. We know this because man even in his lowest and darkest manifestation has always this characteristic of physical and psychological unity. His identity continues long enough to see the end of many of his own acts; he cannot be cut off from his past with a hatchet; as he sows so shall he reap.

This then is the basis of all tragedy, this living and perilous continuity which does not exist in the lower creatures. This is the basis of tragedy, and this is certainly the basis of *Macbeth*. The great ideas of *Macbeth,* uttered in the first few scenes with a tragic energy which has never been equalled perhaps in Shakespeare or out of him, is the idea of the enormous mistake a man makes if he supposes that one decisive act will clear his way. Macbeth's ambition, though selfish and someway sullen, is not in itself criminal or morbid. He wins the title of Glamis in honourable war; he deserves and gets the title of Cawdor; he is rising in the world and has a not ignoble exhilaration in doing so. Suddenly a new ambition is presented to him (of the agency and atmosphere which presents it I shall speak in a moment) and he realizes that nothing lies across his path to the Crown of Scotland except the sleeping body of Duncan. If he does that one cruel thing, he can be infinitely kind and happy.

Here, I say, is the first and most formidable of the great actualities of *Macbeth.* You cannot do a mad thing in order to reach sanity. Macbeth's mad resolve is not a cure even for his own irresolution. He was indecisive before his decision. He is, if possible, more indecisive after he has decided. The crime does not get rid of the problem. Its effect is so bewildering that one may say that the crime does not get rid of the temptation. Make a morbid decision and you will only become more morbid; do a lawless thing and you will only get into an atmosphere much more suffocating than that of law. Indeed, it is a mistake to speak of a man as "breaking out". The lawless man never breaks out; he breaks in. He smashes a door and finds himself in another room, he smashes a wall and finds himself in a yet smaller one. The more he shatters the more his habitation shrinks. Where he ends you may read in the end of *Macbeth.*

For us, moderns, therefore, the first philosophical significance of the play is this; that our life is one thing and that our lawless acts limit us; every time we break a law we make a limitation. In some strange way hidden in the deeps of human psychology, if we build our palace on some unknown wrong it turns very slowly into our prison. Macbeth at the end of the play is not merely a wild beast; he is a caged wild beast. But if this is the thing to be put in a primary position there is something else that demands at least our second one. The second idea in the main story of *Macbeth* is, of course, that of the influence of evil suggestion upon the soul, particularly evil suggestion of a mystical and transcendental kind. In this connection the mystical character of the promptings is not more interesting than the mystical character of the man to whom they are especially sent. Mystical promptings are naturally sweet to a mystic. The character of Macbeth in this regard has been made the matter of a great deal of brilliant and futile discussion. Some critics have represented him as a burly silent soldier because he won battles for his country. Other critics have represented him as a feverish and futile decadent because he makes long practical speeches full of the most elaborate imagery. In the name of commonsense let it be remembered that Shakespeare lived before the time when unsuccessful poets thought it poetical to be decadent and unsuccessful soldiers thought it military to be silent. Men like Sidney and Raleigh and Essex could have fought as well as Macbeth and could have ranted as well as Macbeth. Why should Shakespeare shrink from making a great general talk poetry when half the great generals of his time actually wrote great poetry?

The whole legend, therefore, which some critics have based on the rich rhetoric of *Macbeth:* the legend that Macbeth was a febrile and egotistical coward because he liked the sound of his own voice, may be dismissed as a manifestation of the diseases of later days. Shakespeare meant Macbeth for a fine orator for he made fine speeches; he also meant him for a fine soldier because he made him not only win battles bravely, but what is much more to the point, lose battles bravely; he made him, when overwhelmed by enemies in heaven and earth, die the death of a hero. But Macbeth is meant to be among other things an orator and a poet; and it is to Macbeth in this capacity that the evil supernatural appeal is made. If there be any such thing as evil influences coming from beyond the world, they have never been so suggestively indicated as they are here. They appeal, as evil always does, to the existence of a coherent and comprehensible scheme. It is the essence of a nightmare that it turns the whole cosmos against us. Two of their prophecies have been fulfilled; may it not be assumed then that the third will also be fulfilled?

Also they appeal, as evil always does (being slavish itself and believing all men slaves) to the inevitable. They put Macbeth's good fortune before him as if it were not so much a fortune as a fate. In the same way imperialists sought to salve the consciences of Englishmen by giving them the offer of gold and empire with all the gloom of predestination. When the devil, and the witches who are the servants of the devil, wish to make a weak man snatch a crown that does not belong to him, they are too cunning to come to him and say, "Will you be King?" They say without further parley, "All hail, Macbeth, that shall be king hereafter." This weakness Macbeth really has; that he is easily attracted by that kind of spiritual fatalism which relieves the human creature of a great part of his responsibility. In this way there is a strange and sinister appropriateness in the way in which the promises of the evil spirits end in new fantasies; end, so to speak, as mere diabolical jokes. Macbeth accepts as a piece of unreasoning fate first his crime and then his crown. It is appropriate that this fate which he has accepted as external and irrational should end in incidents of mere extravagant bathos, in the walking forest and strange birth of Macduff. He has once surrendered himself with a kind of dark and evil faith, to a machinery of destiny that he can neither respect nor understand, and it is the proper sequel of this that the machinery should produce a situation which crushes him as something useless.

Shakespeare does not mean that Macbeth's emotionalism and rich rhetoric prove him to be unmanly in any ordinary sense. But Shakespeare does mean, I think, to suggest that the man, virile in his essential structure, has this weak spot in his artistic temperament; that fear of the mere strength of destiny and of unknown spirits, of their strength as apart from their virtue, which is the only proper significance of the word superstition. No man can be superstitious who loves his God, even if the god be Mumbo-Jumbo. Macbeth has something of this fear and fatalism; and fatalism is exactly the point at which rationalism passes silently into superstition. Macbeth, in short, has any amount of physical courage, he has even a great deal of moral courage. But he lacks what may be called spiritual courage; he lacks a certain freedom and dignity of the human soul in the universe, a freedom and dignity which one of the scriptural writers expresses as the difference between the servants and the sons of God.

But the man Macbeth and his marked but inadequate manliness, can only be expressed in connection with the character of his wife. And the question of Lady Macbeth immediately arouses again the controversies that have surrounded this play. Miss Ellen Terry and Sir Henry Irving acted *Macbeth* upon the theory that Macbeth was a feeble and treacherous man and that Lady Macbeth was a frail and clinging woman. A somewhat similar view of Lady Macbeth has been, I believe, consistently uttered by a distinguished American actress. The question as commonly stated, in short, is the question of whether Macbeth was really masculine, and second, of whether Lady Macbeth was not really feminine. The old critics assumed that because Lady Macbeth obviously ruled her husband she must have been a masculine woman. The whole inference of course is false. Masculine women may rule the Borough Council, but they never rule their husbands. The women who rule their husbands are the feminine women and I am entirely in accord with those who think that Lady Macbeth must have been a very feminine woman. But while some critics rightly insist on the feminine character of Lady Macbeth they endeavour to deprive Macbeth of that masculine character which is obviously the corollary of the other. They think Lady Macbeth must be a man because she rules. And on the same idiotic principle they think that Macbeth must be a woman or a coward or a decadent or something odd because he is ruled. The most masculine kind of man always is ruled. As a friend of mine once said, very truly, physical cowards are the only men who are not afraid of women.

The real truth about Macbeth and his wife is somewhat strange but cannot be too strongly stated. Nowhere else in all his wonderful works did Shakespeare describe the real character of the relations of the sexes so sanely, or so satisfactorily as he describes it here. The man and the woman are never more normal than they are in the abnormal and horrible story. *Romeo and Juliet* does not better describe love than this describes marriage. The dispute that goes on between Macbeth and his wife about the murder of Duncan is almost word for word a dispute which goes on at any suburban breakfast-table about something else. It is merely a matter of changing "Infirm of purpose, give me the daggers" into "Infirm of purpose, give me the postage stamps." And it is quite a mistake to suppose that the woman is to be called masculine or even in any exclusive sense strong. The strengths of the two partners differ in kind. The woman has more of that strength on the spot which is called industry. The man has more of that strength in reserve which is called laziness.

But the acute truth of this actual relation is much deeper even than that. Lady Macbeth exhibits one queer and astounding kind of magnanimity which is quite peculiar to women. That is, she will take something that her husband dares not do but which she knows he wants to do and she will become more fierce for it than he is. For her, as for all very feminine souls (that is, very strong ones) selfishness is the only thing which is acutely felt as sin: she will commit any crime if she is not committing it only for herself. Her husband thirsts for the crime egotistically and therefore vaguely, darkly, and subconsciously, as a man becomes conscious of the beginnings of physical thirst. But she thirsts for the crime altruistically and therefore clearly and sharply, as a man perceives a public duty to society. She puts the thing in plain words, with an acceptance of extremes. She has that perfect and splendid cynicism of women which is the most terrible thing God has made. I say it without irony and without any undue enjoyment of its slight element of humour.

If you want to know what are the permanent relations of the married man with the married woman you cannot read it anywhere more accurately than in the little domestic idyll of Mr. and Mrs. Macbeth. Of a man so male and a woman so female, I cannot believe anything except that they ultimately save their souls. Macbeth was strong in every masculine sense up to the very last moment; he killed himself in battle. Lady Macbeth was strong in the very female sense which is perhaps a more courageous sense; she killed herself, but not in battle. As I say, I cannot think that souls so strong and so elemental have not retained those permanent possibilities of humility and gratitude which ultimately place the soul in heaven. But wherever they are they are together. For alone among so many of the figures of human fiction, they are actually married.

The Repetition of Rosalind

In numberless modern novels and magazine stories, the heroine is apparently complimented by being described as "boyish". Doubtless there will soon be another fashion in fiction, in which the hero will always be described as girlish. Fettered as we are with an antiquated Victorian prejudice of the equality of the sexes, we cannot quite understand why one should be a compliment any more than the other. But, anyhow, the present fashion offers a much deeper difficulty. For the girl is being complimented on her boyishness by people who obviously know nothing at all about boys. Nothing could possibly be more unlike a boy than the candid, confident, unconventional and somewhat shallow sylph who swaggers up to the unfortunate hero of the novel *à la mode.* So far from being unconventional and shallow, the boy is commonly conventional because he is secretive. He is much more sullen outside and much more morbid inside. Who then is this new Pantomime Boy, and where did she come from? In truth she comes out of a very old pantomime.

About three hundred years ago William Shakespeare, not knowing what to do with his characters, turned them out to play in the woods, let a girl masquerade as a boy and amused himself with speculating on the effect of feminine curiosity freed for an hour from feminine dignity. He did it very well, but he could do something else. And the popular romances of today cannot do anything else. Shakespeare took care to explain in the play itself that he did *not* think that life should be one prolonged picnic. Nor would he have thought that feminine life should be one prolonged piece of private theatricals. But Rosalind, who was then unconventional for an hour, is now the convention of an epoch. She was then on a holiday; she is now very hard-worked indeed. She has to act in every play, novel or short story, and always in the same old pert pose. Perhaps she is even afraid to be herself: certainly Celia is now afraid to be herself.

We should think it rather a bore if all tragic youths wore black cloaks and carried skulls in imitation of Hamlet, or all old men waved wands and clasped enormous books in imitation of Prospero. But we are almost as much tied to one type of girl in popular fiction today. And it is getting very tiresome. A huge human success is banking up for anybody bold enough to describe a quiet girl, a girl handicapped by good manners and a habit of minding her own business. Even a sulky girl would be a relief.

The moral is one we often draw; that the family is the real field for personality. All the best Shakespearian dramas are domestic dramas; even when mainly concerned with domestic murders. So far from freedom following on the decay of the family, what follows is uniformity. The Rosalinds become a sort of regiment; if it is a regiment of vivandières. They wear uniform of shingled hair and short skirts; and they seem to stand in a row like chorus girls. Not till we have got back within the four walls of the home shall we have any great tragedy or great comedy. The attempts to describe life in a Utopia of the future are alone enough to prove that there is nothing dramatic about an everlasting picnic.

Men and women must stand in some serious and lasting relation to each other for great passions and great problems to arise; and all this anarchy is as bad for art as it is for morals. Rosalind did not go into the wood to look for her freedom; she went into the wood to look for her father. And all the freedom; and even all the fun of the adventure really arises from that fact. For even an adventure must have an aim. Anyhow, the modern aimlessness has produced a condition in which we are so bored with Rosalind that we almost long for Lady Macbeth.

The Heroines of Shakespeare

It is an odd thing that the words hero and heroine have in their constant use in connection with literary fiction entirely lost their meaning. A hero now means merely a young man sufficiently decent and reliable to go through a few adventures without hanging himself or taking to drink. The modern realistic novelist introduces us to a weak-kneed young suburban gentleman who varies dull respectability with duller vice, and consumes three thick volumes before he has decided which woman he will marry. And by the strange, blasphemous perversion of words, he is called "The Hero". He might just as well, in reason, be called "The Saint", or "The Prophet", or "The Messiah". A hero means a man of heroic stature, a demigod, a man on whom rests something of the mystery which is beyond man. Now, the great and striking thing about heroines like Portia and Isabella and Rosalind is that they are heroines, that they do represent a certain dignity, a certain breadth, which is distinct from the mere homely vigour of the Shakespearian men. You could not slap Portia on the back as you could Bassanio. There may or may not be a divinity that doth hedge a king, but there is certainly a divinity that doth hedge a queen. To understand this heroic quality in the Shakespearian women it is necessary to grasp a little the whole Elizabethan, and especially the whole Shakespearian, view of this matter.

The great conception at the back of the oldest religions in the world is, of course, the conception that man is of divine origin, a sacred and splendid heir, the eldest son of the universe. But humanity could not in practice carry out this conception that everyone was divine. The practical imagination recoils from the idea of two gods swindling each other over a pound of cheese.

The mind refuses to accept the idea of sixty bodies, each filled with a blazing divinity, elbowing each other to get into an omnibus. This mere external difficulty causes men in every age to fall back upon the conception that certain men preserved for other men the sanctity of man. Certain figures were more divine because they were more human. In primitive times of folklore, and in some feudal periods, this larger man was the conquering hero, the strong man who slew dragons and oppressors. To the old Hebrews this sacred being was the prophet; to the men of the Christian ages it was the saint. To the Elizabethans this sacred being was the pure woman.

The heroic conception of womanhood comes out most clearly in Shakespeare because of his astonishing psychological imagination, but it exists as an ideal in all Elizabethans. And the precise reason why the heroines of Shakespeare are so splendid is because they stand alone among all the characters as the embodiments of the primal ages of faith. They are the high and snowy peaks which catch the last rays of the belief in the actual divinity of man. We feel, as we read the plays, that the women are more large, more typical, belong more to an ideal and less to a realistic literature. They are the very reverse of abstractions; considered merely as women they are finished down to the finest detail. Yet there is something more in them that is not in the men. Portia is a good woman and Bassanio is a good man. But Portia is more than a woman: Portia is Woman and Bassanio is not Man. He is merely a very pleasant and respectable individual.

There are Elizabethan plays so dark and frightful that they read like the rubbish from the wastepaper basket of a madhouse. No one but a prophet possessed of devils, one might fancy, could produce incidents so abrupt and so sombre, could call up scenes so graphic and so unmeaning. In one play a man is forced to watch the murder of those he loves and cannot speak because his tongue is nailed to the floor with a dagger. In another a man is torn with red-hot pincers; in another a man is dropped through a broken floor into a cauldron. With horrible cries out of the lowest hell it is proclaimed that man cannot be continent, that man cannot be true, that he is only the filthiest and the funniest of monkeys. And yet the one belief that all these dark and brutal men admit, is the belief in the pure woman. In this one virtue, in this one sex, something heroic and holy, something in the highest sense of that word, fabulous, was felt to reside. Man was natural, but woman was supernatural.

Now it is quite clear that this was the Elizabethan view of woman. Portia is not only the most splendid and magnanimous woman in literature. She is not only the heroine of the play, she is the play. She is the absolute heroic ideal upon which the play is built. Shakespeare had conceived, with extraordinary force, humour and sympathy, a man to express the ideal of technical justice, formal morality, and the claim of a man to his rights: the man was Shylock. Over against him he set a figure representing the larger conception of generosity and persuasion, the justice that is fused of a score of genial passions, the compromise that is born of a hundred worthy enthusiasms. Portia had to represent the ideal of magnanimity in law, morality, religion, art and politics. And Shakespeare made this figure a good woman because, to the mind of his day, to make it a good woman was to ring it with a halo and arm it with a sword.

Louisa Alcott

It is very good for a man to talk about what he does not understand; as long as he understands that he does not understand it. Agnosticism (which has, I am sorry to say, almost entirely disappeared from the modern world) is always an admirable thing, so long as it admits that the thing which it does not understand may be much superior to the mind which does not understand it. Thus if you say that the cosmos is incomprehensible, and really mean (as most moderns do) that it is not worth comprehending; then it would be much better for your Greek agnosticism if it were called by its Latin name of ignorance. But there is one thing that any man can fairly consider incomprehensible, and yet in some ways superior. There is one thing that any man may worry about, and still respect; I mean any woman. The deadly and divine cleavage between the sexes has compelled every woman and every man, age after age, to believe without understanding; to have faith without any knowledge.

Upon the same principle it is a good thing for any man to have to review a book which he cannot review. It is a good thing for his agnosticism and his humility to consider a book which may be much better than he can ever understand. It is good for a man who has seen many books which he could not review because they were so silly, to review one book which he cannot review because it is so wise. For wisdom, first and last, is the characteristic of women. They are often silly, they are always wise. Commonsense is uncommon among men; but commonsense is really and literally a common sense among women. And the sagacity of women, like the sagacity of saints, or that of donkeys, is something outside all questions of ordinary cleverness and ambition. The whole truth of the matter was revealed to Mr. Rudyard Kipling when the spirit of truth suddenly descended on him and he said: "Any woman can manage a clever man; but it requires a rather clever woman to manage a fool."

The wisdom of women is different; and this alone makes the review of such books by a man difficult. But the case is stronger. I for one will willingly confess that the only thing on earth I am frightfully afraid of is a little girl. Female children, she babies, girls up to the age of five are perfectly reasonable; but then all babies are reasonable. Grown girls and women give us at least glimpses of their meaning. But the whole of the period between a girl who is six years old and a girl who is sixteen is to me an abyss not only of mystery, but of terror. If the Prussians were invading England, and I were holding a solitary outpost, the best thing they could do would be to send a long rank or regiment of Prussian girls of twelve, from which I should fly, screaming.

Now the famous books of Miss Alcott are all about little girls. Therefore, my first impulse was to fly screaming. But I resisted this impulse, and I read the books; and I discovered, to my immeasurable astonishment, that they were extremely good. *Little Women* was written by a woman for women—for little women. Consequently it anticipated realism by twenty or thirty years; just as Jane Austen anticipated it by at least a hundred years. For women are the only realists; their whole object in life is to pit their realism against the extravagant, excessive, and occasionally drunken idealism of men. I do not hesitate. I am not ashamed to name Miss Alcott and Miss Austen. There is, indeed, a vast division in the matter of literature (an unimportant matter), but there is the same silent and unexplained assumption of the feminine point of view. There is no pretence, as most unfortunately occurred in the case of another woman of genius, George Eliot, that the writer is anything else but a woman, writing to amuse other women, with her awful womanly irony. Jane Austen did not call herself George Austen; nor Louisa Alcott call herself George Alcott. These women refrained from that abject submission to the male sex which we have since been distressed to see; the weak demand for masculine names and for a part in merely masculine frivolities; parliaments, for instance. These were strong women; they classed parliament with the public-house. But for another and better reason, I do not hesitate to name Miss Alcott by the side of Jane Austen; because her talent, though doubtless inferior, was of exactly the same kind. There is an unmistakable material truth about the thing; if that material truth were not the chief female characteristic, we should most of us find our houses burnt down when we went back to them. To take but one instance out of many, and an instance that a man can understand, because a man was involved, the account of the quite sudden and quite blundering proposal, acceptance, and engagement between Jo and the German professor under the umbrella, with parcels falling off them, so to speak, every minute, is one of the really human things in human literature; when you read it you feel sure that human beings have experienced it often; you almost feel that you have experienced it yourself. There is something true to all our own private diaries in the fact that our happiest moments have happened in the rain, or under some absurd impediment of absurd luggage. The same is true of a hundred other elements in the story. The whole affair of the children acting the different parts in *Pickwick,* forming a childish club under strict restrictions, in order to do so; all that is really life, even where it is not literature. And as a final touch of human truth, nothing could be better than the way in which Miss Alcott suggests the borders and the sensitive privacy of such an experiment. All the little girls have become interested, as they would in real life, in the lonely little boy next door; but when one of them introduces him into their private club in imitation of *Pickwick,* there is a general stir of resistance; these family fictions do not endure being considered from the outside.

All that is profoundly true; and something more than that is profoundly true. For just as the boy was an intruder in that club of girls, so any masculine reader is really an intruder among this pile of books. There runs through the whole series a certain moral philosophy, which a man can never really get the hang of. For

instance, the girls are always doing something, pleasant or unpleasant. In fact, when they have not to do something unpleasant,
they deliberately do something else. A great part, perhaps the
more godlike part, of a boy's life, is passed in doing nothing at all.
Real selfishness, which is the simplest thing in the world to a boy
or man, is practically left out of the calculation. The girls may
conceivably oppress and torture each other; but they will not
indulge or even enjoy themselves—not, at least, as men understand indulgence or enjoyment. The strangest things are taken for
granted; as that it is wrong in itself to drink champagne. But two
things are quite certain; first, that even from a masculine standpoint,
the books are very good; and second, that from a feminine standpoint they are so good that their admirers have really lost sight
even of their goodness. I have never known, or hardly ever
known, a really admirable woman who did not confess to having
read these books. Haughty ladies confessed (under torture) that
they liked them still. Stately Suffragettes rose rustling from the
sofa and dropped *Little Women* on the floor, covering them with
public shame. At learned ladies' colleges, it is, I firmly believe,
handed about secretly, like a dangerous drug. I cannot understand
this strange and simple world, in which unselfishness is natural, in
which spite is easier than self-indulgence. I am the male intruder,
like poor Mr. Laurence and I withdraw. I back out hastily, bowing.
But I am sure that I leave a very interesting world behind me.

PART FOUR

FATHERS & MOTHERS

* * *

And the business done in the home is nothing less than the shaping of the bodies and souls of humanity. The family is the factory that manufactures mankind.

"The Policeman as a Mother", in *The New Witness,*
November 14, 1919

There was hugely more sense in the old people who said that a wife and a husband ought to have the same religion than there is in all the contemporary gushing about sister souls and kindred spirits and auras and identical colour. As a matter of fact, the more the sexes are in violent contrast the less likely they are to be in violent collision. The more incompatible their tempers are the better. . . . There are very few marriages of identical taste and temperament; they are generally unhappy. But to have the same fundamental theory, to think the same thing a virtue, whether you practice or neglect it, to think the same thing a sin, whether you punish or pardon or laugh at it, in the last extremity to call the same thing duty and the same thing disgrace—this really is necessary to a tolerably happy marriage; and it is much better represented by a common religion than it is by affinities and auras.

A Miscellany of Men

We are superiors by that silliest and most snobbish of all superiorities, the mere aristocracy of time. All works must become thus old and

141

insipid which have ever tried to be 'modern', which have consented to smell of time rather than of eternity. Only those who have stopped to be in advance of their time will ever find themselves behind it.

We are never oppressed by old things; it is recent things that can really oppress us.

George Bernard Shaw

The Head of the House

. . . $\mathbf{T}$his notion of the head of a house may seem at first sight somewhat mystical and despotic. It is not despotic, but it is mystical. It all arises from this perfectly simple and primal fact, which everyone seems to forget in the discussion. I mean the fact that the family is older than the State; and this means that agreement is older than coercion. No doubt there was much coercion mixed up with it. A man may have dragged a woman to a wedding as a nigger-driver drives a nigger to a plantation. But there are at least an impressive number of instances in which the woman will want rather less dragging than the nigger. A man may have put his own sons to death under the old Roman law; but the very fact that the tale is told of him proves that the thing was startling and unnatural. It proves that the sons were not put to death by the father as the modern prisoners are put to death by the modern judge—that is, hurriedly, carelessly, and with a frivolous formality. Children may hate and murder their parents, as in the "Electra" of Euripides; but even Euripides thought it a tragedy.

The family is primarily supposed to rest upon consent—that is, on certain spontaneous attachments such as occur in animals and plants. It is for this reason that the father of a family has never been called "the king of the house" or "the priest of the house," or again, "the pope of the house." His power was not dogmatic or definite enough for that. He was called "the head of the house." The man is the head of the house, while the woman is the heart of the house. The definition of the head is that it is the thing that talks.

The head of an arrow is not more necessary than the shaft of it;

perhaps not so much. The head of an axe is not more necessary
than the handle; for mere fighting I would sooner have the handle
alone than the blade alone. But the head of axe and arrow is the
thing that enters first; the thing that speaks. If I kill a man with an
arrow I send the arrow-head as an ambassador, to open the question.
If I split a man's skull with an axe, it is the blade of the axe that
opens the question—and the head.

   Now the old human family, on which civilisation is built,
meant this when it talked about its "head." It has nothing to do
with detailed despotism or the control of other people's daily
lives. That is quite another and later idea, arising out of the crazy
complexity of all high civilisations. If authority means power
(which it does not), I think the wife has more of it than the
husband. If I look round any ordinary room at all the objects—at
their colour, choice and place—I feel as if I were a lonely and
stranded male in a world made wholly by women. All the same, if
a canvasser comes to urge the cause of the Conservative-Radicals,
or of the Radical-Conservatives, it is I who ought to see him. If a
drunkard has wandered into my front garden and lain down on
the principal flower-bed, it is I who ought to inspect him. If a
burglar wanders about the house at night, it is I who ought to
parley with him. Because I am the head; I am the tiresome
excrescence that can talk to the world.

Where Should the Mother Be?

The recent controversy about the professional position of married women was part of a much larger controversy, which is not limited to professional women or even to women. It involves a distinction that controversialists on both sides commonly forget. As it is conducted, it turns largely on the query about whether family life is what is called a "whole-time job" or a "half-time job." But there is also another distinction between a whole job and a half job, or a hundredth part of a job. It has nothing to do with the time that is occupied, but only with the ground that is covered. An industrial expert once actually boasted that it took twenty men to make a pin; and I hope he sat down on the pin. But the man making the twentieth part of the pin did not only work for the twentieth part of an hour. He might perfectly well be working for twelve hours—indeed, he might have been working for twenty-four hours for all the happy industrial expert generally cared. He might work for the whole of a lifetime, but he never made the whole of a pin.

Now there are lingering still in the world a number of lunatics, among whom I have the honour to count myself, who think it a good thing to preserve as many whole jobs as possible. We congratulate ourselves, in our crazy fashion, whenever we find anybody personally and completely doing anything. We rejoice when we find remaining in the world any cases in which the individual can see the beginning and the end of his own work. We are well aware that this is often incompatible with modern scientific civilisation, and the fact has sometimes moved us to say what we think about modern scientific civilisation. But anyhow, whether we are right or wrong, that is an important distinction not always remembered; and that is the important distinction that ought to be most remembered, and is least remembered, in this modern debate about the occupation of women.

Probably there must be a certain number of people doing work which they do not complete. Perhaps there must be some people doing work which they do not comprehend. But we do not want to multiply those people indefinitely, and then cover it all by shouting emancipation and equality. It may be emancipation to allow a woman to make part of a pin, if she really wants to make part of a pin. It may be equality if she is really filled with a furious jealousy of her husband, who has the privilege of making part of a pin. But we question whether it is really a more human achievement to make part of a pin than to make the whole of a pinafore. And we even go further, and question whether it is more human to make the whole of a pinafore than to look after the whole of a child. The point about the "half-time job" of motherhood is that it is at least one of the jobs that can be regarded as a whole, and almost as an end in itself. A human being is in some sense an end in himself. Anything that makes him happy or high-minded is, under God, a thing directed to an ultimate end. It is not, like nearly all the trades and professions, merely a machinery and a means to an end. And it is a thing which can, by the constitution of human nature, be pursued with positive and unpurchased enthusiasm. Whether or not it is a half-time job, it need not be a half-hearted job.

Now, as a matter of fact, there are not so many jobs which normal and ordinary people can pursue with enthusiasm for their own sakes. The position is generally falsified by quoting the exceptional cases of specialists who achieve success. There may be a woman who is so very fond of swimming the Channel that she can go on doing it until she breaks a record. There may be, for that matter, a woman who is so fond of discovering the North Pole that she goes on doing it long after it has been discovered. Such sensational successes naturally bulk big in the newspapers, because they are sensational cases. But they are not the question of whether women are more free in professional or domestic life. To answer that question, we must assume all the sailors on the Channel boats to be women, all the fishermen in the herring fleet to be women, all the whalers in the North Sea to be women, and then consider whether the worst paid and hardest worked of all those workers were really having a happier or a harder life. It will be at once apparent that the vast majority of them must be under orders; and that perhaps a considerable minority of them would be under orders which they did not entirely understand. There could not be a community in which the average woman was in command of a ship. But there can be a community in which the average woman is in command of a house.

To take a hundred women out of a hundred houses and give them a hundred ships would be obviously impossible, unless all the ships were canoes. And that would be carrying to rather fanatical lengths the individualist ideal of people paddling their own canoes. To take the hundred women out of the hundred houses and put them on ten ships, or more probably on two ships, is obviously to increase vastly the number of servants and diminish the number of mistresses. The only ship I remember that was so manned (or perhaps we should say womanned) was the ship of the Bab Ballad commanded by Lieutenant Bellay. And even there it might be said that the young ladies who sailed with him had ultimately rather a domestic than a professional ideal. But that naval commander was not very professional himself, and, it will be remembered, excused his sailors from most of their duties and amused himself by firing off his one big gun.

I fear that the experience of more subordinate women in shops and factories is a little more strenuous. I have taken an extremely elementary and crude example, but I am not the first rhetorician who has found it convenient to discuss the State under the bright and original similitude of a ship. But the principle does apply quite as much to a shop as to a ship. It applies with especial exactitude to the modern shop which is almost larger than the modern ship. A shop or a factory must consist of a very large majority of servants and one of the few human institutions in which there need be no such enormous majority of servants is the human household. I still think, therefore, that for the lady interested in ships the most supreme and symbolical moment is the moment when her ships come home. And I think there are some sort of symbolic ships that had much better come home and stay there.

I know all about the necessary modifications and compromises produced by the accidental conditions of today. I am not unreasonable about them. But what we are discussing is not the suggestion that the ideal should be modified. It is the suggestion that the ideal should be abolished. It is the suggestion that a new test or method of judgment should be applied to the affair, which is not the test of whether the thing is a whole job, in the sense of a self-sufficing and satisfactory job, but of whether it is what is called a half-time job—that is, a thing to be measured by the mechanical calculation of modern employment.

There have been household gods and household saints and household fairies. I am not sure that there have yet been any factory gods or factory saints or factory fairies. I may be wrong, as I am no commercial expert, but I have not heard of them as yet. And we think that the reason lies in the distinction which I made at the beginning of these remarks. The imagination and the religious instinct and the human sense of humour have free play when people are dealing with something which, however small, is rounded and complete like a cosmos.

The place where babies are born, where men die, where the drama of mortal life is acted, is not an office or a shop or a bureau. It is something much smaller in size and much larger in scope. And while nobody would be such a fool as to pretend that it is the only place where women should work, it has a character of unity and universality that is not found in any of the fragmentary experiences of the division of labour.

The Glory of Home and Family

Modern moral controversy reels to and fro, to such an extent that men seem sometimes to change weapons, as in the duel in "Hamlet," or even change places, as in the game of Puss-in-the-Corner. I admit that I quote the facts at second-hand, but from a very moderate and reliable paper; and it would seem that in a recent discussion on that totally new topic, the True Position of Woman, some rather remarkable manifestations were made. It seems that Mr. Henry Ford, the very incarnation of swift progress and practical industrialism, has been saying that Woman's only place is the Home. And it seems that Mr. Bertrand Russell, the very champion of Feminism, has been saying that American civilisation is over-feminised. The report in question sums up his view by saying that "American women are over-romantic, and that the American family is disintegrating in consequence, since it is regarded primarily as the vehicle of sentimental compatibility and not as a child-rearing unit." The language is a little pedantic; but on the whole it serves to show that everybody has a sane spot somewhere, even Cambridge philosophers and scientific millionaires. But the philosopher is more philosophical than the millionaire, for it is the wrong way of putting it to say that Woman should be confined to the Home, as if it were a Home for Incurables. The Home is not a prison, or even an asylum; nor is the case for the Home the idea that certain people should be locked up in it because they are weak-minded or incapable. It is as if men had said that the Priestess of Delphi should be kept in her place, which was to sit on a tripod and deliver nice little oracles. Or it is as if Miss Maude Royden were accused of saying that a woman should be locked up in the pulpit and not allowed to pollute the rest of the church. Those who believe in the dignity of the domestic tradition, who happen to be the overwhelming majority of mankind, regard the home as a sphere of vast social importance and supreme spiritual significance; and to talk of being confined to it is like talking of being chained to a throne, or set in the seat of judgment as if it were the stocks. There may be women who are uncomfortable in family life, as there have been certainly men who were uncomfortable on thrones. There are wives who do not want to be mothers; and there are lawyers who do not want to be judges. But, taking normal human nature and historic tradition as a whole, we cannot be expected to start the discussion by assuming that these human dignities are not the object of human desires. We cannot simply take it for granted that kings are humiliated by being crowned. We cannot accept it as a first principle that a man is made judge because he is a fool. And we cannot assume, as both sides in this curious controversy so often do assume, that bringing forth and rearing and ruling the living beings of the future is a servile task suited to a silly person.

It is, however, a curious example of the way in which a modern tendency will often cut its own throat. People begin by saying that it is an antiquated tyranny to ask women to form part of "a child-rearing unity." They encourage them to talk sham psychology about compatibility and affinity, and all the rest of it, with the result, as Mr. Bertrand Russell sees, that the view of the whole thing becomes pestiferously sentimental. Then they find that, in introducing the New Woman who shall appeal to posterity, they have in fact introduced a very old-fashioned sort of woman, as fastidious, hysterical, and irresponsible as any silly spinster in a Victorian novel; and above all, that, so far as she is concerned, there is no posterity to appeal to. Meanwhile, by this ingenious *détour,* they have managed to lose the other opportunity altogether. They cannot get the female energy harnessed again to the human and creative purposes of the family, because they have started by denouncing and deriding those purposes as slavish and superstitious. They began by saying that only silly women are domestic; then they went off with the sensible women and watched them turning silly; and now they cannot get anybody to go in for what they originally deprecated as silliness. It is as if they had spat upon all work as being servile work, created a whole generation that could do no work, and then clamoured in vain for somebody to do the work although it was servile. There is no hope for them, except to begin again at the beginning; and consider the paradox that free men can labour or that free women can be at home, even at home.

I have never understood myself how this superstition arose: the notion that a woman plays a lowly part in the home and a loftier part outside the home. There may be all sorts of excellent reasons for individuals doing or not doing either; but I cannot understand how the domestic thing can be considered inferior in the nature of the thing done. Most work done in the outer world is pretty mechanical work; some of it is decidedly dirty work. There seems no possible sense in which it is intrinsically superior to domestic work. Nine times out of ten, the only difference is that the one person is drudging for people she does care for and the other drudging for people she does not care for. But allowing for the element of drudgery in both cases, there is rather more element of distinction, and even dictatorship, in the domestic case. The most fully trusted official must very largely go by the rules and regulations established by superiors. The mother of a family makes her own rules and regulations; and they are not merely mechanical rules, but often very fundamental moral ones. Nor are they merely monotonous in their application. Mr. Ford is reported, rightly or wrongly, as saying that the woman should not be in the business of the outer world, because business people have to make decisions. I should say that mothers have to make many more decisions. A great part of a big business goes by routine; and all the technical part of Mr. Ford's business goes, quite literally, on oiled wheels. It is the very boast of such a system that its products are made rapidly because rigidly, upon a regular pattern, and can be trusted ninety-nine times out of a hundred to turn out according to plan. The little boy does not, by any means, always turn out according to plan. The little boy will present a series of problems in the course of twenty-four hours which could correspond to a Ford car bursting like a bomb or flying out of the window like an aeroplane. The little boy is individual; he cannot be mended with spare parts from another little boy. The mother cannot order another little boy at the same works, and make the experiment work. The domestic woman really is called upon to make decisions, real or moral decisions, and she jolly well does. Some have even complained that her decisions were too decisive.

I suppose the prejudice must have sprung merely from the fact that domestic operations occur in a small space, and on private premises. Even that is illogical enough, in an age that is so proud of the experimental history of science. The most epoch-making scientific feats have been performed in a space no larger than a parlour or a nursery. A baby is bigger than a bacillus; and even the little boy is larger and more lively than a germ under the microscope. And the science that is studied in the home is the greatest and most glorious of all sciences, very inadequately indicated by the word education, and nothing less, at least, than the mystery of the making of men. It does not seem to me in the least odd that so mysterious and momentous a business should have been surrounded by virtues of vigilance and loyalty, as by an armed guard; or that the partners in it should have a sealed and sacred relationship. We may or may not be content with the frigid phrase that the family is a child-rearing unit. But it is not unreasonable to expect a unit to have unity.

Turning Inside Out

When the author of "If Winter Comes" brought out another book about the life of the family, it was almost as much criticized as the first book was praised. I do not say that there was nothing to criticize, but I do say that I was not convinced by the abstract logic of the criticism. Probably the critics would have accepted it as a true story if the author had not been so incautious as to give it a true moral. And the moral is not fashionable in the Press at the moment; for it is to the effect that a woman may gain a professional success at the price of a domestic failure. And it is the convention of journalism at this moment to support what is feminist against what is feminine. Anyhow, while the story might be criticized, the criticisms can certainly be criticized. It is not really conclusive to say that a woman may be ambitious in business without her children going to the bad. It is just as easy to say that a woman may be ambitious in politics without helping to murder an old gentleman in his bed. But that does not make "Macbeth" either inartistic or untrue. It is just as easy to say that a woman may be ambitious in society without tricking her husband into a debtor's prison, so that she may spend the time with a bald-headed nobleman with red whiskers. But that does not make the great scene in "Vanity Fair" unconvincing either in detail or design. The question in fiction is not whether that thing must occur, but whether that sort of thing may occur, and whether it is significant of larger things. Now this business of the woman at work and the woman at home is a very large thing, and this story about it is highly significant.

For in this matter the modern mind is inconsistent with itself. It has managed to get one of its rather crude ideals in flat contradiction to the other. People of the progressive sort are perpetually telling us that the hope of the world is in education. Education is everything. Nothing is so important as training the rising generation. Nothing is really important except the rising generation. They tell us this over and over again, with slight variations of the same formula, and never seem to see what it involves. For if there be any word of truth in all this talk about the education of the child, then there is certainly nothing but nonsense in nine-tenths of the talk about the emancipation of the woman. If education is the highest function in the State, why should anybody want to be emancipated from the highest function in the State? It is as if we talked of commuting the sentence that condemned a man to be President of the United States; or a reprieve coming in time to save him from being Pope. If education is the largest thing in the world, what is the sense of talking about a woman being liberated from the largest thing in the world? It is as if we were to rescue her from the cruel doom of being a poet like Shakespeare; or to pity the limitations of an all-round artist like Leonardo da Vinci. Nor can there be any doubt that there is truth in this claim for education. Only precisely the sort of which it is particularly true is the sort called domestic education. Private education really is universal. Public education can be comparatively narrow. It would really be an exaggeration to say that the schoolmaster who takes his pupils in freehand drawing is training them in all the uses of freedom. It really would be fantastic to say that the harmless foreigner who instructs a class in French or German is talking with all the tongues of men and angels. But the mother dealing with her own daughters in her own home does literally have to deal with all forms of freedom, because she has to deal with all sides of a single human soul. She is obliged, if not to talk with the tongues of men and angels, at least to decide how much she shall talk about angels and how much about men.

In short, if education is really the larger matter, then certainly domestic life is the larger matter; and official or commercial life the lesser matter. It is a mere matter of arithmetic that anything taken from the larger matter will leave it less. It is a mere matter of

simple subtraction that the mother must have less time for the
family if she has more time for the factory. If education, ethical
and cultural, really were a trivial and mechanical matter, the
mother might possibly rattle through it as a rapid routine, before
going about her more serious business of serving a capitalist for
hire. If education were merely instruction, she might briefly
instruct her babies in the multiplication tables, before she mounted
to higher and nobler spheres as the servant of a Milk Trust or the
secretary of a Drug Combine. But the moderns are perpetually
assuring us that education is not instruction; they are perpetually
insisting that it is not a mechanical exercise, and must on no
account be an abbreviated exercise. It must go on at every hour. It
must cover every subject. But if it must go on at all hours, it must
not be neglected in business hours. And if the child is to be free to
cover every subject, the parent must be free to cover every subject
too.

For the idea of a non-parental substitute is simply an illusion of
wealth. The advanced advocate of this inconsistent and infinite
education for the child is generally thinking of the rich child; and
all this particular sort of liberty should rather be called luxury. It
is natural enough for a fashionable lady to leave her little daughter
with the French governess or the Czecho-Slovakian governess or
the Ancient Sanskrit governess, and know that one or other of
these sides of the infant's intelligence is being developed; while
she, the mother, figures in public as a money-lender or some other
modern position of dignity. But among poorer people there
cannot be five teachers to one pupil. Generally there are about
fifty pupils to one teacher. There it is impossible to cut up the soul
of a single child and distribute it among specialists. It is all we can
do to tear in pieces the soul of a single schoolmaster, and distribute
it in rags and scraps to a whole mob of boys. And even in the case
of the wealthy child it is by no means clear that specialists are a
substitute for spiritual authority. Even a millionaire can never be
certain that he has not left out one governess, in the long procession of governesses perpetually under his marble portico; and the
omission may be as fatal as that of the king who forgot to ask the

bad fairy to the christening. The daughter, after a life of ruin and despair, may look back and say, "Had I but also had a Lithuanian governess, my fate as a diplomatist's wife in Eastern Europe would have been very different." But it seems rather more probable, on the whole, that what she would miss would not be one or other of these special accomplishments, but some common sense code of morals or general view of life. The millionaire could, no doubt, hire a mahatma or mystical prophet to give his child a general philosophy. But I doubt if the philosophy would be very success-ful even for the rich child, and it would be quite impossible for the poor child. In the case of comparative poverty, which is the common lot of mankind, we come back to a general parental responsibility, which is the common sense of mankind. We come back to the parent as the person in charge of education. If you exalt the education, you must exalt the parental power with it. If you exaggerate the education, you must exaggerate the parental power with it. If you depreciate the parental power, you must depreciate education with it. If the young are always right and can do as they like, well and good; let us all be jolly, old and young, and free from every kind of responsibility. But in that case do not come pestering us with the importance of education, when nobody has any authority to educate anybody. Make up your mind whether you want unlimited education or unlimited emancipation, but do not be such a fool as to suppose you can have both at once.

There is evidence, as I have noted, that the more hard-headed people, even of the most progressive sort, are beginning to come back to realities in this respect. The new work of Mr. Hutchinson's is only one of many indications among the really independent intelligences, working on modern fiction, that the cruder culture of merely commercial emancipation is beginning to smell a little stale. The work of Miss Clemence Dane and even of Miss Sheila Kaye-Smith contains more than one suggestion of what I mean. People are no longer quite so certain that a woman's liberty consists of having a latch-key without a house. They are no longer wholly convinced that every housekeeper is dull and prosaic, while every bookkeeper is wild and poetical. And among the intelligent the reaction is actually strengthened by all the most modern excitements about psychology and hygiene. We cannot insist that every trick of nerves or train of thought is important enough to be searched for in libraries and laboratories, and not important enough for anybody to watch by simply staying at home. We cannot insist that the first years of infancy are of supreme importance, and that mothers are not of supreme importance; or that motherhood is a topic of sufficient interest for men, but not of sufficient interest for mothers. Every word that is said about the tremendous importance of trivial nursery habits goes to prove that being a nurse is not trivial. All tends to the return of the simple truth that the private work is the great one and the public work the small. The human house is a paradox, for it is larger inside than out.

But in the problem of private versus public life there is another neglected truth. It is true of many masculine problems as well as of this feminine problem. Indeed, feminism falls here into exactly the same mistake as militarism and imperialism. I mean that anything on a grand scale gives the illusion of a grand success. Curiously enough, multiplication acts as a concealment. Repetition actually disguises failure. Take a particular man, and tell him to put on a particular kind of hat and coat and trousers, and to stand in particular attitudes in the back garden; and you will have great difficulty in persuading yourself (or him) that he has passed through a triumph and transfiguration. Order four hundred such hats, and eight hundred such trousers, and you will have turned the fancy costume into a uniform. Make all the four hundred men stand in the special attitudes on Salisbury Plain, and there will rise up before you the spirit of a regiment. Let the regiment march past, and, if you have any life in you above the brutes that perish, you will have an overwhelming sense that something splendid has just happened, or is just going to begin. I sympathize with this moral emotion in militarism; I think it does symbolize something great in the soul, which has given us the image of St. Michael. But I also realize that in practical relations that emotion can get mixed up with an illusion. It is not really possible to know the characters of all the four hundred men in the marching column as well as one might know the character of the one man attitudinizing in the back garden. If all the four hundred men were individual failures, we could still vaguely feel that the whole thing was a success. If we know the one man to be a failure, we cannot think him a success.

That is why a footman has become rather a foolish figure, while a foot-soldier remains rather a sublime one. Or rather, that is one of the reasons; for there are others much more worthy. Anyhow, footmen were only formidable or dignified when they could come in large numbers like foot-soldiers—when they were in fact the feudal army of some great local family, having some of the loyalty of local patriotism. Then a livery was as dignified as a uniform, because it really was a uniform. A man who said he served the Nevilles or rode with the Douglases could once feel much like a man fighting for France or England. But military feeling is mob feeling, noble as mob feeling may be. Parading one footman is like lunching on one pea, or curing baldness by the growth of one hair. There ought not to be anything but a plural for flunkeys, any more than for measles or vermin or animalculae or the sweets called hundreds and thousands. Strictly speaking, I suppose that a logical Latinist could say, "I have seen an animalcula"; but I never heard of a child having the moderation to remark, "I have eaten a hundred and thousand." Similarly, any one of us can feel that to have hundreds and thousands of slaves, let alone soldiers, might give a certain imaginative pleasure in magnificence. To have one slave reveals all the meanness of slavery. For the solitary flunkey really is the man in fancy dress, the man standing in the back garden in the strange and the fantastic coat and breeches. His isolation reveals our illusion. We find our failure in the back garden, when we have been dreaming a dream of success in the market-place. When you ride through the streets amid a great mob of vassals (you may have noticed) you have a genial and not ungenerous sense of being at one with them all. You cannot remember their names or count their numbers, but their very immensity seems a substitute for intimacy. That is what great men have felt at the head of great armies; and the reason why Napoleon or Foch would call his soldiers *"mes enfants."* He feels at that moment that they are a part of him, as if he had a million arms and legs. But it is very different if you disband your army of lackeys; or if (as is, after all, possible) you have not got an army of lackeys. It is very different if you look at one lackey; one solitary solemn footman standing in your front hall. You never have the sense of being caught up into a rapture of unity with *him.* All your sense of social solidarity with your social inferiors has dropped from you. It is only in public that people can be so intimate as that. When you look into the eyes of the lonely footman, you see that his soul is far away.

In other words, you find yourself at the foot of a steep and staggering mountain crag, that is the real character and conscience of a man. To be really at one with that man, you would have to solve real problems and believe that your own solutions were real. In dealing with the one man you would really have a far huger and harder job than in dealing with your throng of thousands. And *that* is the job that people run away from when they wish to escape from domesticity to public work, especially educational work. They wish to escape from a sense of failure which is simply a sense of fact. They wish to recapture the illusion of the marketplace. It is an illusion that departs in the dark interiors of domesticity, where the realities dwell. As I have said, I am very far from condemning it altogether; it is a lawful pleasure, and a part of life, in its proper proportion, like any other. But I am concerned to point out to the feminists and the faddists that it is not an approach to truth, but rather the opposite. Publicity is rather of the nature of a harmless romance. Public life at its very best will contain a great deal of harmless romancing, and much more often a very harmful romancing. In other words, I am concerned with pointing out that the passage from private life to public life, while it may be right or wrong, or necessary or unnecessary, or desirable or undesirable, is always of necessity a passage from a greater work to a smaller one, and from a harder work to an easier one. And that is why most of the moderns do wish to pass from the great domestic task to the smaller and easier commercial one. They would rather provide the liveries of a hundred footmen than be bothered with the love-affairs of one. They would rather take the salutes of a hundred soldiers than try to save the soul of one. They would rather serve out income-tax papers or telegraph forms to a hundred men than meals, conversation, and moral support to one. They would rather arrange the educational course in history or geography, or correct the examination papers in algebra or trigonometry, for a hundred children, than struggle with the whole human character of one. For anyone who makes himself responsible for one small baby, as a whole, will soon find that he is wrestling with gigantic angels and demons.

In another way there is something of illusion, or of irresponsibility, about the purely public function, especially in the case of public education. The educationist generally deals with only one section of the pupil's mind. But he always deals with only one section of the pupil's life. The parent has to deal, not only with the whole of the child's character, but also with the whole of the child's career. The teacher sows the seed, but the parent reaps as well as sows. The schoolmaster sees more children, but it is not clear that he sees more childhood; certainly he sees less youth and no maturity. The number of little girls who take prussic acid is necessarily small. The boys who hang themselves on bedposts, after a life of crime, are generally the minority. But the parent has to envisage the whole life of the individual, and not merely the school life of the scholar. It is not probable that the parent will exactly anticipate crime and prussic acid as the crown of the infant's career. But he will anticipate hearing of the crime if it is committed; he will probably be told of the suicide if it takes place. It is quite doubtful whether the schoolmaster or schoolmistress will ever hear of it at all. Everybody knows that teachers have a harassing and often heroic task, but it is not unfair to them to remember that in this sense they have an exceptionally happy task. The cynic would say that the teacher is happy in never seeing the results of his own teaching. I prefer to confine myself to saying that he has not the extra worry of having to estimate it from the other end. The teacher is seldom in at the death. To take a milder theatrical metaphor, he is seldom there on the night. But this is only one of many instances of the same truth: that what is called public life is not larger than private life, but smaller. What we call public life is a fragmentary affair of sections and seasons and impressions; it is only in private life that dwells the fullness of our life bodily.

PART FIVE

THE INNOCENCE OF
THE CHILD

✳ ✳ ✳

As Jupiter could be hidden from all-devouring Time, as the Christ Child could be hidden from Herod—so the child unborn is still hidden from the omniscient oppressor. He who lives not yet, he and he alone is left; and they seek his life to take it away.

Eugenics and Other Evils

What was wonderful about childhood is that anything in it was a wonder. It was not merely a world full of miracles; it was a miraculous world. What gives me this shock is almost anything I really recall; not the things I should think most worth recalling. This is where it differs from the other great thrill of the past, all that is connected with first love and the romantic passion; for that, though equally poignant, comes always to a point; and is narrow like a rapier piercing the heart, whereas the other was more like a hundred windows opened on all sides of the head.

Autobiography

The devil can quote Scripture for his purpose; and the text of Scripture which he now most commonly quotes is, 'the kingdom of heaven is within you.' That text has been the stay and support of more Pharisees and prigs and self-righteous spiritual bullies than all the dogmas in creation; it has served to identify self-satisfaction with the peace that passes all understanding. And the text to be quoted in answer to it is that which declares that no man can receive the kingdom except as a little child. What we are to have inside is the childlike spirit; but the childlike spirit is not entirely concerned about what is inside. It is the first mark of possessing it that one is interested in what is outside. The most childlike thing about a child is his curiosity and his appetite and his power to wonder at the world. We might say that the whole advantage of having the kingdom within is that we look for it somewhere else.

What I Saw in America

I begin with a little girl's hair. That I know is a good thing at any rate. Whatever else is evil, the pride of a good mother in the beauty of her daughter is good. It is one of those adamantine tenderness which are the touchstones of every age and race. If other things are against it, other things must go down. If landlords and laws and sciences are against it, landlords and laws and sciences must go down. With the red hair of one she-urchin in the gutter I will set fire to all modern civilisation. Because a girl should have long hair, she should have clean hair; because she should have clean hair, she should not have an unclean home; because she should not have an unclean home, she should have a free and leisured mother; because she should have a free mother, she should not have an usurious landlord; because there should not be an usurious landlord, there should be a redistribution of property; because there should be a redistribution of property, there shall be a revolution. (...) Her mother may bid her bind her hair, for that is a natural authority; but the Emperor of the Planet shall not bid her to cut it off. She is the human and sacred image; all around her the social fabric shall sway and split and fall; the pillars of society shall be shaken, and the roofs of ages come rushing down; and not one hair of her head shall be harmed.

What's Wrong with the World

.

By the Babe Unborn

If trees were tall and grasses short,
    As in some crazy tale,
If here and there a sea were blue
    Beyond the breaking pale,

If a fixed fire hung in the air
    To warm me one day through,
If deep green hair grew on great hills,
    I know what I should do.

In dark I lie: dreaming that there
    Are great eyes cold or kind,
And twisted streets and silent doors,
    And living men behind.

Let storm-clouds come: better an hour,
    And leave to weep and fight,
Than all the ages I have ruled
    The empires of the night.

I think that if they gave me leave
    Within the world to stand,
I would be good through all the day
    I spent in fairyland.

They should not hear a word from me
    Of selfishness or scorn,
If only I could find the door,
    If only I were born.

Our Birthday

As this is a Birthday Number, I propose to write about birthdays in a futile and irresponsible manner, as befits a festive occasion; and to leave for a later issue some of the serious questions that are raised in this one. I remember that long ago, in one of my countless controversies with Mr. Bernard Shaw, I commented on a scornful remark of his that he did not keep his own birthday and would not be bothered with anybody else's; and I argued that this exactly illustrates the one point upon which he is really wrong; and that if he had only kept his birthday, he might have kept many other things along with it. It will be noted that, with the magnificent magnanimity in which he has never failed, especially in dealing with me and my romantic delusions, he has contributed to this special number an article dealing with very vital matters. I hope to answer that article, in greater detail, in due course; here I will only give a very general reply upon the particular aspect which is excellently and exactly represented by Birthdays.

For one happy hour, in talking about Birthdays, I shall not stoop to talk about Birth-Control. But when Mr. Shaw asks why I doubt that he and I, not to mention Mr. H. G. Wells and Mr. Bertrand Russell, can form a committee to produce a creed, not to say a cosmos—my general answer is that the difference begins with the very birth of the conception. A Birthday embodies certain implicit ideas; with some of which he agrees and is right; with others of which he disagrees and is wrong. In some matters the difference between us seems to amount to this: that I very respectfully recognise that he disagrees with me; but he will not even allow me to disagree with him. But there is one fundamental truth in which I have never for a moment disagreed with him.

166

Whatever else he is, he has never been a pessimist; or in spiritual matters a defeatist. He is at least on the side of Life, and in that sense of Birth. When the Sons of God shout for joy, merely because the creation is in being, Mr. Shaw's splendid Wagnerian shout or bellow will be mingled with my less musical but equally mystical song of praise. I am aware that in the same poem the patriarch Job, under the stress of incidental irritations, actually curses the day he was born; prays that the stars of its twilight be dark and that it be not numbered among the days of the year; but I am sure that G.B.S. will not carry his contempt for birthday celebrations to that length. The first fact about the celebration of a birthday is that it is a way of affirming defiantly, and even flamboyantly, that it is a good thing to be alive. On that matter, and it is a basic matter, there really is a basis of agreement; and Mr. Shaw and I, giving our performance as morning stars that sing together, will sing in perfect harmony if hardly with equal technique.

But there is a second fact about Birthdays, and the birth-song of all creation, a fact which really follows on this; but which, as it seems to me, the other school of thought almost refuses to recognise. The point of that fact is simply that it is a fact. In being glad about my Birthday, I am being glad about something which I did not myself bring about. In being grateful for my birth, I am grateful for something which has already happened; which happened, sad as it may seem to some, quite a long time ago. Now it seems to me that Mr. Shaw and his school start almost everything in the spirit of people who are saying, "I shall myself select the 17th of October as the date of my birth. I propose to be born at Market Harborough; I have selected for my father a very capable and humane dentist, while my mother will be trained as a high-class headmistress for the tremendous honour and responsibility of her position; before that, I think I shall send her to Girton. The house I have selected to be born in faces a handsome ornamental park, etc., etc." In other words, it seems to me that modern thinkers of this kind have simply no philosophy or poetry or possible attitude at all, towards the things which they *receive* from the real world that exists already; from the past; from the parent; from the patriotic tradition or the moral philosophy of mankind. They only talk about making things; as if they could make themselves as well as everything else. They are always talking about making a religion; and cannot get into their heads the very notion of receiving a revelation. They are always talking about making a creed; without seeing that it involves making a cosmos. But even then, we could not possibly make the cosmos that has made us. Now nobody who knows anything about my little tastes and prejudices will say that I am not in sympathy with the notion of making things. I believe in making thousands of things; making jokes, making pictures, making (as distinct from faking) goods, making books, and even articles (of which, as the reader will sadly perceive, there is no end), making toys, making tools, making farms, making homes, making churches, making sacred images; and, incidentally also, making war on people who would prevent me from doing these things. But the workshop, vast as it is, is only one half of the world. There is a whole problem of the human mind, which is necessarily concerned with the things that it did not make; with the things that it could not make; including itself. And I say it is a narrow view of life, which leaves out the whole of that aspect of life; all receptivity, all gratitude, all inheritance, all worship. Unless a philosopher has a philosophy, which can make tolerable and tenable his attitude towards all the actualities that are around him and before him and behind him — then he has only half a philosophy; and, though he is the wittiest man in the world, he is in that sense half-witted.

Mr. Bernard Shaw is certainly one of the wittiest men in the world, and about whole huge aspects of life, one of the wisest. But if I am to sit down with him at a committee of evolutionists, to draw up a creed for humanity, I fancy I foresee that this is the line along which I shall eventually come to issue my Minority Report. I shall find myself the representative, and I suspect the only representative, of *all* the implications of my Birthday. I do not even mind calling it the pride of birth, which of course has nothing to do with the pride of rank; so long as it involves the humility of birth also.

Blasphemy and the Baby

I have so very much admiration for Mr. A. P. Herbert, and so very little admiration for the decisions of the Anglican Bishops at their recent Council, that I have no natural impulse to defend the latter against the former. But as he has attacked them from the other side, I should like to point out one or two curiously neglected facts that are very evident to our side; in the business called Birth Control. First of all, may I implore Mr. Herbert to avoid a logomachy about the word "natural," which arises accidentally out of a modern use of that word. He elaborately explains that shaving is artificial, being the result of human action on a non-human part of nature. Now really, Mr. Herbert, with his brilliant and genial personality, must have a number of Catholic friends and acquaintances; he must know that many of them are people capable of the use of reason, and guided by some sort of coherent philosophy, right or wrong. Lastly, with his shrewd and exact observation of life, to which we all owe so much, he must have noticed that Catholics put up umbrellas when it rains, put down doormats where it is muddy, summon fire brigades during a fire and send out lifeboats to a shipwreck. In other words, they do not mean by being "natural" that we must leave every non-human process in the cosmos to complete itself as if there were no human beings. It is in a very much deeper and more vital sense that we call contraception unnatural. Roughly speaking, it was not till Victorian times that this conception of Nature, as the non-human order of things, was turned into a sort of impersonal person. The Victorian agnostic insisted sternly that it must be called She, and must on no account be called He. But to apply this to the Catholic and the other older philosophies is to make a historical mistake about the use of words. When Aristotle said that man is by nature a political animal, he was not thinking of the nineteenth century nightmare about Nature red in tooth and claw. When Catholics talk, as they have always talked, about the natural law, they mean something which could be better translated into modern English as the human law. They mean the law of man's moral status, as it can be perceived by man's natural reason, even without supernatural aid. And when they say that contraception is unnatural, they mean it as they mean that sexual perversion is unnatural. That is, it is unnatural in man, and not merely unnatural in nature. It is something which his own instincts, conscience and imaginative foresight tell him is unworthy of his human dignity; not merely something that interferes with what comes from outside, like a shower of rain or a thunderbolt. There is no space here to do justice to our very vivid sense of this moral fact; so I will content myself for the moment with a parallel, which has always struck me as very exact, except that the subject is less serious. If an epicure decided that he could lunch at the Ritz six times a day, and sup at the Savoy seven times in the same evening, by the simple operation of taking emetics between the meals, I should have a very strong conviction that he was following an unwholesome course of life. I should think that unlimited gluttony, even when not followed by digestion (or indigestion) would probably in the long run be bad for his body, and would quite certainly be bad for his mind. I think the same of unlimited lust without its natural consequences, as of unlimited gluttony without its natural consequences. I think it would have other and much less natural consequences.

One proof of its unnatural character is that the theory starts everybody on an unnatural way of thinking; even Mr. A. P. Herbert. For instance, I feel it to be utterly unnatural, though it is already quite stale and conventional, to talk in this queer contemptuous way about the birth of a child. Mr. Herbert breaks out into a sort of romantic, not to say sentimental, indignation against the remark that the chief object of marriage is the procreation of children. He calls it all sorts of funny things which are supposed to be withering; such as masculine and mediaeval and smacking of the stud farm; an odd thing to associate with what is mediaeval, since the eugenic fancy is peculiarly modern. Well, Catholics will not resent being called masculine and are used to being called mediaeval. But what strikes me as truly extraordinary is the implication that there is something low about the objective being the birth of a child. Whereas it is obvious that this great natural miracle is the one creative, imaginative and disinterested part of the whole business. The creation of a new creature, not ourselves, of a new conscious centre, of a new and independent focus of experience and enjoyment, is an immeasurably more grand and godlike act even than a real love affair; how much more superior to a momentary physical satisfaction. If creating another self is not noble, why is pure self-indulgence nobler?

I regret to see a man like Mr. Herbert getting into the rut of this vulgar but very conventional convention. He has the misfortune to live in an age of journalese, in which anything done inside a house is called "drudgery," while anything done inside an office is called "enterprise." This convention forces him to talk of the most incredible creative power in man, more amazing than any work of art, as if it were drudgery and too degrading a thing to be the object of marriage. Of course there are other objects, which those may enjoy who miss this one by no fault of their own. But I cannot for the life of me see why this one is not worthy to be called the greatest and the first. I will not debate here the other aspects connected with economics and genetics; merely remarking for the present that the enemies of child-birth have never even begun to prove their case, though they have often tried in public to prove it. I am only concerned with the human and instinctive ideals implied by Mr. Herbert himself; and I humbly but firmly state that they do not really come from Mr. Herbert himself, but from the cheap popular science and dull fashionable fatalism which have, in this particular matter prevented him from using his mind.

Babies and Distributism

I hope it is not a secret arrogance to say that I do not think I am exceptionally arrogant; or if I were, my religion would prevent me from being proud of my pride. Nevertheless, for those of such a philosophy, there is a very terrible temptation to intellectual pride, in the welter of wordy and worthless philosophies that surround us to-day. Yet there are not many things that move me to anything like a personal contempt. I do not feel any contempt for an atheist, who is often a man limited and constrained by his own logic to a very sad simplification. I do not feel any contempt for a Bolshevist, who is a man driven to the same negative simplification by a revolt against very positive wrongs. But there is one type of person for whom I feel what I can only call contempt. And that is the popular propagandist of what he or she absurdly describes as Birth-Control.

I despise Birth-Control first because it is a weak and wobbly and cowardly word. It is also an entirely meaningless word; and is used so as to curry favour even with those who would at first recoil from its real meaning. The proceeding these quack doctors recommend does not *control* any birth. It only makes sure that there shall never be any birth to control. It cannot, for instance, determine sex, or even make any selection in the style of the pseudo-science of Eugenics. Normal people can only act so as to produce birth; and these people can only act so as to prevent birth. But these people know perfectly well that they dare not write the plain word Birth-Prevention, in any one of the hundred places where they write the hypocritical word Birth-Control. They know as well as I do that the very word Birth-Prevention would strike a chill into the public, the instant it was blazoned on headlines, or proclaimed on platforms, or scattered in advertisements like any other quack medicine. They dare not call it by its name, because its name is very bad advertising. Therefore they use a conventional and unmeaning word, which may make the quack medicine sound more innocuous.

Second, I despise Birth-Control because it is a weak and wobbly and cowardly thing. It is not even a step along the muddy road they call Eugenics; it is a flat refusal to take the first and most obvious step along the road of Eugenics. Once grant that their philosophy is right, and their course of action is obvious; and they dare not take it; they dare not even declare it. If there is no authority in things which Christendom has called moral, because their origins were mystical, then they are clearly free to ignore all difference between animals and men; and treat men as we treat animals. They need not palter with the stale and timid compromise and convention called Birth-Control. Nobody applies it to the cat. The obvious course for Eugenists is to act towards babies as they act towards kittens. Let all the babies be born; and then let us drown those we do not like. I cannot see any objection to it; except the moral or mystical sort of objection that we advance against Birth-Prevention. And that would be real and even reasonable Eugenics; for we could then select the best, or at least the healthiest, and sacrifice what are called the unfit. By the weak compromise of Birth-Prevention, we are very probably sacrificing the fit and only producing the unfit. The births we prevent may be the births of the best and most beautiful children; those we allow, the weakest or worst. Indeed, it is probable; for the habit discourages the early parentage of young and vigorous people; and lets them put off the experience to later years, mostly from mercenary motives. Until I see a real pioneer and progressive leader coming out with a good, bold, scientific programme for drowning babies, I will not join the movement.

But there is a third reason for my contempt, much deeper and therefore much more difficult to express; in which is rooted all my reasons for being anything I am or attempt to be; and above all, for being a Distributist. Perhaps the nearest to a description of it is to say this: that my contempt boils over into bad behaviour when I hear the common suggestion that a birth is avoided because people want to be "free" to go to the cinema or buy a gramophone or a loud-speaker. What makes me want to walk over such people like doormats is that they use the word "free." By every act of that sort they chain themselves to the most servile and mechanical system yet tolerated by men. The cinema is a machine for unrolling certain regular patterns called pictures; expressing the most vulgar millionaires' notion of the taste of the most vulgar millions. The gramophone is a machine for recording such tunes as certain shops and other organisations choose to sell. The wireless is better; but even that is marked by the modern mark of all three; the impotence of the receptive party. The amateur cannot challenge the actor; the householder will find it vain to go and shout into the gramophone; the mob cannot pelt the modern speaker, especially when he is a loud-speaker. It is all a central mechanism giving out to men exactly what their masters think they should have.

Now a child is the very sign and sacrament of personal freedom. He is a fresh free will added to the wills of the world; he is something that his parents have freely chosen to produce and which they freely agree to protect. They can feel that any amusement he gives (which is often considerable) really comes from him and from them, and from nobody else. He has been born without the intervention of any master or lord. He is a creation and a contribution; he is their own creative contribution to creation. He is also a much more beautiful, wonderful, amusing and astonishing thing than any of the stale stories or jingling jazz tunes turned out by the machines. When men no longer feel that he is so, they have lost the appreciation of primary things, and therefore all sense of proportion about the world. People who prefer the mechanical pleasures, to such a miracle, are jaded and enslaved. They are preferring the very dregs of life to the first fountains of life. They are preferring the last, crooked, indirect, borrowed, repeated and exhausted things of our dying Capitalist civilisation, to the reality which is the only rejuvenation of all civilisation. It is they who are hugging the chains of their old slavery; it is the child who is ready for the new world.

The Terror of a Toy

It would be too high and hopeful a compliment to say that the world is becoming absolutely babyish. For its chief weak-mindedness is an inability to appreciate the intelligence of babies. On every side we hear whispers and warnings that would have appeared half-witted to the Wise Men of Gotham. Only this Christmas I was told in a toy-shop that not so many bows and arrows were being made for little boys; because they were considered dangerous. It might in some circumstances be dangerous to have a little bow. It is always dangerous to have a little boy. But no other society, claiming to be sane, would have dreamed of supposing that you could abolish all bows unless you could abolish all boys. With the merits of the latter reform I will not deal here. There is a great deal to be said for such a course; and perhaps we shall soon have an opportunity of considering it. For the modern mind seems quite incapable of distinguishing between the means and the end, between the organ and the disease, between the use and the abuse; and would doubtless break the boy along with the bow, as it empties out the baby with the bath.

But let us, by way of a little study in this mournful state of things, consider this case of the dangerous toy. Now the first and most self-evident truth is that, of all the things a child sees and touches, the most dangerous toy is about the least dangerous thing. There is hardly a single domestic utensil that is not much more dangerous than a little bow and arrow. He can burn himself in the fire, he can boil himself in the bath, he can cut his throat with the carving-knife, he can scald himself with the kettle, he can choke himself with anything small enough, he can break his neck off anything high enough. He moves all day long amid a murderous machinery, as capable of killing and maiming as the wheels of the most frightful factory. He plays all day in a house fitted up with engines of torture like the Spanish Inquisition. And while he thus dances in the shadow of death, he is to be saved from all the perils of possessing a piece of string, tied to a bent bough or twig. When he is a little boy it generally takes him some time even to learn how to hold the bow. When he does hold it, he is delighted if the arrow flutters for a few yards like a feather or an autumn leaf. But even if he grows a little older and more skilful, and has yet not learned to despise arrows in favour of aeroplanes, the amount of damage he could conceivably do with his little arrows would be about one hundredth part of the damage that he could always in any case have done by simply picking up a stone in the garden.

Now you do not keep a little boy from throwing stones by preventing him from ever seeing stones. You do not do it by locking up all the stones in the Geological Museum, and only issuing tickets of admission to adults. You do not do it by trying to pick up all the pebbles on the beach, for fear he should practise throwing them into the sea. You do not even adopt so obvious and even pressing a social reform as forbidding roads to be made of anything but asphalt, or directing that all gardens shall be made on clay and none on gravel. You neglect all these great opportunities opening before you; you neglect all these inspiring vistas of social science and enlightenment. When you want to prevent a child from throwing stones, you fall back on the stalest and most sentimental and even most superstitious methods. You do it by trying to preserve some reasonable authority and influence over the child. You trust to your private relation with the boy, and not to your public relation with the stone. And what is true of the natural missile is just as true, of course, of the artificial missile; especially as it is a very much more ineffectual and therefore innocuous missile. A man could be really killed, like St. Stephen, with the stones in the road. I doubt if he could be really killed, like St. Sebastian, with the arrows in the toyshop. But anyhow the very plain principle is the same. If you can teach a child not to throw a stone, you can teach him when to shoot an arrow; if you cannot teach him anything, he will always have something to throw. If he can be persuaded not to smash the Archdeacon's hat with a heavy flint, it will probably be possible to dissuade him from transfixing that head-dress with a toy arrow. If his training deters him from heaving half a brick at the postman, it will probably also warn him against constantly loosening shafts of death against the policeman. But the notion that the child depends upon particular implements, labelled dangerous, in order to be a danger to himself and other people, is a notion so nonsensical that it is hard to see how any human mind can entertain it for a moment. The truth is that all sorts of faddism, both official and theoretical, have broken down the natural authority of the domestic institution, especially among the poor; and the faddists are now casting about desperately for a substitute for the thing they have themselves destroyed. The normal thing is for the parents to prevent a boy from doing more than a reasonable amount of damage with his bow and arrow; and for the rest, to leave him to a reasonable enjoyment of them. Officialism cannot thus follow the life of the individual boy, as can the individual guardian. You cannot appoint a particular policeman for each boy, to pursue him when he climbs trees or falls into ponds. So the modern spirit has descended to the indescribable mental degradation of trying to abolish the abuse of things by abolishing the things themselves; which is as if it were to abolish ponds or abolish trees. Perhaps it will have a try at that before long. Thus we have all heard of savages who try a tomahawk for murder, or burn a wooden club for the damage it has done to society. To such intellectual levels may the world return.

There are indeed yet lower levels. There is a story from America about a little boy who gave up his toy cannon to assist the disarmament of the world. I do not know if it is true, but on the whole I prefer to think so; for it is perhaps more tolerable to imagine one small monster who could do such a thing than many more mature monsters who could invent or admire it. There were some doubtless who neither invented nor admired. It is one of the peculiarities of the Americans that they combine a power of producing what they satirize as "sob-stuff" with a parallel power of satirizing it. And of the two American tall stories, it is sometimes hard to say which is the story and which the satire. But it seems clear that some people did really repeat this story in a reverential spirit. And it marks, as I have said, another stage of cerebral decay. You can (with luck) break a window with a toy arrow; but you can hardly bombard a town with a toy gun. If people object to the mere model of a cannon, they must equally object to the picture of a cannon, and so to every picture in the world that depicts a sword or a spear. There would be a splendid clearance of all the great art-galleries of the world. But it would be nothing to the destruction of all the great libraries of the world, if we logically extended the principle to all the literary masterpieces that admit the glory of arms. When this progress had gone on for a century or two, it might begin to dawn on people that there was something wrong with their moral principle. What is wrong with their moral principle is that it is immoral. Arms, like every other adventure or art of man, have two sides according as they are invoked for the infliction or the defiance of wrong. They have also an element of real poetry and an element of realistic and therefore repulsive prose. The child's symbolic sword and bow are simply the poetry without the prose; the good without the evil. The toy sword is the abstraction and emanation of the heroic, apart from all its horrible accidents. It is the soul of the sword, that will never be stained with blood.

The Library of the Nursery

A glance at recent publishing announcements shows that a great many children's books of the more modern and artistic type are being issued and re-issued. Edward Lear, one of the most thoroughly original men of the nineteenth century, as original in his own way as Darwin or Carlyle, and all the imitators of Edward Lear, whose name is legion, are apparently planning a new invasion of the nursery. A vast and very honourable revolution is expressed in the fact that there are a fair number of modern places of residence in which the nursery is the best room in the house. It represents a very genuine and self-sacrificing ideal of the aesthetic education of children. To the majority of our ancestors the sacrifice of a large and artistic room to infancy would have appeared outrageous. It would have seemed like making the dog-kennel bigger than the house, or giving the cow the unrestricted use of the drawing-room. While minds more strenuous than our own are discussing whether the world is growing better or worse, it cannot be amiss to point out that this age has really invented this great artistic sacrifice to children, this costly loan to posterity, who is the most bankrupt of all debtors. The moral credit of this act is not affected even if we choose to think that it is a mistake to place really ingenious poetry and really decorative art before infants. It may possibly be true that subtle aesthetics are unsuited to the simple mind. It may be that when we present Walter Crane's illustrations in a nursery book we are acting like a person who should put a very abstruse selection from Wagner into a baby's musical box. It may be that a child can no more realise the best art than he can realise the best algebra. We do not think ourselves that he is at all inferior in this particular. But even if he is, the toil undertaken for the literary education of children remains equally stirring and reassuring to all who are discussing the moral development of humanity. It is the latest movement of the religious instinct, which is the instinct of trust.

Before the throne of the modern child the best treasures of art and literature are unrolled: the worship of the Child (an essential part of Christian religious art) is carried in these days even further than it was carried by the most careful colour and gold-leaf of the medieval craftsman. No sacrifices are spared and no reward is demanded. The offerings made to the old Pagan gods, who were the personifications of power, fall far short of the prodigality and richness of the offerings made to this god, who is the personification of impotence. None of the old literary patrons who could drive a poet into beggary or put his fingers into the treasury of the king is so well treated as this new patron, who can neither smite nor reward, whose vengeance consists in throwing a brick and his gratitude in offering, in a somewhat hesitating manner, a portion of a partly consumed chocolate.

In honour of the child the nineteenth century has made one real discovery, the discovery of what are called Nonsense Books. They are so entirely the creation of our time that we ought to value them like electricity or compulsory education. They constitute an entirely new discovery in literature, the discovery that incongruity itself may constitute a harmony, that as there is a beauty in the wings of a bird because they evoke aspiration, so also there may be a beauty in the wings of a rhinoceros because they evoke laughter. Lewis Carroll is great in this lyric insanity. Mr. Edward Lear is, to our mind, even greater. But it is only fair to say that this invention may be criticised in its educational aspect. We must avoid, above all things, confusing those aspects of childhood which are pleasing to children with those which are pleasing to us.

The great literature of Nonsense has enormous value, but it may at least be reasonably maintained that this value exists chiefly for grown-up people. Nonsense is a thing of Meredithian subtlety. It is not children who ought to read the words of Lewis Carroll;

they are far better employed making mud-pies; it is rather sages and grey-haired philosophers who ought to sit up all night reading *Alice in Wonderland* in order to study that darkest problem of metaphysics, the borderland between reason and unreason, and the nature of the most erratic of spiritual forces, humour, which eternally dances between the two. That we do find a pleasure in certain long and elaborate stories, in certain complicated and curious forms of diction, which have no intelligible meaning whatever, is not a subject for children to play with; it is a subject for psychologists to go mad over. It is we mature persons, with our taste for something lawless, who invented nonsense. We indulged ourselves in Jabberwocky and the Yongy Bongy Bo just as we indulged ourselves in spiritualism and the Celtic fairy tales, because we had an everlasting impatience with our own humdrum earth. But the child is in an immeasurably finer position. To him the earth is not humdrum; for him there is no need of books. That element of the wild and the poetic which is stirred in us by the Dong with the Luminous Nose is stirred in him by any ordinary uncle. It is not necessary to the child to awaken the sense of the strange and humorous by giving a man a luminous nose. To the child (type of the true philosopher, who is not yet born) it is sufficiently strange and humorous to have a nose at all.

If any one of us casts back his mind to his childhood, he will remember that the sense of the supernatural clung as often as not round some entirely trivial and material object, round a particular landing on the stairs, round a particular tree in the park, round a way of cutting cardboard or the hair of a Japanese doll. The child has no need of nonsense: to him the whole universe is nonsensical, in the noblest sense of that noble word. A tree is something top-heavy and fantastic, a donkey is as exciting as a dragon. All objects are seen through a great magnifying glass; the daisy in the meadow is as large as a tree of the Hesperides, and the pebbles littered about a puddle will serve for the Islands of the Blest. A child has innumerable points of inferiority to ourselves; he has no sense of experience, of self-possession; above all he has no knowledge of deep emotion, no knowledge of those great pains which make life worth living. But he has one real point of superiority. We are going forth continually to discover new aesthetic worlds, and last of all our conquests we have discovered this world of nonsense. But he has appreciated this world at a glance, and first glances are best.

This amounts only to a one-sided view, but it is a view which may demand to be stated, if only in justice to the old-fashioned writers for children, who are often denounced in our day. Their moralising is sometimes nauseous, but after all it is grown-up people whom it nauseates. Off children the morality ran like water off a duck's back. What children enjoyed about the old moral tales was that they were realistic tales, and that the authors were, like children, realists, people who were really interested in the phenomena of this world. All readers of the tales of Miss Edgeworth (to take an excellent example) will remember an admirable story about a little girl who wished to possess the vases of coloured liquid which are exhibited in the front of a chemist's shop. The moral of the story, which we only dimly remember, was something about the wrongness of the desire and the vanity of human wishes. But the child who read the story did, as a matter of fact, imbibe a precisely opposite moral to that of the story: he learnt to dream of the vases, to exult in the glory of the primal colours. The didactic pessimism of old-fashioned ethics did not touch the matter; the essential of the matter was that Miss Edgeworth had grasped a glowing fragment of poetry which was missed by Keats and Browning, the fascination of those monstrous and coloured moons which proclaim for yards down the street the mystery of the home of healing.

A Defence of Baby-Worship

The two facts which attract almost every normal person to children are, first, that they are very serious, and, secondly, that they are in consequence very happy. They are jolly with the completeness which is possible only in the absence of humour. The most unfathomable schools and sages have never attained to the gravity which dwells in the eyes of a baby of three months old. It is the gravity of astonishment at the universe, and astonishment at the universe is not mysticism, but a transcendent commonsense. The fascination of children lies in this: that with each of them all things are remade, and the universe is put again upon its trial. As we walk the streets and see below us those delightful bulbous heads, three times too big for the body, which mark these human mushrooms, we ought always primarily to remember that within every one of these heads there is a new universe, as new as it was on the seventh day of creation. In each of those orbs there is a new system of stars, new grass, new cities, a new sea.

There is always in the healthy mind an obscure prompting that religion teaches us rather to dig than to climb; that if we could once understand the common clay of earth we should understand everything. Similarly, we have the sentiment that if we could destroy custom at a blow and see the stars as a child sees them, we should need no other apocalypse. This is the great truth which has always lain at the back of baby-worship, and which will support it to the end. Maturity, with its endless energies and aspirations, may easily be convinced that it will find new things to appreciate; but it will never be convinced, at bottom, that it has properly appreciated what it has got. We may scale the heavens and find new stars

183

innumerable, but there is still the new star we have not found—
that on which we were born.

But the influence of children goes further than its first trifling
effort of remaking heaven and earth. It forces us actually to
remodel our conduct in accordance with this revolutionary theory
of the marvellousness of all things. We do (even when we are
perfectly simple or ignorant)—we do actually treat talking in
children as marvellous, walking in children as marvellous, common intelligence in children as marvellous. The cynical philosopher fancies he has a victory in this matter—that he can laugh
when he shows that the words or antics of the child, so much
admired by its worshippers, are common enough. The fact is that
this is precisely where baby-worship is so profoundly right. Any
words and any antics in a lump of clay are wonderful, the child's
words and antics are wonderful, and it is only fair to say that the
philosopher's words and antics are equally wonderful.

The truth is that it is our attitude towards children that is right,
and our attitude towards grown-up people that is wrong. Our
attitude towards our equals in age consists in a servile solemnity,
overlying a considerable degree of indifference or disdain. Our
attitude towards children consists in a condescending indulgence,
overlying an unfathomable respect. We bow to grown people,
take off our hats to them, refrain from contradicting them flatly,
but we do not appreciate them properly. We make puppets of
children, lecture them, pull their hair, and reverence, love, and
fear them. When we reverence anything in the mature, it is their
virtues or their wisdom, and this is an easy matter. But we
reverence the faults and follies of children.

We should probably come considerably nearer to the true
conception of things if we treated all grown-up persons, of all
titles and types, with precisely that dark affection and dazed
respect with which we treat the infantile limitations. A child has a
difficulty in achieving the miracle of speech, consequently we
find his blunders almost as marvellous as his accuracy. If we only
adopted the same attitude towards Premiers and Chancellors of
the Exchequer, if we genially encouraged their stammering and

delightful attempts at human speech, we should be in a far more wise and tolerant temper. A child has a knack of making experiments in life, generally healthy in motive, but often intolerable in a domestic commonwealth. If we only treated all commercial buccaneers and bumptious tyrants on the same terms, if we gently chided their brutalities as rather quaint mistakes in the conduct of life, if we simply told them that they would 'understand when they were older,' we should probably be adopting the best and most crushing attitude towards the weaknesses of humanity. In our relations to children we prove that the paradox is entirely true, that it is possible to combine an amnesty that verges on contempt with a worship that verges upon terror. We forgive children with the same kind of blasphemous gentleness with which Omar Khayyam forgave the Omnipotent.

The essential rectitude of our view of children lies in the fact that we feel them and their ways to be supernatural while, for some mysterious reason, we do not feel ourselves or our own ways to be supernatural. The very smallness of children makes it possible to regard them as marvels; we seem to be dealing with a new race, only to be seen through a microscope. I doubt if anyone of any tenderness or imagination can see the hand of a child and not be a little frightened of it. It is awful to think of the essential human energy moving so tiny a thing; it is like imagining that human nature could live in the wing of a butterfly or the leaf of a tree. When we look upon lives so human and yet so small, we feel as if we ourselves were enlarged to an embarrassing bigness of stature. We feel the same kind of obligation to these creatures that a deity might feel if he had created something that he could not understand.

But the humorous look of children is perhaps the most endearing of all the bonds that hold the Cosmos together. Their top-heavy dignity is more touching than any humility; their solemnity gives us more hope for all things than a thousand carnivals of optimism; their large and lustrous eyes seem to hold all the stars in their astonishment; their fascinating absence of nose seems to give to us the most perfect hint of the humour that awaits us in the kingdom of heaven.

PART SIX

THE ASSASSINS OF
THE FAMILY

* * *

For sex cannot be admitted to a mere equality among elementary emotions or experiences like eating and sleeping. The moment sex ceases to be a servant it becomes a tyrant. There is something dangerous and disproportionate in its place in human nature, for whatever reason; and it does really need a special purification and dedication. The modern talk about sex being free like any other sense, about the body being beautiful like any tree or flower, is either a description of the Garden of Eden or a piece of thoroughly bad psychology, of which the world grew weary two thousand years ago.

St. Francis of Assisi

For the next great heresy is going to be simply an attack on morality; and especially on sexual morality. And it is coming, *not* from a few Socialists surviving from the Fabian Society, but from the living exultant energy of the rich resolved to enjoy themselves at last, with neither Popery nor Puritanism nor Socialism to hold them back. . . . The madness of tomorrow is *not* in Moscow, but much more in Manhattan.

"The Next Heresy", in *G.K.'s Weekly,* June 19, 1926

187

Sex is an instinct that produces an institution; and it is positive and not negative, noble and not base, creative and not destructive, because it produces that institution. That institution is the family; a small state or commonwealth which has hundreds of aspects, when it is once started, that are not sexual at all. It includes worship, justice, festivity, decoration, instruction, comradeship, repose. Sex is the gate of that house; and romantic and imaginative people naturally like looking through a gateway. But the house is very much larger than the gate. There are indeed a certain number of people who like to hang about in the gate and never get any further.

G.K.'s Weekly, January 29, 1927

A free lover is worse than a profligate. For a profligate is serious and reckless even in his shortest love; while a free lover is cautious and irresponsible even in his longest devotion.

Tremendous Trifles

But if it be true that Socialism attacks the family in theory, it is far more certain that Capitalism attacks it in practice.

The Superstition of Divorce

This domestic institution doubtless is now seen under great disadvantages; battling for its life and almost battered to pieces by the forces of capitalism and materialism. I will not say it is not at its best; for I suppose this human institution, like humanity, is never at its best. It always falls short of a divine plan; and there was no complete human family except the Holy Family.

G.K.'s Weekly, January 29, 1927

The answer to anyone who talks about the surplus population is to ask him whether he is the surplus population, or if he is not, how he knows he is not.

Introduction to *A Christmas Carol*

The normal and real birth control is called self control.

Social Reform versus Birth Control

An Agreement

Mr. William Clissold regards Birth-Control as the test of liberality: those against it are reactionary: those in favour are for the progressive revolution.

Where you have laid it, let the sword divide:
And your unmotherly Medea be
Here sundered from our human trinity,
The Mother and the Virgin and the Bride.

Why should we falter? Ours shall be the mirth
And yours the amaze when you have thinned away
Your starving serfs to fit their starveling pay
And see the meek inheriting the earth.

That Christ from his creative purity
Came forth your sterile appetites to scorn.
Lo: in her house Life without Lust was born,
So in your house Lust without Life shall die.

Three Foes of the Family

I t was certainly a very brilliant lightning-flash of irony by which Mr. Aldous Huxley lit up the whole loathsome landscape of his satirical Utopia, of synthetic humanity and manufactured men and women, by the old romantic quotation of "Brave New World". The quotation comes, of course, from that supreme moment of the magic of youth, nourished by the magic of old age, when Miranda the marvellous becomes Miranda the marvelling, at the unique wonder of first love. To use it for the very motto of a system which, having lost all innocence, would necessarily lose all wonder, was a touch of very withering wit. And yet it will be well to remember that, in comparison with some other worlds, where the same work is done more weakly and quite as wickedly, the Utopia of the extremists really has something of the intellectual integrity which belongs to extremes, even of madness. In that sense the two ironical adjectives are not merely ironical. The horrible human, or inhuman, hive described in Mr. Huxley's romance is certainly a base world, and a filthy world, and a fundamentally unhappy world. But it is in one sense a new world; and it is in one sense a brave world. At least a certain amount of bravery, as well as brutality, would have to be shown before anything of the sort could be established in the world of fact. It would need some courage, and even some self-sacrifice, to establish anything so utterly disgusting as that.

But the same work is being done in other worlds that are not particularly new, and not in the least brave. There are people of another sort, much more common and conventional, who are not only working to create such a paradise of cowardice, but who actually try to work for it through a conspiracy of cowards. The attitude of these people towards the Family and the tradition of its Christian virtues is the attitude of men willing to wound and yet afraid to strike; or ready to sap and mine so long as they are not called upon to fire or fight in the open. And those who do this cover much more than half, or nearly two-thirds, of the people who write in the most respectable and conventional Capitalist newspapers. It cannot be too often repeated that what destroyed the Family in the modern world was Capitalism. No doubt it might have been Communism, if Communism had ever had a chance, outside that semi-Mongolian wilderness where it actually flourishes. But, so far as we are concerned, what has broken up households, and encouraged divorces, and treated the old domestic virtues with more and more open contempt, is the epoch and power of Capitalism. It is Capitalism that has forced a moral feud and a commercial competition between the sexes; that has destroyed the influence of the parent in favour of the influence of the employer; that has driven men from their homes to look for jobs; that has forced them to live near their factories or their firms instead of near their families; and, above all, that has encouraged, for commercial reasons, a parade of publicity and garish novelty, which is in its nature the death of all that was called dignity and modesty by our mothers and fathers. It is not the Bolshevist but the Boss, the publicity man, the salesman and the commercial advertiser who have, like a rush and riot of barbarians, thrown down and trampled under foot the ancient Roman statue of Verecundia. But because the thing is done by men of this sort, of course it is done in their own muggy and muddle-headed way; by all the irresponsible tricks of their foul Suggestion and their filthy Psychology. It is done, for instance, by perpetually guying the old Victorian virtues or limitations which, as they are no longer there, are not likely to retaliate. It is done more by pictures than by printed words; because printed words are supposed to make some sense and a man may be answerable for printing them. Stiff and hideous effigies of women in crinolines or bonnets are paraded, as if *that* could possibly be all there was to see when Maud came into the garden, and was saluted by such a song. Fortunately, Maud's friends, who would have challenged the pressman and photographer to a duel, are all dead; and these satirists of Victorianism are very careful to find out that all their enemies are dead. Some of their bold caricaturists have been known to charge an old-fashioned bathing-machine as courageously as if it were a machine-gun. It is convenient thus courageously to attack bathing-machines, because there are no bathing-machines to attack. Then they balance these things by photographs of the Modern Girl at various stages of the nudist movement; and trust that anything so obviously vulgar is bound to be popular. For the rest, the Modern Girl is floated on a sea of sentimental sloppiness; a continuous gush about her frankness and freshness, the perfect naturalness of her painting her face or the un-precedented courage of her having no children. The whole is diluted with a dreary hypocrisy about comradeship, far more sentimental than the old-fashioned sentiment. When I see the Family sinking in these swamps of amorphous amorous futility, I feel inclined to say, "Give me the Communists." Better Bolshevist battles and the Brave New World than the ancient house of man rotted away silently by such worms of secret sensuality and individual appetite. "The coward does it with a kiss; the brave man with a sword."

But there is, curiously enough, a third thing of the kind, which I am really inclined to think that I dislike even more than the other two. It is not the Communist attacking the family or the Capitalist betraying the family; it is the vast and very astonishing vision of the Hitlerite defending the family. Hitler's way of defending the independence of the family is to make every family dependent on him and his semi-Socialist State; and to preserve the authority of parents by authoritatively telling all the parents what to do. His notion of keeping sacred the dignity of domestic life is to issue peremptory orders that the grandfather is to get up at five in the morning and do dumb-bell exercises, or the grandmother to march twenty miles to a camp to procure a Swastika flag. In other words, he appears to interfere with family life more even than the Bolshevists do; and to do it in the name of the sacredness of the family. It is not much more encouraging than the other two social manifestations; but at least it is more entertaining.

Social Reform versus Birth Control

The real history of the world is full of the queerest cases of notions that have turned clean head-over-heels and completely contradicted themselves. The last example is an extraordinary notion that what is called Birth Control is a social reform that goes along with other social reforms favoured by progressive people.

It is rather like saying that cutting off King Charles' head was one of the most elegant of the Cavalier fashions in hair-dressing. It is like saying that decapitation is an advance on dentistry. It may or may not be right to cut off the King's head; it may or may not be right to cut off your own head when you have the toothache. But anybody ought to be able to see that if we once simplify things by head-cutting we can do without hair-cutting; that it will be needless to practise dentistry on the dead or philanthropy on the unborn—or the unbegotten. So it is not a provision for our descendants to say that the destruction of our descendants will render it unnecessary to provide them with anything. It may be that it is only destruction in the sense of negation; and it may be that few of our descendants may be allowed to survive. But it is obvious that the negation is a piece of mere pessimism, opposing itself to the more optimistic notion that something can be done for the whole family of man. Nor is it surprising to anybody who can think, to discover that this is exactly what really happened.

The story began with Godwin, the friend of Shelley, and the founder of so many of the social hopes that are called revolutionary. Whatever we think of his theory in detail, he certainly filled the more generous youth of his time with that thirst for social justice and equality which is the inspiration of Socialism and other ideals.

What is even more gratifying, he filled the wealthy old men of his time with pressing and enduring terror; and about three-quarters of the talk of Tories and Whigs of that time consists of sophistries and excuses invented to patch up a corrupt compromise of oligarchy against the appeal to fraternity and fundamental humanity made by men like Godwin and Shelley.

Malthus: An Answer to Godwin

The old oligarchs would use any tool against the new democrats; and one day it was their dismal good luck to get hold of a tool called Malthus. Malthus wrote avowedly and admittedly an answer to Godwin. His whole dreary book was only intended to be an answer to Godwin. Whereas Godwin was trying to show that humanity might be made happier and more humane, Malthus was trying to show that humanity could never by any possibility be made happier or more humane. The argument he used was this: that if the starving man were made tolerably free or fairly prosperous, he would marry and have a number of children, and there would not be food for all. The inference was, evidently, that he must be left to starve. The point about the increase of children he fortified by a fantastically mathematical formula about geometrical progression, which any living human being can clearly see is inapplicable to any living thing. Nothing depending on the human will can proceed by geometrical progression, and population certainly does not proceed by anything of the sort.

But the point is here, that Malthus meant his argument as an argument against all social reform. He never thought of using it as anything else, except an argument against all social reform. Nobody else ever thought in those more logical days of using it as anything but an argument against social reform. Malthus even used it as an argument against the ancient habit of human charity. He warned people against any generosity in the giving of alms. His theory was always thrown as cold water on any proposal to give the poor man property or a better status. Such is the noble story of the birth of Birth Control.

The only difference is this: that the old capitalists were more sincere and more scientific, while the modern capitalists are more hypocritical and more hazy. The rich man of 1850 used it in theory for the oppression of the poor. The rich man of 1927 will only use it in practice for the oppression of the poor. Being incapable of theory, being indeed incapable of thought, he can only deal in two things: what he calls practicality and what I call sentimentality. Not being so much of a man as Malthus, he cannot bear to be a pessimist, so he becomes a sentimentalist. He mixes up this old plain brutal idea (that the poor must be forbidden to breed) with a lot of slipshod and sickly social ideals and promises which are flatly incompatible with it. But he is after all a practical man, and he will be quite as brutal as his forbears when it comes to practice. And the practical upshot of the whole thing is plain enough. If he can prevent his servants from having families, he need not support those families. Why the devil should he?

A Simple Test

If anybody doubts that this is the very simple motive, let him test it by the very simple statements made by the various Birth-Controllers like the Dean of St. Paul's. They never do say that we suffer from a *too* bountiful supply of bankers or that cosmopolitan financiers must not have such large families. They do not say that the fashionable throng at Ascot wants thinning, or that it is desirable to decimate the people dining at the Ritz or the Savoy. Though, Lord knows, if ever a thing human could look like a sub-human jungle, with tropical flowers and very poisonous weeds, it is the rich crowd that assembles in a modern Americanized hotel.

But the Birth-Controllers have not the smallest desire to control that jungle. It is much too dangerous a jungle to touch. It contains tigers. They never do talk about a danger from the comfortable classes, even from a more respectable section of the comfortable classes. The Gloomy Dean is not gloomy about there being too many Dukes; and naturally not about there being too many Deans. He is not primarily annoyed with a politician for having a whole population of poor relations, though places and public salaries have to be found for all the relations. Political Economy means that everybody except politicians must be economical.

The Birth-Controller does not bother about all these things, for the perfectly simple reason that it is not such people that he wants to control. What he wants to control is the populace, and he practically says so. He always insists that a workman has no right to have so many children, or that a slum is perilous because it is producing so many children. The question he dreads is "Why has not the workman a better wage? Why has not the slum family a better house?" His way of escaping from it is to suggest, not a larger house but a smaller family. The landlord or the employer says in his hearty and handsome fashion: "You really cannot expect me to deprive myself of my money. But I will make a sacrifice, I will deprive myself of your children."

One of a Class

Meanwhile, as the Malthusian attack on democratic hopes slowly stiffened and strengthened all the reactionary resistance to reform in this country, other forces were already in the field. I may remark in passing that Malthus, and his sophistry against all social reform, did not stand alone. It was one of a whole class of scientific excuses invented by the rich as reasons for denying justice to the poor, especially when the old superstitious glamour about kings and nobles had faded in the nineteenth century. One was talking about the Iron Laws of Political Economy, and pretending that somebody had proved somewhere, with figures on a slate, that injustice is incurable. Another was a mass of brutal nonsense about Darwinism and a struggle for life, in which the devil must catch the hindmost. As a fact it was struggle for wealth, in which the devil generally catches the foremost. They all had the character of an attempt to twist the new tool of science to make it a weapon for the old tyranny of money.

But these forces, though powerful in a diseased industrial plutocracy, were not the only forces even in the nineteenth century. Towards the end of that century, especially on the Continent, there was another movement going on, notably among Christian Socialists and those called Catholic Democrats and others. There is no space to describe it here; its interest lies in being the exact reversal of the order of argument used by the Malthusian and the Birth-Controller. This movement was not content with the test of what is called a Living Wage. It insisted specially on what it preferred to call a Family Wage. In other words, it maintained that no wage is just or adequate unless it does envisage and cover the man, not only considered as an individual, but as the father of a normal and reasonably numerous family. This sort of movement is the true contrary of Birth Control and both will probably grow until they come into some tremendous controversial collision. It amuses me to reflect on that big coming battle, and to remember that the more my opponents practise Birth Control, the fewer there will be of them to fight us on that day.

The Conflict

What I cannot get my opponents in this matter to see, in the strange mental confusion that covers the question, is the perfectly simple fact that these two claims, whatever else they are, are contrary claims. At the very beginning of the whole discussion stands the elementary fact that limiting families is a reason for lowering wages and not a reason for raising them. You may like the limitation for other reasons, as you may dislike it for other reasons. You may drag the discussion off to entirely different questions, such as, whether wives in normal homes are slaves. You may compromise out of consideration for the employer or for some other reason, and meet him half-way by taking half a loaf or having half a family. But the claims are in principle opposite. It is the whole truth in that theory of the class war about which the newspapers talk such nonsense. The full claim of the poor would be to have what they considered a full-sized family. If you cut this down to suit wages you make a concession to fit the capitalist conditions. The practical application I shall mention in a moment; I am talking now about the primary logical contradiction. If the two methods can be carried out, they can be carried out so as to contradict and exclude each other. One has no need of the other; one can dispense with or destroy the other. If you can make the wage larger, there is no need to make the family smaller. If you can make the family small, there is no need to make the wage larger. Anyone may judge which the ruling capitalist will probably prefer to do. But if he does one, he need not do the other.

There is of course a great deal more to be said. I have dealt with only one feature of Birth Control—its exceedingly unpleasant origin. I said it was purely capitalist and reactionary; I venture to say I have proved it was entirely capitalist and reactionary. But there are many other aspects of this evil thing. It is unclean in the light of the instincts; it is unnatural in relation to the affections; it is part of a general attempt to run the populace on a routine of quack medicine and smelly science; it is mixed up with a muddled idea that women are free when they serve their employers but slaves when they help their husbands; it is ignorant of the very existence of real households where prudence comes by free-will and agreement. It has all those aspects, and many of them would be extraordinarily interesting to discuss. But in order not to occupy too much space, I will take as a text nothing more than the title.

A Piece of Humbug

The very name of "Birth Control" is a piece of pure humbug. It is one of those blatant euphemisms used in the headlines of the Trust Press. It is like "Tariff Reform." It is like "Free Labour." It is meant to mean nothing, that it may mean anything, and especially something totally different from what it says. Everybody believes in birth control, and nearly everybody has exercised some control over the conditions of birth. People do not get married as somnambulists or have children in their sleep. But throughout numberless ages and nations, the normal and real birth control is called self control. If anybody says it cannot possibly work, I say it does. In many classes, in many countries where these quack nostrums are unknown, populations of free men have remained within reasonable limits by sound traditions of thrift and responsibility. In so far as there is a local evil of excess, it comes with all other evils from the squalor and despair of our decaying industrialism. But the thing the capitalist newspapers call birth control is not control at all. It is the idea that people should be, in one respect, completely and utterly uncontrolled, so long as they can evade everything in the function that is positive and creative, and intelligent and worthy of a free man. It is a name given to a succession of different expedients (the one that was used last is always described as having been dreadfully dangerous) by which it is possible to filch the pleasure belonging to a natural process while violently and unnaturally thwarting the process itself.

The nearest and most respectable parallel would be that of the Roman epicure, who took emetics at intervals all day so that he might eat five or six luxurious dinners daily. Now any man's common sense, unclouded by newspaper science and long words, will tell him at once that an operation like that of the epicures is likely in the long run even to be bad for his digestion and pretty certain to be bad for his character. Men left to themselves have sense enough to know when a habit obviously savours of perversion and peril. And if it were the fashion in fashionable circles to call the Roman expedient by the name of "Diet Control," and to talk about it in a lofty fashion as merely "the improvement of life and the service of life" (as if it meant no more than the mastery of man over his meals), we should take the liberty of calling it cant and saying that it had no relation to the reality in debate.

The Mistake

The fact is, I think, that I am in revolt against the conditions of industral capitalism and the advocates of Birth Control are in revolt against the conditions of human life. What their spokesmen can possibly mean by saying that I wage a "class war against mothers" must remain a matter of speculation. If they mean that I do the unpardonable wrong to mothers of thinking they will wish to continue to be mothers, even in a society of greater economic justice and civic equality, then I think they are perfectly right. I doubt whether mothers could escape from motherhood into Socialism. But the advocates of Birth Control seem to want some of them to escape from it into capitalism. They seem to express a sympathy with those who prefer "the right to earn outside the home" or (in other words) the right to be a wage-slave and work under the orders of a total stranger because he happens to be a richer man. By what conceivable contortions of twisted thought this ever came to be considered a freer condition than that of companionship with the man she has herself freely accepted, I never could for the life of me make out. The only sense I can make of it is that the proletarian work, though obviously more servile and subordinate than the parental, is so far safer and more irresponsible because it is not parental. I can easily believe that there are some people who do prefer working in a factory to working in a family; for there are always some people who prefer slavery to freedom, and who especially prefer being governed to governing someone else. But I think their quarrel with motherhood is not like mine, a quarrel with inhuman conditions, but simply a quarrel with life. Given an attempt to escape from the nature of things, and I can well believe that it might lead at last to something like "the nursery school for our children staffed by other mothers and single women of expert training."

I will add nothing to that ghastly picture, beyond speculating pleasantly about the world in which women cannot manage their own children but can manage each other's. But I think it indicates an abyss between natural and unnatural arrangements which would have to be bridged before we approached what is supposed to be the subject of discussion.

On the Fallacy of Eugenics

I shall go down to my neglected pauper's grave continuing to praise, honour, and glorify the name of Mr. H. G. Wells; even if he is by that time himself in the great Cosmic Crematorium and Pagan Pantheon, where will stand the sacred urns of the founders of the New State. And this will not be merely for the obvious reasons. It is not only, though it is very largely, because he filled my youth with the fairy-tales of science, which are so much more delightful when you have really discovered that they are fairy-tales. It will not be only because he has interpreted the mind of the Englishman who, even by the confession of the modern newspapers, has been turned by modern conditions into what is called a Little Man. Alas, it is indeed his manhood that has become little. He is not allowed to have anything else on a small scale, except himself. He is not now allowed to be a small shopkeeper, or a small farmer, or a small craftsman; so, naturally, he has become a small man. But what H. G. Wells did bring out, in burning colours of reality, is the fact that even that small man can also be great. For though the Machine may grind the work of man's hands into a dust of indistinguishable atoms, it cannot alter the fact that Man is not a small thing. It cannot alter the fact that the Man is greater than the Machine, even at the moment when the Machine has killed him. Nor, again, is it merely because Mr. Wells has brought out this great truth, of the greatness of apparently trivial people, by a most delightful comedy of contrasts in the characters of those people. It is not even because he created the character of the aunt of the hero of *Tono-Bungay;* I have forgotten her name, but I still know her nature. I know her very well; and she was one of the consolations of life; a real triumph of tenderness and power. It is not even

because he disposed of a celebrated Continental Pacifist with a
vigorous phrase I have never forgotten: " '*Au-dessus de la mêlée,*' "
as the man up the tree said while the wild bull was goring his
sister. At the moment, at least, it is for none of these things that I
fell impelled to pour out a pagan libation before that dignified
pagan urn, if the time should ever come (may it be far distant)
when he has provided himself with an urn. My gratitude is
grounded on the grand and impressive fact that it was Mr. H. G.
Wells, and not any of us poor slaves of superstition, who long ago
pointed out the gaping and ghastly scientific fallacy in almost all
that is now being revived, under the labels of Eugenics and
Heredity.

The point is this; and it has never been answered. To judge by
the way in which politicians and publicists discuss such matters, it
has never even been understood. The fact is that it is totally
impossible to argue from the fact of physical inheritance to any
sort of result other than the very simplest physical features. We all
know that a positive physical element, which is also an entirely
simple element, may be inherited; though even then it is unsafe to
prophesy that it will be inherited. We all know what is meant by
saying that the Robinsons run to tall men; or that red hair is for
some reason recurrent and even frequent in the family of Pickleby.
But nobody wants indefinite length as such, or humanity measured by the yard; and red hair may accompany any cast of
features from that of Judas Iscariot to that of Bernard Shaw. All
the things that are worth having, such as health and beauty and
happiness and virtue, are all, without exception, things produced
by a particular proportion between different things. It is said of a
newborn baby with affection that he has his mother's eyes, with
tolerance that he has his father's nose, with faint alarm that he has
his great-uncle's jaw. But even if his mother were as beautiful as
Helen of Troy, her eyes would not make him as beautiful as Paris
or Apollo. Beauty in a face depends on how the eyes and other
features fit in with each other; and if all is devastated by Uncle
Humphrey's jaw, the result will be disastrous even if Uncle
Humphrey himself was a very handsome, though trying, old

gentleman. For these harmonies which we human beings value, as beauty or virtue or the rest, do indeed form part (as some of us superstitiously believe) of the ultimate purpose of God, but they do not form part of what may be called the obvious and ostensible purpose of Nature. So far as that is concerned, they are only tunes or melodies that we happen to like; combinations of colour and form which we happen to admire. Yet the same is true even of what seems so simple and natural a thing as health. It is quite useless for eugenists to tell us that healthy parents always have healthy children; and especially that mentally healthy parents always have mentally healthy children. If we have lived long enough in the real world, we simply know that it is not true.

But the point is that the reason is really the same. Mental sanity, like bodily beauty, is not a separate positive concrete character that can be carried on like a pattern of big bones or a racial colouring of black curly hair. The question about any individual, born of any family, is not whether he inherits elements from that family; as no doubt he does. It is, as Shakespeare said, the question of whether "the elements were so mixed in him" as to produce a success or failure by our special standard of spiritual values. There is nobody with any wide circle of acquaintances, who does not know families in which the father and the mother are both normal, sane, and even splendid specimens, but in which for some reason something has gone wrong with the full psychological development of one or two of the children. But what has gone wrong is not the inheritance of a positive quality. It is not even the inheritance of a negative quality; such as is implied in the very vague phrase about feeble-mindedness; for it is often obvious that the father and mother and the family generally were not in the least feeble-minded. What has gone wrong in some manner, we can only suppose, is the tendency to achieve proportion. There has been too much of something; too little of something else, and the combination necessary for normal activity is thrown out of balance. The son of a sane man is often mad, because he has the right scruples in the wrong place. The son of a handsome man is often ugly, because he has the right features in the wrong face.

Now it is true that Mr. Wells, in the early work to which I refer, did not go into all this matter as I have done; nor do I make him for a moment responsible for my own irresponsible speculations. But he did, all that long time ago (I think it was in the book called *Mankind in the Making*), point out the essential fact which all the eugenists seem to have forgotten all over again. We breed cows for milk; and not for a moral balance of particular virtues in the cow. We breed pigs to turn them into pork, not to exhibit their portraits as pictures of perfect and harmonious beauty. In other words, we can breed cows and pigs precisely because we cannot really criticize cows and pigs. We cannot judge them from the point of view of the Cow Concept or the Pig Ideal. Therefore we cannot, and do not, criticize them in the way in which we criticize our fellow-creatures (always provided, of course, that they are our poorer fellow-creatures) when we call them feeble-minded; or when we betray our own feeble-mindedness by calling them Unfit. For the very word Unfit reveals the weakness of the whole of this pseudo-scientific position. We should say that a cow is fit to provide us with milk; or that a pig is unfit to provide us with pork. But nobody would call a cow fit without naturally adding what she was fit for. Nobody would call up the insanely isolated vision of the Unfit Pig in the abstract. But when we talk about human beings, we are bound to break off the sentence in the middle; we are bound to call them Unfit in the abstract. For we know how varied, how complex, and how controversial are the questions that arise about the functions for which they should be fitted. All this is very obvious, and very old; I said it all myself twenty years ago; and Mr. Wells, as I have noted, said part of it much better than I could. But since there seems to be a queer revival of such things, a belated and benighted renascence of these fads I fancied were forgotten, it is as well to repeat our unanswered answer to the creed behind such barbarous tricks; for they are not confined to the curious commonwealth of Mr. Hitler.

The Pessimist and the Birthday-Book

In the course of this week, which is apparently called Baby Week, there will probably be repeated countless times in countless towns an anecdote which is supposed to illustrate the pathetic pig-headedness of the working classes—an anecdote about a poor old woman who said she ought to understand children, as "she had buried eight." As I have said more than once, when others have more than once made this anecdote an argument, there is another side to it. At least, to put it brutally, the old woman did have to bury all the babies she killed. She had the responsibility and expense, and some have even fancied they found traces of human sorrow in such social types. But a semi-official reformer, flying round with a fad, might kill eighty babies without having to bury any of them. It is, moreover, probable, for those who care about such things, that the old woman really did bury them, with quaint old forms of respect, and even vaguely remembered where they were buried. Whereas I have met many a social reformer who would be capable, at his mildest, of cremating and, at his keenest, of dissecting them. Of course the people roped in for Baby Week are not like this; many of them are as kind and disinterested as dupes can be; but they are like it to this extent, that they would never think the domestic experience of the working-class of any value *at all* as against any man who could use long words. If he said that standing a child in the corner produced obliquity of vision, they would swallow it, without once reflecting that even mothers might by this time have noticed if nearly all children had a squint. Past experience, if it be only popular experience, now goes for literally nothing. For the rest, we have no objection to Baby Week except it is Baby Week. The two words contain the two great fallacies involved. The first is that we ought to be content with helping babies, as distinct from helping men and women to their rights and natural relation to babies. The second is that the sort of person who will consider babies as a mob for a week will "organise" them better than those who have to consider them individually for years and years. Beyond that, I am not here concerned with the scheme, but with a larger matter of which it is but an illustration, and that is the futility of culture without custom.

Popular custom is the only real popular rule. Without popular custom we are wretchedly reduced to popular education, which should rather be called anti-popular education. The Germans call it culture; and it is culture, by many English tests taken from Matthew Arnold, or perhaps from the misunderstanding of Matthew Arnold. To explain what I mean by culture and custom, I will take a larger aspect of the same example of birth and childhood. Suppose some incurable sceptic in Baby Week should push the debate about birth a stage further back to fundamentals. Suppose he asked a question asked by many philosophers, especially German philosophers—the question of whether any baby gets any good by being born at all. Now if we went only by culture, "the best that has been written," etc., I am far from sure we should always hit on the healthiest answers. Birthday-books are full of classic quotations, but few of them are quotations about birthdays. I have seldom seen the birthday-book of anybody, however cultured, bearing as a blazon and motto what is probably the grandest piece of pure literature on the subject of a birthday. "Let the day perish wherein I was born, and the night in which it was said, There is a man child conceived," and all that sublime inverted imagery about the lost day and the dark stars, that turns Nothing itself into a vision. The Book of Job is certainly among "the best that has been written," etc., and there is something compact and contented in the thought that the best blasphemy is in the Bible. Swift, I believe, said something of the same sombre sort about his birthday, and Swift was, perhaps, the strongest, nay in some ways the noblest, intellect of the eighteenth

century. If we look only at the peaks, they will sometimes seem to
be under a cloud. Culture will not always understand those that
carry the cloud most lightly; Goethe took Homer for a pessimist,
as Shaw took Shakespeare. Literature as well as learning may
mislead us here; a mere man of letters, even if he is a poet and not a
pedant, may be too much attracted by the paradox of pessimism.
Indeed, what we call "letters" are in this literally literal. We see the
black lettering and we forget the white page.

Now what can we really pit against a poem like that of Job to
express a saner sentiment about a man's birthday? There are few
poems directly dealing with the subject; there are no nobler
poems dealing with any subject. The best answer to it is not any
individual composition; it is a universal custom. It is the simple
fact that men do keep birthdays and keep them as feast-days. The
answer is in all the birthdays of men and even in the celestial
paradox of the birthday of God. Christmas Day is the real answer
to the Book of Job. The nativity even of a true Man of Sorrows is
itself a day of joys, and even of jokes. But Christmas Day is not a
book; it is a custom. All birthdays are a custom; but many would
dispute their claim to be a culture. The occasional verses privately
written for birthdays are generally commonplace. The Birthday
Odes written by Laureates are proverbially commonplace. We
should have to read, not a choice library of the best that has been
written, but a paper wilderness of the very worst that has been
written, before we could cover a corner of the huge human
communion in this idea. But the whole point of it, as a practical
reply to pessimism, is that it is commonplace because it is common.
It is perhaps a less sublime literary achievement to say "Many
happy returns of the day" than "May the day perish wherein I was
born." But the whole point of it is that, apart from the many
happy returns of the day, there will certainly be many happy
returns of the remark. The birthday is a dogma no normal men
deny, a formula of fundamental confession; and it thanks Heaven
by implication for our creation, preservation and all the blessings
of this life. It is expressed by ritual, which is often much larger
than reason, for it includes the subconsciousness. The pessimist

philosophy is written, at best sung, like a poem. The optimist philosophy acted like a play, a huge pageant in which millions take their many-coloured parts. The reversal of that ritual would startle us as much as the sky turning green or the grass blue. If men really thought a baby unlucky for being born, they would have behaved otherwise from the beginning; they would have black-edged cards instead of birthday cards, black bread instead of birthday cake, readings from Schopenhauer instead of Birthday Odes or the more delicate of a man's friends might avoid alluding to his father's son having been born, as they would to his father having been hanged.

Now, the culture which is a curse is a certain modern spirit; the spirit that would think everything of encouraging everybody to read the best pessimist poets but would think nothing of discouraging the popular custom of birthdays. It does not matter on what ground they would be discouraged; it might be an optimist and not a pessimist sophistry; it might insist on the abstract equality of the three hundred and sixty-five days. It might say the excitement of a special day disturbed the hygienic rhythm of the organism. It might be part of some grand platonic plan, by which a man should be cured of superstition by not knowing when he was born, as well as cured of patriotism by not knowing where he was born. It might say that birthday presents make children individualistic, or merely that birthday cake makes them ill. It might say anything. But the mark of it is that the multitudinous human habit would go for *nothing*. The officials would not have the faintest idea of what a forest they were attacking in attacking such festivals; any more than they have any idea of what an ocean they are attacking in attacking ale. They cannot see that ale is an institution, and that simply because it is a popular institution; they cannot believe that haymakers, for instance, have had a scheme of recurrent refreshment founded on their own experience and industry, exactly as civilised and in the real sense cultured as any ritual of a gentleman about his courses or his costumes. Where such customs can rule, the people can rule; where such customs are disregarded, the people does not rule, and never will.

Finally, this truth is most applicable to the question of the Trades Union traditions, and any attempt to find a substitute for them. Those customs are defective in many ways; they fall short of the full creative character of the old lads of the mediaeval Guilds; they may be enlarged and altered to advantage, so long as they are enlarged and altered by those who made them. They are fragmentary customs, but they are customs—that is, they were made by the common people; they can only be kept by the common people, and only through such customs can the common people have any real power. No paper constitution, no political machinery, no shaky representation or sham partnership, can ever be a substitute for a living habit of human beings. A man cannot watch a distant representative as he watches his daily work; he cannot look after his indirect partnership as he looks after his pay. If he accepts such substitutes, he has sold a birthright which is as personal as a birthday. And he has sold his birthright for something much worse than a mess of pottage; he has sold it for a mess of politics. For surely he must know by this time that politics may truly be called a mess.

"The Hopeful One"

I could fill this book with examples of the universal, unconscious assumption that life and sex must live by the laws of "business" or industrialism, and not vice versa; examples from all the magazines, novels, and newspapers. In order to make it brief and typical, I take one case of a more or less Eugenist sort from a paper that lies open in front of me—a paper that still bears on its forehead the boast of being peculiarly an organ of democracy in revolt. To this a man writes to say that the spread of destitution will never be stopped until we have educated the lower classes in the methods by which the upper classes prevent procreation. The man had the horrible playfulness to sign his letter "Hopeful." Well, there are certainly methods by which people in the upper classes prevent procreation; one of them is what used to be called "platonic friendship," till they found another name for it at the Old Bailey. I do not suppose the hopeful gentleman hopes for this; but some of us find the abortion he does hope for almost as abominable. That, however, is not the curious point. The curious point is that the hopeful one concludes by saying, "When people have large families and small wages, not only is there a high infantile death-rate, but often those who do live to grow up are stunted and weakened by having had to share the family income for a time with those who died early. There would be less unhappiness if there were no unwanted children." You will observe that he tacitly takes it for granted that the small wages and the income, desperately shared, are the fixed points, like day and night, the conditions of human life. Compared with them marriage and maternity are luxuries, things to be modified to suit the wage-market. There are unwanted children; but unwanted by whom?

This man does not really mean that the parents do not want to have them. He means that the employers do not want to pay them properly. Doubtless, if you say to him directly, "Are you in favour of low wages?" he would say, "No." But I am not, in this chapter, talking about the effect on such modern minds of a cross-examination to which they do not subject themselves. I am talking about the way their minds work, the instinctive trick and turn of their thoughts, the things they assume before argument, and the way they faintly feel that the world is going. And, frankly, the turn of their mind is to tell the child he is not wanted, as the turn of my mind is to tell the profiteer he is not wanted. Motherhood, they feel, and a full childhood, and the beauty of brothers and sisters, are good things in their way, but not so good as a bad wage. About the mutilation of womanhood and the massacre of men unborn, he signs himself "Hopeful." He is hopeful of female indignity, hopeful of human annihilation. But about improving the small bad wage he signs himself "Hopeless."

Birth and Brain Control

A correspondent has written to us last week complaining of the article signed "Heretic," which condemned Birth Control not from a religious but a purely rationalist standpoint. The correspondent, Mr. Victor Neuburg, appears to give himself considerable airs of superiority because he is unable to believe in anything (except in Mrs. Stopes) and this is interesting, as illustrating a not uncommon combination of the incapacity for believing with the incapacity for thinking. It will be quite sufficient to quote about four lines of his letter, which contain more complicated contradictions and inconsequences than we have ever seen in such a space; and which end with one of those abrupt abysses of the entire absence of humour which is more laughable than the best humour in the world.

He says that a man does not practise Birth Control "in order to indulge his passions, as a Heretic slipshoddly affirms; but in order that his quite natural (and therefore legitimate) sexual passion may have no unforeseen and undesired results."

Why he should repudiate the indulging of his passion if his passion is quite legitimate, and why he should want to make the indulgence safe except in order to indulge it, the Lord only knows. He will pardon this theological expression; which we apologise for not putting in quotation marks, as he so haughtily presents all theological expressions. But the muddle is much more amusing than that. The passion, let it be noted, is not natural *and* legitimate; he distinctly says it is natural and *therefore* legitimate. In other words everything that is natural is legitimate. So far so good. It is natural for a man to wish to rush out of a burning theatre, even if he tramples on women and children; it is natural and therefore it is legitimate. It is natural for a man called upon to face death or tortures for the truth (of Mrs. Stopes, let us say) to run away and hide; it is natural and therefore it is legitimate. That is quite understood; and so far we are all getting along nicely. But if everything that is natural is right, why in the world is not the birth of a baby as natural as the growth of a passion? If it is unnatural to control appetite, why is it not unnatural to control birth? They are both obviously parts of the same natural process, which has a natural beginning and a natural end. And Mr. Neuburg, who thinks all natural things legitimate, has no possible reason for interrupting it at one stage more than at another. As Nature is infallible, we must not question what progeny she produces. If Nature is not infallible, we have a right to question the passions that she inspires.

And then comes the joyous culmination and collapse; of calling a baby an unforeseen consequence of getting married. It would be entertaining to wander through the world with Mr. Neuburg, sharing all the unforeseen consequences of the most ordinary actions. Life must be full of surprises for him; he strikes a match and is indignant that it burns the sulphur; he throws a stone into a puddle and is irritated that it makes a splash; he keeps bees and is furious because they fertilise flowers; he breeds dogs and stands astounded before the unforeseen consequence of puppies. Wonder is a wonderful thing and, with less irritation, might be a beautiful thing. But we rather doubt whether anyone who argues like this has any right to a tone of such extreme intellectual arrogance.

Who Is the Ascetic?

A masterpiece of horrible if unconscious humour was produced by Professor Julian Huxley, in a recent article on Sterilisation in the *News-Chronicle.* His remarks were doubtless very exact and even reliable about everything connected with the facts of his own subject and his own business; but like so many scientific men of his school, he could not be persuaded to mind his own business. He was weirdly impelled from within to mind our business; the business of believers or traditional Christians. Not to ask about our business; far from it. Not to study our business; God forbid. But simply to mind it; to take charge of it, as if he knew all about it by the light of nature; to explain to the world, briefly and brightly, what it really is; as if he at least was in a position to explain it, even if the world needed to have it explained. And the result was the following astonishing statement.

Professor Huxley said that "the ascetical element in Christianity" was what led to the moral protest against Sterilisation. It is a grisly and repulsive subject to joke about; but this is quite unquestionably an exceedingly good joke; an exceedingly funny joke. "Asceticism," whether it be good or bad, can only mean the rejection of some earthly joys and jollities, which it is the general human desire to enjoy. In logic, therefore, we could only infer that Professor Huxley thinks sterilising other people so ordinary a form of fun and festivity, that to refuse it is like forbidding the dance or dashing down the wine-cup. "Thou hast conquered, O pale Galilean; the world has grown grey with thy breath"; being deprived not only of wine, woman and song, but of their natural accompaniment of performing surgical operations on poor people, alleged to be of deficient intellect. Because we are virtuous, the scientists can have no more cakes and ale and castrating expeditions among their fellow-citizens. Thus do we frown upon the gayer and more frivolous side of life; denying to the medical profession its natural form of merriment. This is what would be meant by what he unquestionably said; if he had thought what he was saying. Of course, it is not what he meant; because he did not think what he was saying. No laborious conscientious sceptical man of science ever does think what he is saying, when he says anything on that particular subject of Christianity and its ascetical element. If it were any other subject, it would stare him in the face that allowing people to love and marry and have children, in such cases, whether it be right or wrong, cannot possibly be ascetical. If anybody is the ascetic, it is obviously the man who wants to prevent people from having babies to love in the normal way: in other words, it is the Steriliser.

But no such writer ever bothers about what any Christian code does teach; or about any other parts of it, except what he has heard mentioned in abuse of it. By Christianity he probably means Catholicism; and he has never heard of any other element in Catholicism except the ascetical element. So the notion of protecting natural procreation and parenthood must somehow or other be ascetical; even when it is quite obviously the very opposite. It is true that Professor Huxley adds some very vague and mysterious words about asceticism producing the idea that sex is sacred; and therefore under the control of religion. But why should it be ascetic to think that sex is sacred; and how can it possibly be ascetic to think that sex should pursue its natural course? Were the rites of Priapus ascetic; they were certainly sacred? The simple fact is that the modern agnostic knows less about the modern Catholic than he would know about the most savage priest of a Phallic prehistoric cult.

In truth, besides the ascetical element (which of course he entirely misunderstands), and bulking far bigger as a buttress and central citadel of the old Christian system, is its universal teaching about the sanity of observing the Natural Law. By the way, the Natural Law does not mean the Law of Nature; which moderns talk about when they mean the Lawlessness of Nature. It means the truth which Man can perceive even through his own nature; without the supernatural that is above nature. Nine-tenths of the battles the Church has fought have been on behalf of Nature against the unnatural "ascetical element" of the Catharist and the Manichee. Quite logically must be classed with these the battle of the Church against the Steriliser or the Birth-Controller. We need not notice the idiots who insist that we must mean noninterference with common external growth; as if no Catholic could cut down a tree. The point is that these moderns have collided, *not* with our "ascetical element," but with our ancient and universal element of belief in Creation and Nature and Life. We are the only real worshippers of the Life-Force.

This queer fact, that those presumed to be the prophets of the Life-Force, the professors who study Nature to encourage health or humanitarianism, should be so incredibly ignorant of a whole huge aspect of the root religion of their own culture, has an application that is not religious, but political and practical. It is extraordinary that they will not see this other side of Christianity, considering that it is against this other side that they have just hurled themselves with a crash. They will go on assuming theoretically, and in the air, that our asceticism is only pessimism; though they are occupied practically in attacking something that they might call sentimentalism; but which, even if it is wrong, can only be wrong by an excess of optimism. We are more hopeful for human families, and their power of finding happiness, than are the Birth-Preventionists; we may be mistaken, but we cannot be morbid. Yet they cannot even talk of us except in terms of morbidity. The truth is that the morbidity and the pessimism are all on their side and not on ours, and this, as I have said, applies to political as well as moral ideas. We believe in liberty more than they do; in love more than they do; in local common sense more than they do; and we are therefore consistent in more often trusting abnormal children to their normal families; or thinking that most people would be happier with families than without. We have the same attitude to the idea of trusting the common people with private property and political liberty. And our chief enemy is the "ascetical element" in the scientists and sociologists, who have really no notions except the negative ones of amputation and annihilation. That school has offered us a series of cures by cutting things off; beginning with cutting off our beer and ending, for all I know, with cutting off our ears and noses. They might say that men henceforward can do without the sense of smell, as they often do say that they can do without the sense of ownership. But these fads are failures; and a very big civilisation has just discovered that men will not even do without the beer. I have taken this case to show the indifference to the Life-Force among the Evolutionists; I hope to deal later with the parallel indifference to Liberty among the Liberals.

An Attack from the Altars

It is possible to criticise quite frankly the Conference of Modern Churchmen without the fear of stirring up religious controversy, because religion, as any normal Christian, or Buddhist, or Hindu understands the word, hardly entered into its deliberations. Nevertheless, we do not deny a definite element of tradition to the Modern Churchmen. Traditions are founded quickly in these days, when they decay so fast; and already it is a tradition that the month of August is reserved for thinkers in the new science, who are assured that their corrupting statements will be written large for the innocent and the ignorant of the world to read. We cheerfully assert that various opinions expressed by the Modern Churchmen would cause an archangel to be cast out of Heaven, a schoolboy to be sent home with a birching, and a younger child to have his mouth washed out with soap.

In this there is no exaggeration. The Modern Churchmen were pleased to tickle their palates with investigations into the subjects of marriage, birth control, and divorce, not, it would appear, in the light of any fixed body of beliefs, some not with any sense of responsibility as the fathers of a civilised community, not even with a care for the truth of statements made or with any regard for the laws which govern thought, but rather with the ambition to outdo one another carelessly in originality, to challenge whatever conceptions of morality were observed by their fathers, to prove to those poor sheep over whom they claim to be set as spiritual pastors that the State rules all our lives and our destinies.

From the reports given in the more serious daily papers, which we assume to be either accurate, word by word, or else substantially accurate digests of opinions expressed, we shall quote some sentences in which the reader may detect perhaps loose thought, or unwelcome moral teaching, or an attack upon what he has known as the tradition of his people.

A speaker on "Principles of Sexual Conduct" argued "that on the ratio of the sexes depended the reasonableness of monogamy." Again: "From the national point of view, I do not see that infantile mortality matters very much, except for its effect upon the balance of the sexes." Another speaker: "Unwanted children, whether in or out of marriage, are undesirable products, misfortunes alike to themselves and their parents." Again: "To insist that the Christian Church, and still more the Christian State, must legislate in accordance with the letter of Christ's teaching was not to act in accordance with the spirit of Christ." Another speaker: "We rub our hands whenever an old belief is destroyed, and I doubt whether we have it in us to be creative; but the rising generation will perform that miracle for us. The disintegration of morality is a sign that things are moving." Another speaker: "Outside the countries which were still unhappily under the influence of the Latin Church, the marriage law of England was undoubtedly the worst in the world."

It may be that not one of these sayings will strike the reader unaccustomed to fixed standards and rules of thought as a statement in any way immoral or immoderate. Then he may admit some lack of moderation in the following remarks by a clergyman ordained in the Church of England:—

He said that there were plenty of men at the present time who were not merely unemployed, but had almost always been unemployed and intended almost always to be unemployed as long as they lived.

"Yet those people," he added, "are able, if they choose, to go on having children year after year, knowing that they cannot maintain them and that they will be looked after by the State. As each child comes along, it will increase the particular claim which the man has on State maintenance.

"If the State assumes the axiom that every child born has a

claim upon the State for maintenance, then there must go along with that the claim on the part of the State to say whether a child shall be born or not."

A licence to have a child should not, of course, be unreasonably withheld. People should satisfy the State that they were physically fit to produce healthy offspring, and that they were economically capable of supporting their offspring.

"What can be done in regard to punishment for disobedience?" he continued. "I am speaking quite seriously, and do not wish my remarks to be treated in any humorous way. If, when that position is reached and accepted by the community, there are people who depart from that obligation and have children without being physically fit or economically capable of supporting them, then, I say, is the time for sterilisation, so that the action cannot be repeated a second time."

Is that empty talk, the babbling of a poor *Herod, capax imperii nisi imperasset?*[1] Is it the view of an obscure clergyman, unsupported by any power or opinion in the State? On the contrary, the thing is in our midst. The power and the opinion are at work.

"My advice has recently been sought," declared a doctor at the same meeting, "by a statutory committee charged with the supervision of the blind in their area. This committee, rightly wishing to discountenance the marriage of blind workers under its care, has passed a rule which provides that persons so marrying without the consent of the committee shall cease to receive benefit and employment by the committee unless one or both parties to the marriage can produce a medical certificate that such a marriage will be childless.

"Two blind young couples under the care of this committee have expressed in writing their willingness to undergo sterilization, and so comply with the committee's rule. One of the couples is now married and the other will be married shortly.

"In my opinion, sterilisation is the right method of conception control in such cases. Such married couples do not lose their employment; they do not depend on support from the

[1] "Herod, able to command as long as he would not command."

rates, and the State is safeguarded against the risk of the birth of children by parents who are not able to rear them under normal conditions.

"If statutory committees charged with the care of blind persons in their area are justified in their action, surely the State is justified in requiring that persons who are liable to transmit serious mental or bodily defect to offspring shall also undergo sterilisation."

That is slavery, no more and no less. In the year 1930 slavery is first advocated as a social policy and then described in practice at a Conference of Modern Churchmen. In the first case, men and women dependent on the State are regarded as the property of the State, to be used like cattle. In the second case, men and women dependent upon the "care and supervision" of a committee are threatened with the withdrawal of their means of livelihood unless they consent to humiliation. They are the slaves of the committee if they consent; they become the slaves of the State if they refuse.

We know very well that these are not the official teachings of the Church of England, or of any religious body in the land; but we cannot refrain from attacking the Modern Churchmen's Conference for fear of religious controversy when the Modern Churchmen are themselves attacking the whole structure of our civilisation. We know also that the opinions we have quoted would be rejected with disgust by a majority in the nation if they were regarded as anything more than the talk of the "silly season." But those opinions are already more than the talk of the "silly season." They express the realities of corruption. These men of substantial wealth, of impressive education, of a varied influence, have all the powers of destruction that they may wish to wield. It is not enough to tolerate them. They must be actively opposed.

One by one, the defences of our civilisation are being broken down by a concentrated attack upon the mind. Rome's barbarians were a menace on her borders; ours are also within the State. No camouflage or hypocrisy will hide for long the affinities between the philosophy of the Modern Churchmen (with their fellows who profess no God) and the practice of materialism to be seen in Russia. Shall we begin to fight only when the battle is over?

PART SEVEN

THE SUPERSTITION
OF DIVORCE

* * *

Marriage licenses will be sold like dog licenses, good for a period of
twelve months, with no law against changing dogs or keeping more
than one animal at a time.

> Aldous Huxley, Preface to *Brave New World*

Adultery is bad morals, but divorce is bad metaphysics.

> Charles Williams, *The Forgiveness of Sins*

This triangle of truisms, of father, mother and child, cannot be
destroyed; it can only destroy those civilisations which disregard it.

> *The Superstition of Divorce*

We may not believe in sacraments, as we may not believe in spirits,
but it is quite clear that Christ believed in this sacrament in his own
way and not in any current or contemporary way. He certainly did
not get his argument against divorce from the Mosaic law or the
Roman law or the habits of the Palestinian people. It would appear
to his critics then exactly what it appears to his critics now; an
arbitrary and transcendental dogma coming from nowhere save in
the sense that it came from him. I am not at all concerned here to
defend that dogma; the point here is that it is just as easy to defend

it now as it was to defend it then. It is an ideal altogether outside time; difficult at any period; impossible at no period.

The Everlasting Man

The vow is to the man what the song is to the bird, or the bark to the dog; his voice, whereby he is known. Just as a man who cannot keep an appointment is not fit even to fight a duel, so the man who cannot keep an appointment with himself is not sane enough even for suicide. It is not easy to mention anything on which the enormous apparatus of human life can be said to depend. But if it depends on anything, it is on this frail cord, flung from the forgotten hills of yesterday to the invisible mountains of tomorrow.

The Appetite of Tyranny

Let no one flatter himself that he leaves his family life in search of art, or knowledge; he leaves it because he is fleeing from the baffling knowledge of humanity and from the impossible art of life.

"A Defence of Bores", in *Lunacy and Letters* p. 60

The Tragedies of Marriage

There is one view very common among the liberal-minded which is exceedingly fatiguing to the clear-headed. It is symbolised in the sort of man who says, "These ruthless bigots will refuse to bury me in consecrated ground, because I have always refused to be baptised." A clear-headed person can easily conceive his point of view, in so far as he happens to think that baptism does not matter. But the clear-headed will be completely puzzled when they ask themselves why, if he thinks that baptism does not matter, he should think that burial does matter. If it is in no way imprudent for a man to keep himself from a consecrated font, how can it be inhuman for other people to keep him from a consecrated field? It is surely much nearer to mere superstition to attach importance to what is done to a dead body than to a live baby. I can understand a man thinking both superstitious, or both sacred; but I cannot see why he should grumble that other people do not give him as sanctities what he regards as superstitions. He is merely complaining of being treated as what he declares himself to be. It is as if a man were to say, "My persecutors still refuse to make me king, out of mere malice because I am a strict republican." Or it is as if he said, "These heartless brutes are so prejudiced against a teetotaler, that they won't even give him a glass of brandy."

The fashion of divorce would not be a modern fashion if it were not full of this touching fallacy. A great deal of it might be summed up as a most illogical and fanatical appetite for getting married in churches. It is as if a man should practice polygamy out of sheer greed for wedding cake. Or it is as if he provided his household with new shoes, entirely by having them thrown after

the wedding carriage when he went off with a new wife. There
are other ways of procuring cake or purchasing shoes; and there
are other ways of setting up a human establishment. What is
unreasonable is the request which the modern man really makes of
the religious institutions of his fathers. The modern man wants to
buy one shoe without the other; to obtain one half of a supernatural revelation without the other. The modern man wants to
eat his wedding cake and have it, too.

I am not basing this book on the religious argument, and
therefore I will not pause to inquire why the old Catholic institutions of Christianity seem to be especially made the objects of
these unreasonable complaints. As a matter of fact nobody does
propose that some ferocious Anti-Semite like M. Drumont should
be buried as a Jew with all the rites of the Synagogue. But the
broad-minded were furious because Tolstoi, who had denounced
Russian orthodoxy quite as ferociously, was not buried as orthodox,
with all the rites of the Russian Church. Nobody does insist that a
man who wishes to have fifty wives when Mahomet allowed him
five, must have his fifty with the full approval of Mahomet's
religion. But the broad-minded are extremely bitter because a
Christian who wishes to have several wives when his own promise
bound him to one, is not allowed to violate his vow at the same
altar at which he made it. Nobody does insist on Baptists totally
immersing people who totally deny the advantages of being totally
immersed. Nobody ever did expect Mormons to receive the open
mockers of the Book of Mormon, nor Christian Scientists to let
their churches be used for exposing Mrs. Eddy as an old fraud. It
is only of the forms of Christianity making the Catholic claim
that such inconsistent claims are made. And even the inconsistency is, I fancy, a tribute to the acceptance of the Catholic idea in
a catholic fashion. It may be that men have an obscure sense that
nobody need belong to the Mormon religion and every one does
ultimately belong to the Church; and though he may have made a
few dozen Mormon marriages in a wandering and entertaining
life, he will really have nowhere to go to if he does not somehow
find his way back to the churchyard. But all this concerns the

general theological question and not the matter involved here, which is merely historical and social. The point here is that it is at least superficially inconsistent to ask institutions for a formal approval, which they can only give by an inconsistency.

I have put first the question of what is marriage. And we are now in a position to ask more clearly what is divorce. It is not merely the negation or neglect of marriage; for any one can always neglect marriage. It is not the dissolution of the legal obligation of marriage, or even the legal obligation of monogamy; for the simple reason that no such obligation exists. Any man in modern London may have a hundred wives if he does not call them wives; or rather, if he does not go through certain more or less mystical ceremonies in order to assert that they are wives. He might create a certain social coolness round his household, a certain fading of his general popularity. But that is not created by law, and could not be prevented by law. As the late Lord Salisbury very sensibly observed about boycotting in Ireland, "How can you make a law to prevent people going out of the room when somebody they don't like comes into it?" We cannot be forcibly introduced to a polygamist by a policeman. It would not be an assertion of social liberty, but a denial of social liberty, if we found ourselves practically obliged to associate with all the profligates in society. But divorce is not in this sense mere anarchy. On the contrary divorce is in this sense respectability; and even a rigid excess of respectability. Divorce in this sense might indeed be not unfairly called snobbery. The definition of divorce, which concerns us here, is that it is the attempt to give respectability, and not liberty. It is the attempt to give a certain social status, and not a legal status. It is indeed supposed that this can be done by the alteration of certain legal forms; and this will be more or less true according to the extent to which law as such overawed public opinion, or was valued as a true expression of public opinion. If a man divorced in the large-minded fashion of Henry the Eighth pleaded his legal title among the peasantry of Ireland, for instance, I think he would find a difference still existing between respectability and religion. But the peculiar point here is that many are claiming the sanction of religion as well as of respectability. They would attach to their very natural and sometimes very pardonable experiments a certain atmosphere, and even glamour, which has undoubtedly belonged to the status of marriage in historic Christendom. But before they make this attempt, it would be well to ask why such a dignity ever appeared or in what it consisted. And I fancy we shall find ourselves confronted with the very simple truth, that the dignity arose wholly and entirely out of the fidelity; and that the glamour merely came from the vow. People were regarded as having a certain dignity because they were dedicated in a certain way; as bound to certain duties and, if it be preferred, to certain discomforts. It may be irrational to endure these discomforts; it may even be irrational to respect them. But it is certainly much more irrational to respect them, and then artificially transfer the same respect to the absence of them. It is as if we were to expect uniforms to be saluted when armies were disbanded; and ask people to cheer a soldier's coat when it did not contain a soldier. If you think you can abolish war, abolish it; but do not suppose that when there are no wars to be waged, there will still be warriors to be worshipped. If it was a good thing that the monasteries were dissolved, let us say so and dismiss them. But the nobles who dissolved the monasteries did not shave their heads, and ask to be regarded as saints solely on account of that ceremony. The nobles did not dress up as abbots and ask to be credited with a potential talent for working miracles, because of the austerity of their vows of poverty and chastity. They got inside the houses, but not the hoods, and still less the haloes. They at least knew that it is not the habit that makes the monk. They were not so superstitious as those moderns, who think it is the veil that makes the bride.

What is respected, in short, is fidelity to the ancient flag of the family, and a readiness to fight for what I have noted as its unique type of freedom. I say readiness to fight, for fortunately the fight itself is the exception rather than the rule. The soldier is not respected because he is doomed to death, but because he is ready for death; and even ready for defeat. The married man or woman

is not doomed to evil, sickness or poverty; but is respected for
taking a certain step for better for worse, for richer for poorer, in
sickness or in health. But there is one result of this line of argument which should correct a danger in some arguments on the
same side.

It is very essential that a stricture on divorce, which is in
fact simply a defence of marriage, should be independent of
sentimentalism, especially in the form called optimism. A man
justifying a fight for national independence or civic freedom is
neither sentimental nor optimistic. He explains the sacrifice, but
he does not explain it away. He does not say that bayonet wounds
are pin-pricks, or mere scratches of the thorns on the rose of
pleasure. He does not say that the whole display of firearms is a
festive display of fireworks. On the contrary, when he praises it
most, he praises it as pain rather than pleasure. He increases the
praise with the pain; it is his whole boast that militarism, and even
modern science, can produce no instrument of torture to tame the
soul of man. It is idle, in speaking of war, to pit the realistic against
the romantic, in the sense of the heroic; for all possible realism can
only increase the heroism; and therefore, in the highest sense,
increase the romance. Now I do not compare marriage with war,
but I do compare marriage with law or liberty or patriotism or
popular government, or any of the human ideals which have often
to be defended by war. Even the wildest of those ideals, which
seem to escape from all the discipline of peace, do not escape from
the discipline of war. The Bolshevists may have aimed at pure
peace and liberty; but they have been compelled, for their own
purpose, first to raise armies and then to rule armies. In a word,
however beautiful you may think your own visions of beatitude,
men must suffer to be beautiful, and even suffer a considerable
interval of being ugly. And I have no notion of denying that
mankind suffers much from the maintenance of the standard of
marriage; as it suffers much from the necessity of criminal law or
the recurrence of crusades and revolutions. The only question
here is whether marriage is indeed, as I maintain, an ideal and an
institution making for popular freedom; I do not need to be told

that anything making for popular freedom has to be paid for in vigilance and pain, and a whole army of martyrs.

Hence I am far indeed from denying the hard cases which exist here, as in all matters involving the idea of honour. For indeed I could not deny them without denying the whole parallel of militant morality on which my argument rests. But this being first understood, it will be well to discuss in a little more detail what are described as the tragedies of marriage. And the first thing to note about the most tragic of them is that they are not tragedies of marriage at all. They are tragedies of sex; and might easily occur in a highly modern romance in which marriage was not mentioned at all. It is generally summarised by saying that the tragic element is the absence of love. But it is often forgotten that another tragic element is often the presence of love. The doctors of divorce, with an air of the frank and friendly realism of men of the world, are always recommending and rejoicing in a sensible separation by mutual consent. But if we are really to dismiss our dreams of dignity and honour, if we are really to fall back on the frank realism of our experience as men of the world, then the very first thing that our experience will tell us is that it very seldom is a separation by mutual consent; that is, that the consent very seldom is sincerely and spontaneously mutual. By far the commonest problem in such cases is that in which one party wishes to end the partnership and the other does not. And of that emotional situation you can make nothing but a tragedy, whichever way you turn it. With or without marriage, with or without divorce, with or without any arrangements that anybody can suggest or imagine, it remains a tragedy. The only difference is that by the doctrine of marriage it remains both a noble and a fruitful tragedy; like that of a man who falls fighting for his country, or dies testifying to the truth. But the truth is that the innovators have as much sham optimism about divorce as any romanticist can have had about marriage. They regard their story, when it ends in the divorce court, through as rosy a mist of sentimentalism as anybody ever regarded a story ending with wedding bells. Such a reformer is quite sure that when once the prince and princess are divorced by the fairy godmother, they will live happily ever after. I enjoy romance, but I like it to be rooted in reality; and any one with a touch of reality knows that nine couples out of ten, when they are divorced, are left in an exceedingly different state. It will be safe to say in most cases that one partner will fail to find happiness in an infatuation, and the other will from the first accept a tragedy. In the realm of reality and not of romance, it is commonly a case of breaking hearts as well as breaking promises; and even dishonour is not always a remedy for remorse.

The next limitation to be laid down in the matter affects certain practical forms of discomfort, on a level rather lower than love or hatred. The cases most commonly quoted concern what is called "drink" and what is called "cruelty." They are always talked about as matters of fact; though in practice they are very decidedly matters of opinion. It is not a flippancy, but a fact, that the misfortune of the woman who has married a drunkard may have to be balanced against the misfortune of the man who has married a teetotaler. For the very definition of drunkenness may depend on the dogma of teetotalism. Drunkenness, it has been very truly observed,[1] "may mean anything from *delirium tremens* to having a stronger head than the official appointed to conduct the examination." Mr. Bernard Shaw once professed, apparently seriously, that any man drinking wine or beer at all was incapacitated from managing a motor-car; and still more, therefore, one would suppose, from managing a wife. The scales are weighted here, of course, with all those false weights of snobbishness which are the curse of justice in this country. The working class is forced to conduct almost in public a normal and varying festive habit, which the upper class can afford to conduct in private; and a certain section of the middle class, that which happens to concern itself most with local politics and social reforms, really has or affects a standard quite abnormal and even alien. They might go any lengths of injustice in dealing with the working man or working woman accused of too hearty a taste in beer. To mention but one matter

[1] The late Cecil Chesterton, in the "New Witness."

out of a thousand, the middle class reformers are obviously quite ignorant of the hours at which working people begin to work. Because they themselves, at eleven o'clock in the morning, have only recently finished breakfast and the full moral digestion of the *Daily Mail,* they think a charwoman drinking beer at that hour is one of those arising early in the morning to follow after strong drink. Most of them really do not know that she has already done more than half a heavy day's work, and is partaking of a very reasonable luncheon. The whole problem of proletarian drink is entangled in a network of these misunderstandings; and there is no doubt whatever that, when judged by these generalisations, the poor will be taken in a net of injustices. And this truth is as certain in the case of what is called cruelty as of what is called drink. Nine times out of ten the judgment on a navvy for hitting a woman is about as just as a judgment on him for not taking off his hat to a lady. It is a class test; it may be a class superiority; but it is not an act of equal justice between the classes. It leaves out a thousand things; the provocation, the atmosphere, the harassing restrictions of space, the nagging which Dickens described as the terrors of "temper in a cart," the absence of certain taboos of social training, the tradition of greater roughness even in the gestures of affection. To make all marriage or divorce, in the case of such a man, turn upon a blow is like blasting the whole life of a gentle-man because he has slammed the door. Often a poor man cannot slam the door; partly because the model villa might fall down; but more because he has nowhere to go to; the smoking-room, the billiard-room and the peacock music-room not being yet attached to his premises.

I say this in passing, to point out that while I do not dream of suggesting that there are only happy marriages, there will quite certainly, as things work nowadays, be a very large number of unhappy and unjust divorces. They will be cases in which the innocent partner will receive the real punishment of the guilty partner, through being in fact and feeling the faithful partner. For instance, it is insisted that a married person must at least find release from the society of a lunatic; but it is also true that the scientific reformers, with their fuss about "the feeble-minded," are continually giving larger and looser definitions of lunacy. The process might begin by releasing somebody from a homicidal maniac, and end by dealing in the same way with a rather dull conversationalist. But in fact nobody does deny that a person should be allowed some sort of release from a homicidal maniac. The most extreme school of orthodoxy only maintains that anybody who has had that experience should be content with that release. In other words, it says he should be content with that experience of matrimony, and not seek another. It was put very wittily, I think, by a Roman Catholic friend of mine, who said he approved of release so long as it was not spelt with a hyphen.

To put it roughly, we are prepared in some cases to listen to the man who complains of having a wife. But we are not prepared to listen, at such length, to the same man when he comes back and complains that he has not got a wife. Now in practice at this moment the great mass of the complaints are precisely of this kind. The reformers insist particularly on the pathos of a man's position when he has obtained a separation without a divorce. Their most tragic figure is that of the man who is already free of all those ills he had, and is only asking to be allowed to fly to others that he knows not of. I should be the last to deny that, in certain emotional circumstances, his tragedy may be very tragic indeed. But his tragedy is of the emotional kind which can never be entirely eliminated; and which he has himself, in all probability, inflicted on the partner he has left. We may call it the price of maintaining an ideal or the price of making a mistake; but anyhow it is the point of our whole distinction in the matter; it is here that we draw the line, and I have nowhere denied that it is a line of battle. The battle joins on the debatable ground, not of the man's doubtful past but of his still more doubtful future. In a word, the divorce controversy is not really a controversy about divorce. It is a controversy about re-marriage; or rather about whether it is marriage at all.

And with that we can only return to the point of honour which I have compared here to a point of patriotism; since it is both the smallest and the greatest kind of patriotism. Men have died in torments during the last five years for points of patriotism far more dubious and fugitive. Men like the Poles or the Serbians, through long periods of their history, may be said rather to have lived in torments. I will never admit that the vital need of the freedom of the family, as I have tried to sketch it here, is not a cause as valuable as the freedom of any frontier. But I do willingly admit that the cause would be a dark and terrible one, if it really asked these men to suffer torments. As I have stated it, on its most extreme terms, it only asks them to suffer abnegations. And those negative sufferings I do think they may honourably be called upon to bear, for the glory of their own oath and the great things by which the nations live. In relation to their own nation most normal men will feel that this distinction between release and "re-lease" is neither fanciful nor harsh, but very rational and human. A patriot may be an exile in another country; but he will not be a patriot of another country. He will be as cheerful as he can in an abnormal position; he may or may not sing his country's songs in a strange land; but he will not sing the strange songs as his own. And such may fairly be also the attitude of the citizen who has gone into exile from the oldest of earthly cities.

The Sentimentalism of Divorce

Divorce is a thing which the newspapers now not only advertise, but advocate, almost as if it were a pleasure in itself. It may be, indeed, that all the flowers and festivities will now be transferred from the fashionable wedding to the fashionable divorce. A superb iced and frosted divorce-cake will be provided for the feast, and in military circles will be cut with the co-respondent's sword. A dazzling display of divorce presents will be laid out for the inspection of the company, watched by a detective dressed as an ordinary divorce guest. Perhaps the old divorce breakfast will be revived; anyhow, toasts will be drunk, the guests will assemble on the doorstep to see the husband and wife go off in opposite directions; and all will go merry as a divorce-court bell. All this, though to some it might seem a little fanciful, would really be far less fantastic than the sort of things that are really said on the subject. I am not going to discuss the depth and substance of that subject. I myself hold a mystical view of marriage; but I am not going to debate it here. But merely in the interests of light and logic I would protest against the way in which it is frequently debated. The process cannot rationally be called a debate at all. It is a sort of chorus of sentimentalists in the sensational newspapers, perpetually intoning some such formula as this: "We respect marriage, we reverence marriage, holy, sacred, ineffably exquisite and ideal marriage. True marriage is love, and when love alters, marriage alters, and when love stops or begins again, marriage does the same; wonderful, beautiful, beatific marriage."

Now, with all reasonable sympathy with everything sentimental, I may remark that all that talk is tosh. Marriage is an institution like any other, set up deliberately to have certain functions and

235

limitations; it is an institution like private property, or conscription, or the legal liberties of the subject. To talk as if it were made or melted with certain changing moods is a mere waste of words. The object of private property is that as many citizens as possible should have a certain dignity and pleasure in being masters of material things. But suppose a dog-stealer were to say that as soon as a man was bored with his dog it ceased to be his dog, and he ceased to be responsible for it. Suppose he were to say that by merely coveting the dog, he could immediately morally possess the dog. The answer would be that the only way to make men responsible for dogs was to make the relation a legal one, apart from the likes and dislikes of the moment. Suppose a burglar were to say: "Private property I venerate, private property I revere; but I am convinced that Mr. Brown does not truly value his silver Apostle spoons as such sacred objects should be valued; they have therefore ceased to be his property; in reality they have already become my property, for I appreciate their precious character as nobody else can do." Suppose a murderer were to say: "What can be more amiable and admirable than human life lived with a due sense of its priceless opportunity! But I regret to observe that Mr. Robinson has lately been looking decidedly tired and melancholy; life accepted in this depressing and demoralizing spirit can no longer truly be called life; it is rather my own exuberant and perhaps exaggerated joy of life which I must gratify by cutting his throat with a carving-knife."

It is obvious that these philosophers would fail to understand what we mean by a rule, quite apart from the problem of its exceptions. They would fail to grasp what we mean by an institution, whether it be the institution of law, of property, or of marriage. A reasonable person will certainly reply to the burglar: "You will hardly soothe us by merely poetical praises of property; because your case would be much more convincing if you denied, as the Communists do, that property ought to exist at all. There may be, there certainly are, gross abuses in private property; but, so long as it is an institution at all, it cannot alter merely with moods and emotions. A farm cannot simply float away from a farmer, in proportion as his interest in it grows fainter than it was. A house cannot shift away by inches from a householder, by certain fine shades of feeling that he happens to have about it. A dog cannot drift away like a dream, and begin to belong to somebody else who happens just then to be dreaming of him. And neither can the serious social relation of husband and wife, of mother and father, or even of man and woman, be resolved in all its relations by passions and reactions of sentiment." This question is quite apart from the question of whether there are exceptions to the rule of loyalty, or what they are. The primary point is that there is an institution to which to be loyal. If the new sentimentalists mean what they say, when they say they venerate that institution, they must not suggest that an institution can be actually identical with an emotion. And that is what their rhetoric does suggest, so far as it can be said to suggest anything.

These writers are always explaining to us why they believe in divorce. I think I can easily understand why they believe in divorce. What I do not understand is why they believe in marriage. Just as the philosophical burglar would be more philosophical if he were a Bolshevist, so this sort of divorce advocate would be more philosophical if he were a free-lover. For his arguments never seem to touch on marriage as an institution, or anything more than an individual experience. The real explanation of this strange indifference to the institutional idea is, I fancy, something not only deeper, but wider; something affecting all the institutions of the modern world. The truth is that these sociologists are not at all interested in promoting the sort of social life that marriage does promote. The sort of society of which marriage has always been the strongest pillar is what is sometimes called the distributive society; the society in which most of the citizens have a tolerable share of property, especially property in hand. Everywhere, all over the world, the farm goes with the family and the family with the farm. Unless the whole domestic group hold together with a sort of loyalty or local patriotism, unless the inheritance of property is logical and legitimate, unless the family quarrels are kept out of the courts of officialism, the tradition of family ownership cannot be handed on unimpaired. On the other hand, the Servile State, which is the opposite of the distributive state, has always been rather embarrassed by the institution of marriage. It is an old story that the negro slavery of "Uncle Tom's Cabin" did its worst work in the breaking-up of families. But, curiously enough, the same story is told from both sides. For the apologists of the Slave States, or, at least, of the Southern States, make the same admission even in their own defence. If they denied breaking up the slave family, it was because they denied that there was any slave family to break up.

Free love is the direct enemy of freedom. It is the most obvious of all the bribes that can be offered by slavery. In servile societies a vast amount of sexual laxity can go on in practice, and even in theory, save when now and then some cranky speculator or crazy squire has a fad for some special breed of slaves like a breed of cattle. And even that lunacy would not last long; for lunatics are the minority among slave-owners. Slavery has a much more sane and a much more subtle appeal to human nature than that. It is much more likely that, after a few such fads and freaks, the new Servile State would settle down into the sleepy resignation of the old Servile State; the old pagan repose in slavery, as it was before Christianity came to trouble and perplex the world with ideals of liberty and chivalry. One of the conveniences of that pagan world is that, below a certain level of society, nobody really need bother about pedigree or paternity at all. A new world began when slaves began to stand on their dignity as virgin martyrs. Christendom is the civilization that such martyrs made; and slavery is its returning enemy. But of all the bribes that the old pagan slavery can offer, this luxury and laxity is the strongest; nor do I deny that the influences desiring the degradation of human dignity have here chosen their instrument well.

Questions of Divorce

I have just picked up a little book that is not only brightly and suggestively written, but is somewhat unique, in this sense — that it enunciates the modern and advanced view of Woman in such language as a sane person can stand. It is written by Miss Florence Farr, is called *Modern Woman: her Intentions,* and is published by Mr. Frank Palmer. This style of book I confess to commonly finding foolish and vain. The New Woman's monologue wearies, not because it is unwomanly, but because it is inhuman. It exhibits the most exhausting of combinations: the union of fanaticism of speech with frigidity of soul — the things that made Robespierre seem a monster. The worst example I remember was once trumpeted in a Review: a lady doctor, who has ever afterwards haunted me as a sort of nightmare of spiritual imbecility. I forget her exact words, but they were to the effect that sex and motherhood should be treated neither with ribaldry nor reverence: "It is too serious a subject for ribaldry, and I myself cannot understand reverence towards anything that is physical." There, in a few words, is the whole twisted and tortured priggishness which poisons the present age. The person who cannot laugh at sex ought to be kicked; and the person who cannot reverence pain ought to be killed. Until that lady doctor gets a little ribaldry and a little reverence into her soul, she has no right to have any opinion at all about the affairs of humanity. I remember there was another lady, trumpeted in the same Review, a French lady who broke off her engagement with the excellent gentleman to whom she was attached on the ground that affection interrupted the flow of her thoughts. It was a thin sort of flow in any case to judge by the samples; and no doubt it was easily interrupted.

239

The author of *Modern Woman* is bitten a little by the mad dog of modernity, the habit of dwelling disproportionately on the abnormal and the diseased; but she writes rationally and humorously, like a human being; she sees that there are two sides to the case; and she even puts in a fruitful suggestion that, with its sub-consciousness and its virtues of the vegetable, the new psychology may turn up on the side of the old womanhood. One may say indeed that in such a book as this our amateur philosophizing of to-day is seen at its fairest; and even at its fairest it exhibits certain qualities of bewilderment and disproportion which are somewhat curious to note.

I think the oddest thing about the advanced people is that, while they are always talking of things as problems, they have hardly any notion of what a real problem is. A real problem only occurs when there are admittedly disadvantages in all courses that can be pursued. If it is discovered just before a fashionable wed-ding that the Bishop is locked up in the coal-cellar, that is not a problem. It is obvious to anyone but an extreme anti-clerical or practical joker that the Bishop must be let out of the coal-cellar. But suppose the Bishop has been locked up in the wine-cellar, and from the obscure noises, sounds as of song and dance, etc., it is guessed that he has indiscreetly tested the vintages round him; then, indeed, we may properly say that there has arisen a *problem;* for, upon the one hand, it is awkward to keep the wedding waiting, while, upon the other, any hasty opening of the door might mean an episcopal rush and scenes of the most unforeseen description.

An incident like this (which must constantly happen in our gay and varied social life) is a true problem because there are in it incompatible advantages. Now if woman is simply the domestic slave that many of these writers represent, if man has bound her by brute force, if he has simply knocked her down and sat on her—then there is no problem about the matter. She has been locked in the kitchen, like the Bishop in the coal-cellar; and they both of them ought to be let out. If there is any problem of sex, it must be because the case is not so simple as that; because there is something to be said for the man as well as for the woman; and because there are evils in unlocking the kitchen door, in addition to the obvious good of it. Now, I will take two instances from Miss Farr's own book of problems that are really problems, and which she entirely misses because she will not admit that they are problematical.

The writer asks the substantial question squarely enough: "Is indissoluble marriage good for mankind?" and she answers it squarely enough: "For the great mass of mankind, yes." To those like myself, who move in the old-world dream of Democracy, that admission ends the whole question. There may be exceptional people who would be happier without Civil Government; sensitive souls who really feel unwell when they see a policeman. But we have surely the right to impose the State on everybody if it suits nearly everybody; and if so, we have the right to impose the Family on everybody if it suits nearly everybody. But the queer and cogent point is this; that Miss Farr does not see the real difficulty about allowing exceptions—the real difficulty that has made most legislators reluctant to allow them. I do not say there should be no exceptions, but I do say that the author has not seen the painful problem of permitting any.

The difficulty is simply this: that if it comes to claiming exceptional treatment, the very people who will claim it will be those who least deserve it. The people who are quite convinced they are superior are the very inferior people; the men who really think themselves extraordinary are the most ordinary rotters on earth. If you say, "Nobody must steal the Crown of England," then probably it will not be stolen. After that, probably the next best thing would be to say, "Anybody may steal the Crown of England," for then the Crown might find its way to some honest and modest fellow. But if you say, "Those who feel themselves to have Wild and Wondrous Souls, and they only, may steal the Crown of England," then you may be sure there will be a rush for it of all the rag, tag, and bobtail of the universe, all the quack doctors, all the sham artists, all the demireps and drunken egotists, all the nationless adventurers and criminal monomaniacs of the world.

So, if you say that marriage is for common people, but divorce for free and noble spirits, all the weak and selfish people will dash for the divorce; while the few free and noble spirits you wish to help will very probably (because they are free and noble) go on wrestling with the marriage. For it is one of the marks of real dignity of character not to wish to separate oneself from the honour and tragedy of the whole tribe. All men are ordinary men; the extraordinary men are those who know it.

The weakness of the proposition that marriage is good for the common herd, but can be advantageously violated by special "experimenters" and pioneers, is that it takes no account of the problem of the disease of pride. It is easy enough to say that weaker souls had better be guarded, but that we must give freedom to Georges Sand or make exceptions for George Eliot. The practical puzzle is this: that it is precisely the weakest sort of lady novelist who thinks she is Georges Sand; it is precisely the silliest woman who is sure she is George Eliot. It is the small soul that is sure it is an exception; the large soul is only too proud to be the rule. To advertise for exceptional people is to collect all the sulks and sick fancies and futile ambitions of the earth. The good artist is he who can be understood; it is the bad artist who is always "misunderstood." In short, the great man is a man; it is always the tenth-rate man who is the Superman.

Miss Farr disposes of the difficult question of vows and bonds in love by leaving out altogether the one extraordinary fact of experience on which the whole matter turns. She again solves the problem by assuming that it is not a problem. Concerning oaths of fidelity, etc., she writes: "We cannot trust ourselves to make a real love-knot unless money or custom forces us to 'bear and forbear.' There is always the lurking fear that we shall not be able to keep faith unless we swear upon the Book. This is, of course, not true of young lovers. Every first love is born free of tradition; indeed, not only is first love innocent and valiant, but it sweeps aside all the wise laws it has been taught, and burns away experience in its own light. The revelation is so extraordinary, so unlike anything told by the poets, so absorbing, that it is impossible to believe that the feeling can die out."

Now this is exactly as if some old naturalist settled the bat's place in nature by saying boldly, "Bats do not fly." It is as if he solved the problem of whales by bluntly declaring that whales live on land. There is a problem of vows, as of bats and whales. What Miss Farr says about it is quite lucid and explanatory; it simply happens to be flatly untrue. It is not the fact that young lovers have no desire to swear on the Book. They are always at it. It is not the fact that every young love is born free of traditions about binding and promising, about bonds and signatures and seals. On the contrary, lovers wallow in the wildest pedantry and precision about these matters. They do the craziest things to make their love legal and irrevocable. They tattoo each other with promises; they cut into rocks and oaks with their names and vows; they bury ridiculous things in ridiculous places to be a witness against them; they bond each other with rings, and inscribe each other in Bibles; if they are raving lunatics (which is not untenable), they are mad solely on this idea of binding and on nothing else. It is quite true that the tradition of their fathers and mothers is in favour of fidelity; but it is emphatically not true that the lovers merely follow it; they invent it anew. It is quite true that the lovers feel their love eternal, and independent of oaths; but it is emphatically not true that they do not desire to take the oaths. They have a ravening thirst to take as many oaths as possible. Now this is the paradox; this is the whole problem. It is not true, as Miss Farr would have it, that young people feel free of vows, being confident of constancy; while old people invent vows, having lost that confidence. That would be much too simple; if that were so there would be no problem at all. The startling but quite solid fact is that young people are especially fierce in making fetters and final ties at the very moment when they think them unnecessary. The time when they want the vow is exactly the time when they do not need it. That is worth thinking about.

Nearly all the fundamental facts of mankind are to be found in its fables. And there is a singularly sane truth in all the old stories of the monsters—such as centaurs, mermaids, sphinxes, and the rest. It will be noted that in each of these the humanity, though imperfect in its extent, is perfect in its quality. The mermaid is half a lady and half a fish; but there is nothing fishy about the lady. A centaur is half a gentleman and half a horse. But there is nothing horsey about the gentleman. The centaur is a manly sort of man—up to a certain point. The mermaid is a womanly woman—so far as she goes. The human parts of these monsters are handsome, like heroes, or lovely, like nymphs; their bestial appendages do not affect the full perfection of their humanity—what there is of it. There is nothing humanly wrong with the centaur, except that he rides a horse without a head. There is nothing humanly wrong with the mermaid; Hood put a good comic motto to his picture of a mermaid: "All's well that ends well." It is, perhaps, quite true; it all depends which end. Those old wild images included a crucial truth. Man is a monster. And he is all the more a monster because one part of him is perfect. It is not true, as the evolutionists say, that man moves perpetually up a slope from imperfection to perfection, changing ceaselessly, so as to be suitable. The immortal part of a man and the deadly part are jarringly distinct, and have always been. And the best proof of this is in such a case as we have considered—the case of the oaths of love.

A man's soul is as full of voices as a forest; there are ten thousand tongues there like all the tongues of the trees: fancies, follies, memories, madnesses, mysterious fears, and more mysterious hopes. All the settlement and sane government of life consists in coming to the conclusion that some of those voices have authority and others not. You may have an impulse to fight your enemy or an impulse to run away from him; a reason to serve your country or a reason to betray it; a good idea for making sweets or a better idea for poisoning them. The only test I know by which to judge one argument or inspiration from another is ultimately this: that all the noble necessities of man talk the language of eternity. When man is doing the three or four things that he was sent on this earth to do, then he speaks like one who shall live for ever. A man dying for his country does not talk as if local preferences could change. Leonidas does not say, "In my present mood, I prefer Sparta to Persia." William Tell does not remark, "The Swiss civilization, so far as I can yet see, is superior to the Austrian." When men are making commonwealths, they talk in terms of the absolute, and so they do when they are making (however unconsciously) those smaller commonwealths which are called families. There are in life certain immortal moments, moments that have authority. Lovers are right to tattoo each other's skins and cut each other's names about the world; they do belong to each other, in a more awful sense than they know.

The Ideal Must Be Fixed

I n modern ideal conceptions of society there are some desires
that are possibly not attainable: but there are some desires that
are not desirable. That all men should live in equally beautiful
houses is a dream that may or may not be attained. But that all
men should live in the same beautiful house is not a dream at all; it
is a nightmare. That a man should love all old women is an ideal
that may not be attainable. But that a man should regard all old
women exactly as he regards his mother is not only an unattainable
ideal, but an ideal which ought not to be attained. I do not know
if the reader agrees with me in these examples; but I will add the
example which has always affected me most. I could never conceive or tolerate any Utopia which did not leave to me the liberty
for which I chiefly care, the liberty to bind myself. Complete
anarchy would not merely make it impossible to have any discipline or fidelity; it would also make it impossible to have any fun.
To take an obvious instance, it would not be worth while to bet if
a bet were not binding. The dissolution of all contracts would not
only ruin morality but spoil sport. Now betting and such sports
are only the stunted and twisted shapes of the original instinct of
man for adventure and romance, of which much has been said in
these pages. And the perils, rewards, punishments and fulfilments
of an adventure must be real, or the adventure is only a shifting
and heartless nightmare. If I bet I must be made to pay, or there is
no poetry in betting. If I challenge I must be made to fight, or
there is no poetry in challenging. If I vow to be faithful I must be
cursed when I am unfaithful, or there is no fun in vowing. You
could not even make a fairy tale from the experiences of a man
who, when he was swallowed by a whale might find himself at

the top of the Eiffel Tower, or when he was turned into a frog might begin to behave like a flamingo. For the purpose even of the wildest romance results must be real; results must be irrevocable. Christian marriage is the great example of a real and irrevocable result; and that is why it is the chief subject and centre of all our romantic writing. And this is my last instance of the things that I should ask, and ask imperatively, of any social paradise; I should ask to be kept to my bargain, to have my oaths and engagements taken seriously; I should ask Utopia to avenge my honour on myself.

PART EIGHT

HOME FOR CHRISTMAS

* * *

The world cannot keep its own ideals.

What I Saw in America

A religion is not the church a man goes to but the cosmos he lives in.

Irish Impressions

Joy, which was the small publicity of the pagan, is the gigantic secret of the Christian.

Orthodoxy

All goods look better when they look like gifts.

St. Francis of Assisi

That Christianity is identical with democracy, is the hardest of gospels; there is nothing that so strikes men with fear as the saying that they are all the sons of God.

Twelve Types

And the more I considered Christianity, the more I found that while it had established a rule and order, the chief aim of that order was to give room for good things to run wild.

Orthodoxy

And where the house is a temple it will have rites, like those of Christmas.

"Christmas and the New Negations", in *The New Witness,*
December 12, 1919

Any agnostic or atheist whose childhood has known a real Christmas has ever afterwards, whether he likes it or not, an association in his mind between two ideas that most of mankind must regard as remote from each other; the idea of a baby and the idea of the unknown strength that sustains the stars. His instincts and imagination can still connect them, when his reason can no longer see the need of the connection; for him there will always be some savour of religion about the mere picture of a mother and a baby; some hint of mercy and softening about the mere mention of the dreadful name of God.

The Everlasting Man

Nothing will destroy the sacred triangle; and even the Christian faith, the most amazing revolution that ever took place in the mind, served only in a sense to turn the triangle upside down. It held up the mystical mirror in which the order of the three things was reversed; and added a holy family of child, mother and father to the human family of father, mother and child.

The Superstition of Divorce

The Nativity

The thatch on the roof was as golden,
  Though dusty the straw was and old,
The wind had a peal as of trumpets,
  Though blowing and barren and cold,
The mother's hair was a glory
  Though loosened and torn,
For under the eaves in the gloaming
    A child was born.

Have a myriad children been quickened,
  Have a myriad children grown old,
Grown gross and unloved and embittered,
  Grown cunning and savage and cold?
God abides in a terrible patience,
  Unangered, unworn,
And again for the child that was squandered
    A child is born.

What know we of aeons behind us,
  Dim dynasties lost long ago,
Huge empires, like dreams unremembered,
  Huge cities for ages laid low?
This at least—that with blight and with blessing,
  With flower and with thorn,
Love was there, and his cry was among them,
    "A child is born."

Though the darkness be noisy with systems,
  Dark fancies that fret and disprove,
Still the plumes stir around us, above us
  The wings of the shadow of love:
Oh! princes and priests, have ye seen it
  Grow pale through your scorn;

Huge dawns sleep before us, deep changes,
 A child is born.

And the rafters of toil still are gilded
 With the dawn of the stars of the heart,
And the wise men draw near in the twilight,
 Who are weary of learning and art,
And the face of the tyrant is darkened,
 His spirit is torn,
For a new king is enthroned; yea, the sternest,
 A child is born.

And the mother still joys for the whispered
 First stir of unspeakable things,
Still feels that high moment unfurling
 Red glory of Gabriel's wings.
Still the babe of an hour is a master
 Whom angels adorn,
Emmanuel, prophet, anointed,
 A child is born.

And thou, that art still in thy cradle,
 The sun being crown for thy brow,
Make answer, our flesh, make an answer,
 Say, whence art thou come—who art thou?
Art thou come back on earth for our teaching
 To train or to warn—?
Hush—how may we know?—knowing only
 A child is born.

A Child of the Snows

There is heard a hymn when the panes are dim,
 And never before or again,

When the nights are strong with a darkness long,
  And the dark is alive with rain.

Never we know but in sleet and in snow,
  The place where the great fires are,
That the midst of the earth is a raging mirth
  And the heart of the earth a star.

And at night we win to the ancient inn
  Where the child in the frost is furled,
We follow the feet where all souls meet
  At the inn at the end of the world.

The gods lie dead where the leaves lie red,
  For the flame of the sun is flown,
The gods lie cold where the leaves lie gold,
  And a Child comes forth alone.

The House of Christmas

There fared a mother driven forth
Out of an inn to roam;
In the place where she was homeless
All men are at home.
The crazy stable close at hand,
With shaking timber and shifting sand,
Grew a stronger thing to abide and stand
Than the square stones of Rome.

For men are homesick in their homes,
And strangers under the sun,
And they lay their heads in a foreign land
Whenever the day is done.
Here we have battle and blazing eyes,

And chance and honour and high surprise,
But our homes are under miraculous skies
Where the yule tale was begun.

A Child in a foul stable,
Where the beasts feed and foam;
Only where he was homeless
Are you and I at home;
We have hands that fashion and heads that know,
But our hearts we lost—how long ago!
In a place no chart nor ship can show
Under the sky's dome.

This world is wild as an old wives' tale,
And strange the plain things are,
The earth is enough and the air is enough
For our wonder and our war;
But our rest is as far as the fire-drake swings
And our peace is put in impossible things
Where clashed and thundered unthinkable wings
Round an incredible star.

To an open house in the evening
Home shall men come,
To an older place than Eden
And a taller town than Rome.
To the end of the way of the wandering star,
To the things that cannot be and that are,
To the place where God was homeless
And all men are at home.

The Spirit of Christmas

I have rather rashly undertaken to write of the Spirit of Christmas; and it presents a preliminary difficulty about which I must be candid. People are very curious nowadays in their way of talking about "the spirit" of a thing. There is, for example, a particular sort of prig who is always lecturing us about having the spirit of true Christianity, apart from all names and forms. As far as I can make out, he means the very opposite of what he says. He means that we are to go on using the names "Christian" and "Christianity," and so on, for something in which it is quite specially the spirit that is not Christian; something that is a sort of combination of the baseless optimism of an American atheist with the pacifism of a mild Hindoo. In the same way, we read a great deal about the Spirit of Christmas in modern journalism or commercialism; but it is really a reversal of the same kind. So far from preserving the essentials without the externals, it is rather preserving the externals where there cannot be the essentials. It means taking two mere material substances, like holly and mistletoe, and spreading them all over huge and homeless cosmopolitan hotels or round the Doric columns of impersonal clubs full of jaded and cynical old gentlemen; or in any other place where the actual spirit of Christmas is least likely to be. But there is also another way in which modern commercial complexity eats out the heart of the thing, while actually leaving the painted shell of it. And that is the much too elaborate system of dependence on buying and selling, and therefore on bustle and hustle; and the actual neglect of the new things that might be done by the old Christmas.

Normally, if anything were normal nowadays, it would seem a truism to say that Christmas has been a family festival. But it is now possible (as I have had the good or bad luck to discover) to earn a reputation for paradox simply by going on saying that truisms are true. In this case, of course, the reason, the only reasonable reason, was religious. It was concerned with a happy family because it was consecrated to the Holy Family. But it is perfectly true that many men saw the fact without specially feeling the reason. When we say the root was religious, we do not mean that Sam Weller was concentrated on theological values when he told the Fat Boy to "put a bit of Christmas," into some object, probably edible. We do not mean that the Fat Boy had gone into a trance of mystical contemplation like a monk seeing a vision. We do not even mean that Bob Cratchit defended punch by saying he was only looking on the wine when it was yellow; or that Tiny Tim quoted Timothy. We only mean that they, including their author, would have confessed humbly and heartily that there was someone historically quite anterior to Mr. Scrooge, who might be called the Founder of the Feast. But in any case, whatever the reason, all would have agreed about the result. Mr. Wardle's feast centred in Mr. Wardle's family; and none the less because the romantic shadows of Mr. Winkle and Mr. Snodgrass threatened to break it up for the formation of other families.

The Christmas season is domestic; and for that reason most people now prepare for it by struggling in tramcars, standing in queues, rushing away in trains, crowding despairingly into tea-shops, and wondering when or whether they will ever get home. I do not know whether some of them disappear for ever in the toy department or simply lie down and die in the tea-rooms; but by the look of them, it is quite likely. Just before the great festival of the home the whole population seems to have become homeless. It is the supreme triumph of industrial civilisation that, in the huge cities which seem to have far too many houses, there is a hopeless shortage of housing. For a long time past great numbers of our poor have become practically nomadic. We even confess the fact; for we talk of some of them as Street Arabs. But this domestic institution, in its present ironical phase, has gone beyond such normal abnormality. The feast of the family turns the rich as well as the poor into vagabonds. They are so scattered over the bewildering labyrinth of our traffic and our trade, that they sometimes cannot even reach the tea-shop; it would be indelicate, of course, to mention the tavern. They have a difficulty in crowding into their hotels, let alone separating to reach their houses. I mean quite the reverse of irreverence when I say that their only point of resemblance to the archetypal Christmas family is that there is no room for them at the inn.

Now Christmas is built upon a beautiful and intentional paradox; that the birth of the homeless should be celebrated in every home. But the other sort of paradox is not intentional and is certainly not beautiful. It is bad enough that we cannot altogether disentangle the tragedy of poverty. It is bad enough that the birth of the homeless, celebrated at hearth and altar, should sometimes synchronise with the death of the homeless in workhouses and slums. But we need not rejoice in this universal restlessness brought upon rich and poor alike; and it seems to me that in this matter we need a reform of the modern Christmas.

I will now emit another brilliant flash of paradox by remarking that Christmas occurs in the winter. That is, it is not only a feast dedicated to domesticity, but it is one deliberately placed under the conditions in which it is most uncomfortable to rush about and most natural to stop at home. But under the complicated conditions of modern conventions and conveniences, there arises this more practical and much more unpleasant sort of paradox. People have to rush about for a few weeks, if it is only to stay at home for a few hours. Now the old and healthy idea of such winter festivals was this; that people being shut in and besieged by the weather were driven back on their own resources; or, in other words, had a chance of showing whether there was anything in them. It is not certain that the reputation of our most fashionable modern pleasure-seekers would survive the test. Some dreadful exposures would be made of some such brilliant society favourites, if they were cut off from the power of machinery and money. They are quite used to having everything done for them; and even when they go to the very latest American dances, it seems to be mostly the Negro musicians who dance. But anyhow, on the average of healthy humanity I believe the cutting off of all these mechanical connections would have a thoroughly enlivening and awakening effect. At present they are always accused of merely amusing themselves; but they are doing nothing so noble or worthy of their human dignity. Most of them by this time cannot amuse themselves; they are too used to being amused.

Christmas might be creative. We are told, even by those who praise it most, that it is chiefly valuable for keeping up ancient customs or old-fashioned games. It is indeed valuable for both those admirable purposes. But in the sense of which I am now speaking it might once more be possible to turn the truth the other way round. It is not so much old things as new things that a real Christmas might create. It might, for instance, create new games, if people were really driven to invent their own games. Most of the very old games began with the use of ordinary tools or furniture. So the very terms of tennis were founded on the framework of the old inn courtyard. So, it is said, the stumps in cricket were originally only the three legs of the milking-stool. Now we might invent new things of this kind, if we remembered who is the mother of invention. How pleasing it would be to start a game in which we scored so much for hitting the umbrella-stand or the dinner-wagon, or even the host and hostess; of course, with a missile of some soft material. Children who are lucky enough to be left alone in the nursery invent not only whole games, but whole dramas and life-stories of their own; they invent secret languages; they create imaginary families; they laboriously conduct family magazines. That is the sort of creative spirit that we want in the modern world; want both in the sense of desiring and in the sense of lacking it. If Christmas could become more domestic, instead of less, I believe there would be a vast increase in the real Christmas spirit; the spirit of the Child. But in indulging this dream we must once more invert the current convention into the form of a paradox. It is true in a sense that Christmas is the time at which the doors should be open. But I would have the doors shut at Christmas, or at least just before Christmas; and then the world shall see what we can do.

I cannot but remember, with something of a smile, that on an earlier and more controversial page of this book I have mentioned a lady who shuddered at the thought of the things perpetrated by my co-religionists behind closed doors. But my memory of it is mellowed by distance and the present subject, and I feel quite the reverse of controversial. I hope that lady, and all of her way of thinking, may also have the wisdom to close their doors; and discover that only when all the doors are closed the best thing will be found inside. If they are Puritans, whose religion is only based on the Bible, let it for once indeed be a Family Bible. If they are Pagans, who can accept nothing but the winter feast, let it at least be a family feast. The discordance or discomfort complained of by modern critics, in the family reunion, is not due to that mystical focal fire having been left burning, but to its having been left to go cold. It is because cold fragments of a once living thing are clumsily lumped together; it is no argument against making the thing alive. Christmas toys are incongruously dangled before heavy and heathen uncles who wish they were playing golf. But that does not alter the fact that they might become much brighter and more intelligent if they knew how to play with toys; and they are horrible bores about golf. Their dullness is only the last deadly product of the mechanical progress of organised and professional sports, in that rigid world of routine outside the home. When they were children, behind closed doors in the home, it is probable that nearly every one of them had day-dreams and unwritten dramas that belonged to them as much as Hamlet belonged to Shakespeare or Pickwick to Dickens. How much more thrilling it would be if Uncle Henry, instead of describing in detail all the strokes with which he ought to have got out of the bunker, were to say frankly that he had been on a voyage to the end of the world and had just caught the Great Sea-Serpent. How much more truly intellectual would be the conversation of Uncle William if, instead of telling us the point to which he had reduced his handicap, he could still say with conviction that he was King of the Kangaroo Islands, or Chief of the Rango Dango Redskins. These things, projected from within, were in almost all human spirits; and it is not normal that the inspiration of them should be so utterly crushed by the things without. Let it not be supposed for a moment that I also am among the tyrants of the earth, who would impose my own tastes, or force all the other children to play my own games. I have no disrespect for the game of golf; it is an admirable game. I have played it; or rather, I have played at it, which is generally regarded as the very opposite. By all means let the golfers golf and even the organisers organise, if their only conception of an organ is something like a barrel-organ. Let them play golf day after day; let them play golf for three hundred and sixty-four days, and nights as well, with balls dipped in luminous paint, to be pursued in the dark. But let there be one night when things grow luminous from within: and one day when men seek for all that is buried in themselves; and discover, where she is indeed hidden, behind locked gates and shuttered windows, and doors thrice barred and bolted, the spirit of liberty.

The New War on Christmas

Christmas, which in the seventeenth century had to be saved from gloom, in the twentieth century has to be saved from frivolity. The alternative need will seem natural enough if we picture any really poetical combination, as in any of the great Christmas pictures. If a man paints a rich blue sky with a single star blazing white above Bethlehem, the picture is just as much spoilt if you whitewash it and leave it all blank as if you paint out the star and leave it all blue. If there is some glowing Gothic window showing the Three Kings in the flamboyant hues of their holy heraldry, it is just as much lost whether you darken the window and turn it into a wall or smash the window and let in a white glare and a wind of winter. The dancing angels in the medieval picture will be equally limited whether you clip their wings or lame their feet; and the boy bishop ceases even to be amusing if there are no bishops except boys. Christmas, like so many other Christian and Catholic creations, is a wedding. It is the wedding of the wilder spirit of human enjoyment with the higher spirit of humility and the mystical sense. And the parallel of a wedding holds good in more ways than one; because this new danger which threatens Christmas is the same that has long vulgarised and vitiated weddings. It is quite right that there should be pomp and popular rejoicing at a wedding; I do not in the least agree with those who would have it a purely private and personal thing like a proposal or engagement. If a man is not proud of getting married, what is he proud of, and why in the name of nonsense is he getting married at all? But in the normal way all this merry-making is subordinate to the marriage; because it is *in honour* of the marriage. People came there to be married and not to be merry; and they are merry because they did. But in the snobbish society wedding the serious purpose is entirely lost sight of, and nothing remains but frivolity. For frivolity is trying to rejoice with nothing to rejoice over. The result is that at last even the frivolity as frivolity begins to fail. People who began by coming together only for fun end by doing it only for fashion; and there is no more even of faint suggestion of fun but only of fuss.

Similarly people are losing the power to enjoy Christmas through identifying it with enjoyment. When once they lose sight of the old suggestion that it is all about something, they naturally fall into blank pauses of wondering what it is all about. To be told to rejoice on Christmas Day is reasonable and intelligible, if you understand the name, or even look at the word. To be told to rejoice on the twenty-fifth of December is like being told to rejoice at a quarter-past eleven on Thursday week. You cannot suddenly be frivolous unless you believe there is a serious reason for being frivolous. A man might make a feast if he had come into a fortune; and he might make a great many jokes about the fortune. But he would not do it if the fortune were a joke. He would not be so hilarious if his benefactor, with similar hilarity, had left him bundles of bad bank-notes or a cheque book of which all the cheques would be dishonoured. The testator's action, however playful, would not be long an occasion of social festivities and celebrations; nor would the April foolery be so permanent as Christmas fun. You cannot even start a lark about a legacy you believe to be a sham legacy. You cannot start a lark to celebrate a miracle you believe to be a sham miracle. The result of dismissing the divine side of Christmas and demanding only the human, is that you are demanding too much of human nature. You are asking men to illuminate the town for a victory that has not taken place; or which they believe to be the lie of some Jingo journal. You are asking them to go mad with romantic joy because two people they like are being married, at the moment when they are being divorced.

Our modern task therefore is to save festivity from frivolity.

That is the only way in which it will ever again become festive.
Children still understand the feast of Christmas, they still sometimes feast to excess in the matter of plum pudding or a turkey.
But there is never anything in the least frivolous about their
attitude to a plum pudding or a turkey. Still less is there anything
frivolous in their attitude to a stocking or a Christmas tree. They
have the serious and even solemn sense of the great truth; that
Christmas is a time when things happen; things that do not always
happen. But even in children that sanity is in some sense at war
with society. The vivid magic of that night and day is being killed
by the vulgar levity of all the other three hundred and sixty four
days. For this is the age in which everybody incessantly talks
about psychology and nobody apparently thinks about it. Surely
it is the very alphabet of psychology that a child will look more
closely at one Christmas tree than if it stood in a forest of Christmas trees. Surely even a modern psychologist might know enough
of his subject to know that one Father Christmas (whether detected
to be Uncle William or not) is more exciting than a regiment of
Father Christmases all standing in a row and all looking exactly
alike. Yet the moderns are making the whole regiment of the
three hundred and sixty five days look exactly alike, even if they
are disguising them all in the same frivolous masquerade. They
might at least establish one holiday in the year; one wild and
hilarious holiday on which nobody could dance.

The battle against this barbaric blunder in psychology is especially joined in Ireland; and the chances are that the newspapers
will talk great nonsense about it in England. There have been
several signs lately that Ireland intends to be really independent;
that is, that Ireland intends to be really Irish; and in nothing so
much as in a greater restraint in the interpretation of revelry. It is
something of a satire that Ireland was always taunted with being
dependent on America. And now Ireland alone is making some
attempt to be independent of America, while England is allowing
herself to be more and more Americanised. The hard and brassy
hedonism and heathenry of New York will have far less chance in
Dublin than in London or Liverpool. The Irish are already appealing

against jazz and jingle to the tradition of their old national dances, which are comparatively formal and even full of solemnity. The root of the difference is doubtless religious, like everything else; but our Americanised journalists will make another of their native howlers if they imagine that the protest is merely what they would call "clerical." Dignity is deep in the Irish blood and bone; as a priest once said to me, "The Irish have the passion of distinction." It is because the Irishman is an Irishman, and not only because he is a Catholic, that he would always have objected to a young woman in tights and a top-hat becoming the only form of national entertainment. I remember hearing Mr. W. B. Yeats, who is certainly neither a clerical nor a Puritan, saying in a voice of deep indignation: "I hope to see the day when there shall be fights in the street over the attempt to force on our people the vulgarity of the cosmopolitan theatre." It is not impossible that his hope may be realised.

The English Christmas was quite as noble and national a thing as the Irish dance. It was not quite so dignified a thing because it was English and not Irish; but it was, in its very intense and intimate essence, innocent. The whole glory and gaiety of the thing collapses at a touch of anything that is not innocent. Anybody ought to be able to see that, as a mere fact of artistic unity and atmosphere, however much he may himself have lost his innocence; he ought to be able to see what sort of words or suggestions would in fact spoil an old English Carol or spoil a Dickens' story. And those are exactly the elements of that atmosphere that is coming upon us like a roaring and reeking gas out of the yawning and glaring furnace of the new frivolity. It poisons the popular instinct for pleasure, which triumphed in the old popular feasts. It is, very truly, the pace that kills.

The Family

Something startling has happened. A public man had said, not merely something vital, but *the* vital thing about public affairs, which every public man should be saying every day, and which no other public man of our time has hinted at. We are not surprised that it is our King who has said it.

An enthusiastic gentleman praised His Majesty for the elegant delivery of his speech to his people which was broadcast on Christmas Day. And it is true that he spoke with a certain noble simplicity. But our great satisfaction is that the matter was worthy of the manner.

The matter provided the subject of a good many leading articles, some of which displayed the Keyword of the King's speech as their title. But all of them missed the significance of the Keyword.

That Keyword, which unlocks the doors of all politics and all economy, is Family.

The King began by reminding his hearers, his people, that Christmas Day is the festival of the Family. It was plain that he meant that primarily it was the Festival of one particular Family, and of one particular Mother and Child.

It is astounding and yet it is certain that some of his hearers needed to be reminded of this central fact of the world. It is almost equally astounding and yet as certain that far more of them failed to understand him when he went on to speak of his people "all of you who are listening to me, all the peoples of the realm and empire" as "bound to me and to each other by the spirit of one great family." There was the Crib of Bethlehem, and here was this great family of British people. It was the King's urgent desire and hope that the spirit of the One should become the spirit of the Other.

"We have still our own anxieties to face," he went on, "but I am convinced that if we meet them in the spirit of one family we shall overcome them."

That Keyword runs through the speech. The King speaks as a father to his children. And he speaks, says he, "as I sit in my own home."

It is plain enough that he sees the one big British family as a collection of families—not merely families of nations, but millions of individual families listening to him, family by family, each in its own separate home.

We will not take His Majesty farther along the road to Distributism than the words of his speech carry him. But we find it significant when politicians delight in talking of international factors and Weltpolitik (if the recognition of the origin of that second phrase has not made it a trifle unpopular) our King talks of nothing but those homely realities: the family and the home.

The recognition of the family as the unit of the State is the kernel of Distributism. The insistence on ownership to protect its liberty is the shell.

We that are Christians believe that the family has a divine sanction. But any reasonable pagan, if he will work it out, will discover that the family existed before the State and has prior rights; that the State exists only as a collection of families, and that its sole function is to safeguard the rights of each and all of them.

Once admit that the nation is itself one big family with its King as its father, and taking its pattern from one little simple Family, and the step to the central Distributist position seems to us inevitable. The small family is the reality which the King relies upon to give force to his splendid and tremendous figure of speech. He regards his Empire as a League of Families, a League of very little nations.

We do not regard it as remarkable that out King should speak in this familiar homely way which a dictator, still less an expert sociologist, can never hope to reach. There are good republicans among our readers. Yet even they will admit that it is a good thing to have an ordinary man as your chief ruler, since ordinary things are the important ones, and that you are far more likely to get an ordinary man as your King than as your dictator or your Prime Minister.

We need not stress the fact that, as no other secular ruler, a King is dedicated. The thing that springs to the eye is that, when all our politicians and sociologists are losing themselves in big phrases about efficient organisation, our King utters the magical word *family*.

It is as a father of a family that he talks of those unlucky children of his who are dispossessed. He asks that they may be treated in the spirit of their Elder Brother, — as brothers, and not as sociological phenomena.

It is as the father of a family that he speaks of the clash of interests among those more fortunate, or at least more powerful. And what he says admits of easy paraphrase into a call for the spirit of charity, unity and brotherly love.

We imagine that some of his Ministers smiled when they heard his speech, and murmured: "Good, old-fashioned stuff." And of course they are right. It is good, and it is old-fashioned: as old fashioned as man, as man in a garden.

And we imagine that others of his Ministers rubbed their hands, and said: "That's the stuff to give'em." Again they are right. Only they happen to mistake for dope what is doctrine.

At this moment when from all sides the rights of the family are threatened with invasion, and when men and women — and children — of our nation tend to be treated, not as members of separate families, not as brothers and sisters in one great family, but as cyphers, some of them insignificant, or even superfluous cyphers, in a financial statement, it comes with the force of a new revelation that our King has spoken this old-fashioned, homely, familiar, human word.

To a Lady

Light of the young, before you have grown old
The world will have grown weary of its youth.
All its cheap charity and loose-lipped truth
And passion that goes naked—and grows cold.

Tire of a pity so akin to hate
Turn on a truth that is so near to treason,
When Time, the god of traitors, in their season
Marks down for dated all the up-to-date.

Then shall men know by the great grace you are
How something better than blind fear or blunder
Bade us stand back, where we could watch with wonder
Ladies like landscapes, very fair and far.

A crowd shall call your high estrangèd face
A mask of blind reaction and resistance,
Because you have made large the world with distance
As God made large the universe with space.

Yet beautiful your feet upon the mountains
Moving in soundless music shall return,
And they that look into your eyes shall learn—
Having forced up the secret sea in fountains.

And having vulgarised infinity
And splashed their brains against the starry steeps.
In what unfathomable inward deeps
Dwells the last mystery men call Liberty.

When they shall say we corned and held in thrall
Spirits like yours; the mother of the tribe

Slandered, a slave, a butt for slur and gibe,
You shall confound the one great slur of all.

The one great slander answered long ago
By Her that hid all things within her heart,
One speaking when the veil was rent apart
"Women alone can keep a secret so."

BIBLIOGRAPHY

BOOKS BY CHESTERTON

Alarms and Discursions. New York: Dodd, Mead, and Company, 1911.

All I Survey. London: Methuen and Company, Ltd., 1933.

All Things Considered. New York: Sheed and Ward, 1956.

The Appetite of Tyranny in *Collected Works of G. K. Chesterton,* vol. 5. San Francisco: Ignatius Press, 1987.

Autobiography in *Collected Works of G. K. Chesterton,* vol. 16. San Francisco: Ignatius Press, 1988.

Avowals and Denials. London: Methuen, 1934.

The Ball and the Cross. New York: John Lane Company, 1909.

Charles Dickens in *Collected Works of G. K. Chesterton,* vol. 15. San Francisco: Ignatius Press, 1989.

The Club of Queer Trades. Elstree, Hertfordshire: Greenhill Books, 1987.

The Collected Poems of G. K. Chesterton. New York: Dodd, Mead & Co., 1980.

The Coloured Lands. New York: Sheed and Ward, 1938.

The Common Man. New York: Sheed and Ward, 1950.

A Denunciation of Patriotism.

Divorce versus Democracy in *Collected Works of G. K. Chesterton,* vol. 4. San Francisco: Ignatius Press, 1987.

Early Notebooks. (Unpublished; quoted in *G. K. Chesterton* and *Return to Chesterton*).

Eugenics and Other Evils in *Collected Works of G. K. Chesterton,* vol. 4. San Francisco: Ignatius Press, 1987.

The Everlasting Man in *Collected Works of G. K. Chesterton,* vol. 2. San Francisco: Ignatius Press, 1986.

Fancies versus Fads. London: Methuen, 1923.

George Bernard Shaw in *Collected Works of G. K. Chesterton,* vol. 11. San Francisco: Ignatius Press, 1989.

A Handful of Authors. Ed. Dorothy Collins. New York: Sheed and Ward, 1953.

Heretics in *Collected Works of G. K. Chesterton,* vol. 1. San Francisco: Ignatius Press, 1986.

Irish Impressions. New York: John Lane Company, 1920.

Lunacy and Letters. Ed. Dorothy Collins. New York: Sheed and Ward, 1958.

A Miscellany of Men. New York: Dodd, Mead & Co. 1912.

The Napoleon of Notting Hill. London: Bodley Head, 1904, 1961.

Notebook. (Unpublished; quoted in *G. K. Chesterton* and *Return to Chesterton*).

Orthodoxy in *Collected Works of G. K. Chesterton,* vol. 1. San Francisco: Ignatius Press, 1986.

The Queen of the Seven Swords. London and New York: Sheed and Ward, 1933.

Robert Browning. London: Macmillan and Company, Ltd., 1903.

Sidelights on New London and Newer York in *Collected Works of G. K. Chesterton,* vol. 21. San Francisco: Ignatius Press, 1990.

Social Reform versus Birth Control in *Collected Works of G. K. Chesterton,* vol. 4. San Francisco: Ignatius Press, 1987.

The Spice of Life. Ed. Dorothy Collins. Beaconsfield: D. Finlayson, 1964.

St. Francis of Assisi in *Collected Works of G. K. Chesterton,* vol. 2. San Francisco: Ignatius Press, 1986.

The Superstition of Divorce in *Collected Works of G. K. Chesterton,* vol. 4. San Francisco: Ignatius Press, 1987.

The Surprise in *Collected Works of G. K. Chesterton,* vol. 11. San Francisco: Ignatius Press, 1989.

The Thing in *Collected Works of G. K. Chesterton,* vol. 3. San Francisco: Ignatius Press, 1990.

Tremendous Trifles. London: Methuen, 1909.

Twelve Types. London: A. L. Humphreys, 1910

The Uses of Diversity. New York: Dodd, Mead and Company, 1921.

What I Saw in America in *Collected Works of G. K. Chesterton,* vol. 21. San Francisco: Ignatius Press, 1990.

What's Wrong with the World in *Collected Works of G. K. Chesterton,* vol. 4. San Francisco: Ignatius Press, 1987.

The Well and the Shallows in *Collected Works of G. K. Chesterton,* vol. 3. San Francisco: Ignatius Press, 1990.

The Wild Knight. New York: E. P. Dutton & Co. 1914, 4th ed.

PERIODICALS CONTAINING CHESTERTON ARTICLES

G.K.'s Weekly
Illustrated London News
The New Witness
New York American
The Speaker

BOOKS BY OTHER AUTHORS

Aldous Huxley. *Brave New World.* New York and London: Harper & Brothers, 1946.

Greville M. MacDonald. *George MacDonald and His Wife.* London: G. Allen & Unwin, Ltd., 1924.

Robert Louis Stevenson. *Virginibus puerisque.* London: T. Nelson, n.d.

Maisie Ward, *Gilbert Keith Chesterton.* New York: Sheed & Ward, 1943.

Maisie Ward. *Return to Chesterton.* New York: Sheed & Ward, 1952.

Charles Williams. *The Forgiveness of Sins.* Grand Rapids, Michigan: W. B. Eerdmans Pub. Co., 1984.

Karol Wojtyla. *The Jeweler's Shop,* Act III, in *The Collected Plays and Writings on Theater by Karol Wojtyla,* University of California Press, 1987, p. 312.

SOURCES OF SELECTIONS

I. THE WILDEST OF ADVENTURES

II. THE POETRY OF THE HOME

III. MEN & WOMEN, HUSBANDS & WIVES

IV. FATHERS AND MOTHERS

V. THE INNOCENCE OF THE CHILD

VI. THE ASSASSINS OF THE FAMILY

The titles of the selections from the *Illustrated London News* are my own, as is the title given to the excerpt from *Orthodoxy* ("The Ideal Must Be Fixed"). The articles from the *Illustrated London News* appeared as a weekly column called *Our Notebook*. The selections that are editorials and *Top & Tail* columns from *G.K.'s Weekly*, the publication G. K. Chesterton edited, were not signed, but Chesterton wrote most of the editorials from March 21, 1925 (vol. 1, no. 1) to June 1936 (vol. 23, no. 587). He also wrote the *Top & Tail* column from September 2, 1925, to August 10, 1929. Unsigned articles were sometimes written by Bill Titterton. (— Editor.)